Somalis in the Twin Cities and Columbus

Somalis in the Twin Cities and Columbus

*Immigrant Incorporation
in New Destinations*

Stefanie Chambers

TEMPLE UNIVERSITY PRESS
Philadelphia • *Rome* • *Tokyo*

TEMPLE UNIVERSITY PRESS
Philadelphia, Pennsylvania 19122
www.temple.edu/tempress

Library of Congress Cataloging-in-Publication Data

Names: Chambers, Stefanie, author.
Title: Somalis in the Twin Cities and Columbus : immigrant incorporation in
   new destinations / Stefanie Chambers.
Description: Philadelphia : Temple University Press, 2017. | Includes
   bibliographical references and index.
Identifiers: LCCN 2016042256 | ISBN 9781439914410 (hardback : alk. paper) |
   ISBN 9781439914427 (paper : alk. paper) | ISBN 9781439914434 (ebook)
Subjects: LCSH: Somali Americans—Minnesota—Saint Paul. | Somali
   Americans—Ohio—Columbus. | Social integration—Minnesota—Saint Paul. |
   Social integration—Ohio—Columbus. | Immigrants—Minnesota—Saint Paul. |
   Immigrants—Ohio—Columbus. | Saint Paul (Minn.)—Social conditions. |
   Saint Paul (Minn.)—Ethnic relations. | Columbus (Ohio)—Social
   conditions. | Columbus (Ohio)—Ethnic relations. | BISAC: SOCIAL SCIENCE /
   Emigration & Immigration. | POLITICAL SCIENCE / Public Policy / Social
   Policy. | POLITICAL SCIENCE / Civics & Citizenship.
Classification: LCC F614.S4 C56 2017 | DDC 305.893/540776581—dc23
LC record available at https://lccn.loc.gov/2016042256

Printed in the United States of America

9 8 7 6 5 4 3 2 1

For my children, Owen and Olivia,
and my nephew, Sebastian

Contents

List of Figures and Tables

Figures

Tables

Acknowledgments

In 1994, I moved to Columbus, Ohio, to begin my graduate studies at The Ohio State University. During the five years I spent there, I was unaware of the influx of Somalis into my community. I might point to dedication to my studies as one explanation for this oversight, but as I reflect on my graduate education, I realize that it was more likely naiveté that caused my inattention to the demographic changes in the city.

In 2012, I was drawn back to Columbus, a majority white city with a minority mayor (in this case, African American), for an article I was writing on that topic. Much of my fieldwork took place with African American respondents in Columbus. Fond memories of the city and the connection I felt doing research in African American communities made the trips feel like coming home. What surprised me most were the demographic changes in Columbus's historic black neighborhoods: by then, Somalis were an easily identifiable group in these communities and in others that I visited during my trips.

Once my piece on the mayor was published in *21st Century Urban Race Politics: Representing Minorities as Universal Interests* (2013), I started researching Somalis in Columbus. I was intrigued to learn that Columbus was home to the second-largest Somali population in the United States. My interest increased as I explored the reasons for this phenomenon and visualized new lines of research on the Somali experience in Ohio. My research to that point had focused on urban politics and governance, racial and ethnic politics, and urban education policy. Broadening my research to include the migration literature appealed to me as an interesting challenge. Because so many Columbus respondents referenced the Twin Cities and because that region contains the largest Somali population, I decided to design a comparative case study on Somali incorporation in Columbus and the Twin Cities.

As I moved forward with data collection and field research, one of my colleagues encouraged me yet cautioned me about the challenges I might encounter as a woman and a non-Somali. But as it turned out, Somalis in Columbus and in the Twin Cities welcomed me with open arms. Given my inability to speak Somali, my lack of training in the Islamic tradition, and my rudimentary understanding of Somali homeland history, the openness of the Somali respondents in both regions was extraordinary. My respondents encouraged me to ask questions and then patiently educated me on a range of issues. Without their exceptional cooperation and assistance, this book would not have been possible.

At Trinity College, where I have spent the majority of my academic career, I am deeply indebted to several colleagues who helped me develop this project. I am particularly grateful to Zayde Antrim, Diana Evans, Tony Messina, and Abby Williamson, each of whom read draft chapters and provided important feedback. Tony Messina read the entire manuscript and offered his expert guidance on a range of theoretical and practical issues. Serena Laws and my good friend Roger Kittleson, at Williams College, spent considerable time reading sections of the manuscript. Sonia Cardenas, Andy Flibbert, Isaac Kamola, Reo Matsuzaki, Lida Maxwell, Kevin McMahon, and Mary Beth White each played a role in creating a rich intellectual community for me as I worked. President Joanne Berger-Sweeney and Deans Tom Mitzel and Melanie Stein offered vital support and encouraged me to prioritize the research for this book. Trinity College's Faculty Research Committee and the American Political Science Association provided generous funding that made the research possible. I am also extremely grateful to the committee that awarded me the Charles A. Dana Research Associate Professorship.

Rachael Barlow, then the social science data coordinator at Trinity College, was enormously helpful with quantitative data collection and analysis. Dave Tatem, Erin Valentino, and Rob Walsh were also valuable library and IT resources. Several Trinity College research assistants helped me at various stages of the research and writing processes. Nasri Abdulai, Jessica Bosco, Julianna Maisano, and Kyle Pulik each contributed greatly to this project. A special thank-you goes to Will Schreiber-Stainthorp, one of my Posse Scholars. In addition to co-authoring an article with me as an undergraduate, Will read the entire manuscript and provided feedback that was as good as any that I might receive from my colleagues who hold doctoral degrees.

The brilliant scholarship of Ahmed Yusuf—specifically, his book *Somalis in Minnesota*—helped me get my bearings as I expanded this project from Columbus to the Twin Cities. Kadra Abdi and Charley Keys were also incredibly helpful with data collection on Somali homeownership.

A number of friends deserve special mention. During the research for this book, I was diagnosed with cancer. My group of cycling friends showered me with love and helped my entire family cope with the fear and uncertainty we faced. Cathy Curis, Debbie Doucette, Mariann Fiori, Jill Harvey, and Diane Tucker were simply incredible friends. Zayde Antrim, August Kittleson, and Roger Kittleson were always there for us with comforting conversation and reminders of the important things in life. Mandi Hanes, then the senior admissions director at Trinity College, was also a gem. The extended Doucette family, especially Christopher, Claire (my former Trinity College student), and Rick, also helped me during this difficult time. Colleen Keane, even from a distance, also stood by my side, as she has done since we were in kindergarten. I thank them all.

Other friends and colleagues who played a role in the production of this book include Tony Affigne, Laurel Elder, Emily Farris, Melissa Michelson, the late William E. Nelson Jr., Barbara Sicherman, and Evelyn Simien. And, of course, I owe a great deal to my extended family. My mother, Donna Pollock, planted the initial seed that helped me to develop into the scholar I am today. My in-laws, Betty and Jim Chambers, took care of my daughter during several research trips to the Midwest. Bruce and Carol Lambert, my brother-in-law and sister-in-law, made my daughter's time in the Midwest magical. My nephew and niece, Aleksis and Allison Kincaid, put me up on their couch in Minneapolis on more than one occasion.

On the home front, I was fortunate to have an amazing family who understood how important this project was to me. This book would not have come to fruition without their support. My husband, Joe, held down the fort when my research took me away from home. His loving encouragement has always fueled my work, and his keen eye and intellect helped shape this book. My children, Owen and Olivia, each became mini-experts on the Somali experience in America. Owen joined me for a trip to Columbus, and Olivia joined me in the Twin Cities. They made Somali friends, sampled Somali food, sat in on English classes for new refugees, and generally soaked up the experience. Owen and I also wrote together on many occasions—I worked on this book, and he worked on his novel. I love each of them with all my heart.

Last, but not least, I am grateful to Aaron Javsicas, editor-in-chief at Temple University Press, and his entire team for their continued interest in my work. Their efficiency, professionalism, and adherence to deadlines all contribute to my loyalty as a repeat author. This is my second experience publishing a book with the staff at Temple, and I can only sing their praises. I also wish to thank the anonymous reviewers who provided feedback that strengthened the quality of this book. Finally, Heather Wilcox was a fantastic copyeditor.

1 /

Immigrant Incorporation in New Destinations

Every year, thousands of people enter the United States as legal immigrants. They arrive seeking jobs, family, democracy, safety, asylum, or one of the innumerable other desires that push and pull people across the globe. But although it is challenging, successfully migrating to the United States is only the first step in a long path to fulfilling the American dream. To continue their progress—and turn their new land into their new home—immigrants must be incorporated into the society they have entered. Although incorporation exists across many domains, three of the most important are political, economic, and social. Together, these metrics serve as a fairly comprehensive measure of how well immigrants assimilate into the country as a whole. By examining these three metrics, we can better understand how different communities adapt to life in the United States, identify which communities are most vulnerable, and attempt to see why they are vulnerable in an effort to facilitate a smoother transition into American society.

Minneapolis and St. Paul, Minnesota (the Twin Cities), and Columbus, Ohio, are home to the largest Somali communities in the United States. The political, economic, and social positions of Somalis in the

Twin Cities are more promising than those of Somalis in Columbus, Ohio. Several Somali Americans in Minneapolis serve in local elected office, and the Twin Cities boast an impressive group of Somali American economic and intellectual leaders. There are also noteworthy examples of social inclusion and cohesive relationships between Somali and Anglo Minnesotans. In Columbus, Somali incorporation in these realms is less vibrant, and the position of Somali immigrants more stark. No Somali official has been elected at the city or state level, and the community is relatively isolated in terms of economic and social incorporation.

This book examines the question of how two midwestern urban areas with roughly similar Somali refugee populations could end up with quite different levels of Somali incorporation. Understanding the different integration outcomes in areas like Columbus and the Twin Cities is important for policy makers, scholars of immigrant incorporation, Somalis who establish roots in these areas, and residents at large. Recent attention to a few Somali links to terrorist organizations has increased the relevance of this book because of the special challenges of immigrant incorporation during times of security crisis or threat.

Case Selection and Generalizability

The two communities discussed in this book differ in their levels of Somali political, economic, and social incorporation. Somalis arrived slightly earlier in the Twin Cities area (in the early 1990s), and their population increased at a more rapid pace than in Columbus. Today, the area boasts the largest Somali community in the United States. In this book, the term "Twin Cities" is used because of the proximity of the two cities of Minneapolis and St. Paul. Although the majority of Somali organizations and activities occur in Minneapolis, it would be misguided to overlook the role of St. Paul, the state capital, in this portrait. The Twin Cities area has also welcomed other refugee communities, including the Hmong, since the 1970s. Although Minnesota has had some anti-immigrant and conservative politicians, the state is generally known for its progressive political traditions. At the local level, a number of very supportive elected officials in

Minneapolis are members of the Democratic-Farmer-Labor Party. Even some Republican candidates have made direct appeals for the Somali vote. Moreover, the ward-based electoral system has opened doors for Somali elected officials. Under the ward system, candidates who receive the plurality of votes in an individual ward win a seat on an elective body. Minneapolis and St. Paul also use the single-trans-ferrable vote system, allowing voters to rank their candidate choices, something civil rights theorist Lani Guinier advocates as a method for giving underrepresented groups a better chance of winning elections (McClain and Stewart 2010, 62). The regional reputation of "Minnesota Nice" has also created a welcoming environment for new citizens, at least on the surface. Although benefits for Somali immigrants have shrunk significantly since 2000, the state has a reputation for generous social service assistance (Ali 2011; Fennelly 2006b). The Twin Cities also boast a number of Somali and East African community organizations interested in advancing Somali interests or supporting the community. Finally, the union-friendly environment of the area has opened doors for the political mobilization of Somalis through labor organization and apprenticeship programs.

In contrast to the Twin Cities, the Somali refugee population began arriving in Columbus slightly later (in the early to mid-1990s), with the pace of arrival increasing toward the end of this period, especially as Somalis moved from Minneapolis or other cities to Columbus as a secondary destination. Ohio is a more politically conservative state, and the political, economic, and social opportunities available to immigrant groups are somewhat limited when compared to Minneapolis. One demonstration of this can be seen in Ohio's social service benefits, which have traditionally been less substantial than those offered by Minnesota (although, as mentioned above, benefits in Minnesota have been scaled back to levels closer to those in Ohio). Nevertheless, other structural differences in Columbus result in different—and generally poorer—outcomes for Somalis. For example, Columbus has an at-large electoral structure for the city council, making it difficult for minority communities to achieve descriptive representation. Economic organizations that encourage Somali businesses by arranging financial workshops and by making available loans that comply with Islamic law are absent in Columbus, although they play an important role in the Twin Cities. Columbus has its own Somali community organizations, but only a few have succeeded in achieving a stable level of organizational capacity. Along the same lines, very few community organizations without a direct connection to Somalis have any Somali members. Finally, unionization of Somalis in Columbus is low, further limiting the ability of that population to gain experience in political mobilization. In other words, the Somali Columbus community is relatively insulated and faces obstacles to political, economic, and social progress that eclipse those seen in the Twin Cities.

The cities under investigation are similar with respect to the general economic situation of Somalis. Both cities have a modest Somali middle class and a large community subsisting on the margins. Whereas both cities were initially appealing locations for Somali refugees because of low-skill job opportunities in warehouses (Columbus) and in food-processing plants (Twin Cities), chances for upward mobility are limited (Golden, Garad, and Boyle 2011; Horst 2006; H. Samatar 2005; A. Waters 2012). Somali homeownership rates are extremely low in both cities, primarily because of general economic factors and adherence with Islamic legal restrictions on interest-bearing loans (Caeiro 2004). Combined with the fact that Somalis occupy low-paying positions, there is little capacity for building equity in the American tradition. Both communities also lack adequate educational opportunities for immigrant youth (Ali 2011; Fennelly 2006b; A. Waters 2012). In the social realm, Somalis in both cities struggle as "outsiders." They regularly face discrimination based on their religious traditions, dress, status as refugees, and skin color (Ali 2011; A. Waters 2012). As a result, the Somali communities in both areas under investigation experience challenges in terms of housing opportunities, job prospects, and overall inclusion. This de facto discrimination creates significant barriers for the community in general, and for individuals personally. Since 9/11, Somalis have also faced accusations that they are terrorists and have experienced hostility stemming from suspicions about their ties to al-Shabaab, al-Qaeda, and ISIS (Ali 2011; Elliott 2009; A. Waters 2012). The national fear of terrorist threats has increased the negative attention Somalis receive and reinforced misconceptions that Somali Americans are terrorists or sympathizers.

Although this book focuses on Somalis in two midwestern urban areas, the findings are valuable for other American cities where Somalis and other new immigrant communities are growing. A wide range of challenges faced—and continue to face—policy makers in the two urban areas under investigation, yet this study reveals that certain political structures, economic policies, and cultural programs can make the transition for Somalis and their host communities considerably easier. To create policies that facilitate the incorporation of new immigrant communities, policy makers must first understand the ways in which such communities can benefit the host community at large. This understanding is often missing from the political discourse about new immigrant communities, which, unfortunately, is often focused on the perceived "problems" associated with new immigrants. One infamous example of this political shortsightedness was the 2002 plea from Laurier Raymond, the former mayor of Lewiston, Maine, for Somalis to stop coming to his city. That plea aside, Lewiston's economic revival occurred in large part as a result of Somalis' participation in the local economy. Somalis bolstered the labor force by taking low-paying jobs and renting apartments in a housing market with a surplus of vacant rental properties. Despite the challenges that Somalis once faced in Lewiston, they are now viewed as an important part of the community. A June 2014 statement by Domenic Sarno, the mayor of Springfield, Massachusetts, mirrored the unwelcoming message of Lewiston's former mayor a few years earlier: he called on the Massachusetts congressional delegation to help him stop refugee resettlement in his community because of the alleged burden these immigrants had placed on social service delivery (Lefrak 2014). Mayor Sarno's inability to see how new Americans could help revitalize the economy of Springfield, an economically depressed industrial hub, is a concern—especially since the city will need a large supply of blue-collar workers to launch the MGM Casino that was recently approved to be built (Lefrak 2014). The Lewiston and Springfield examples illustrate the continuing need for research that helps policy makers better understand the benefits of a new immigrant community not only to the economy but also to the political and social climates of their cities. Beyond the need for domestic policy makers to understand these issues, there is a growing desire among leaders in other countries with large Somali populations to understand how the Twin Cities have succeeded with Somali incorporation. Understanding the complex reality of this area's "success story" relative to other cities requires a thorough evaluation to determine what has gone right and where there is room for improvement.

The comparative aspect of this book is both novel and immensely valuable for those who wish to understand immigrant incorporation. Minneapolis is viewed around the world, particularly in Scandinavian countries where the Somali diaspora is growing, as a model for Somali integration. Other American mayors, such as the mayor of Portland, Oregon, have visited Minneapolis to learn about policies that can help their cities better address the needs of Somali immigrants. The interest in Minneapolis is important, but challenges to Somali incorporation remain in the Twin Cities that are overlooked by those who view it purely as a Somali-immigrant success story. This study sheds light on the successes *and* on the areas for improvement in the Twin Cities. On the other hand, examining Columbus allows policy makers, scholars, and stakeholders an opportunity to understand how immigrant incorporation has unfolded in a very different political and public-policy climate.

This book assesses the political, economic, and social variations between the Columbus and the Twin Cities to examine how culture and history influenced the incorporation of Somali immigrants and recommends policy changes that can advance the incorporation of Somalis in both areas. Using a combination of qualitative and quantitative data, this two-case ethnographic study on a relatively understudied community establishes a new stream of research. The findings provide a template for scholars and policy makers examining other cities with large refugee populations. Along the same lines, this project offers a model that can conceivably be applied in a larger study that includes multiple cases. As such, it demonstrates the importance of a number of indicators of political incorporation, indicators that could be used in a large-N quantitative study of political incorporation in American cities and towns. The research for this investigation of two Somali communities relied heavily on fieldwork, participant observation, and interviews with Somali residents and policy makers who have sought to increase Somali incorporation in these communities since the population expanded in both areas in the mid-1990s. Particularly when quantitative data were unavailable, these interviews provided essential information necessary to assess the degree to which Somalis have been incorporated. The use of interpretive methods is common in the subfield of racial and ethnic politics, "center[ing] on approaches to political understanding that aim to clarify or illuminate meaning and/or significance of political phenomena" (Schmidt 2015, 367). The voices and perspectives of Somalis in this study complement the data collected in each city and the existent scholarly literature on immigrant incorporation in urban America. Better understanding immigrant incorporation in contemporary urban areas allows policy makers, scholars, and immigrant community leaders the chance to observe the challenges and opportunities new groups face. These observations, in turn, hold the promise that policy can be developed that supports the incorporation of immigrants and benefits the community at large.

Examining the political, economic, and social incorporation of Somalis is a usefully broad method of evaluating various areas of immigrant incorporation. Although they overlap in a variety of ways, these three measures of incorporation provide a robust assessment of the Somali experience in their two largest American destination communities. Examining all three variables is essential, because omitting any one would paint an incomplete picture of the context of Somali incorporation. For example, examining only the political context for Somalis would risk undervaluing the role that local foundations can play in supporting the Somali community (a measure of social incorporation). Similarly, overlooking the ways in which Islamic legal restrictions on interest-bearing loans are related to economic advancement (a measure of economic incorporation) would lead to a failure to understand the ways in which homeownership and home equity are traditionally connected to political opportunities in the United States and, ultimately, political incorporation. Although electoral structures, the number of elected and appointed officials, and governing coalitions are important measures of political incorporation, they are not sufficient to understand the Somali experience in the contemporary urban context. Other factors, such as union influence, party outreach, Somali voting trends, bureaucratic outreach, and the influence of community groups, help contextualize Somali political incorporation.

Previous scholarly literature assumed that after an initial period of transition, new immigrant groups would eventually surmount the barriers to political, economic, and social integration (Park 1928)—the classic, romanticized narrative of nineteenth-century European immigration to the United States. In contrast to the European experience, Somalis came to the United States primarily as part of the fallout from a civil war, often carrying religious and cultural beliefs that have complicated the process of assimilation. Some Somalis have also experienced the impediment of limited English-language skills. Furthermore, American misconceptions about Somalis have created an additional hurdle for their full inclusion in society. The fact that Somalis have settled in several nontraditional or "new" immigrant destinations (e.g., Columbus, Ohio, and Lewiston, Maine) makes examining the factors that help with incorporation particularly compelling. The implications of policies that encourage or impede Somali incorporation in midsize cities are relevant for Somalis and other new immigrant groups with characteristics that differ significantly from the local culture and religious norms in their receiving communities. Minneapolis and St. Paul are considered midsize cities, and they have a history of welcoming immigrant groups. At the same time, their experience with new immigrant communities is just one factor that contributes to Somali incorporation. A range of other factors influence the relatively greater degree of incorporation as well as the ongoing challenges of this community in the Twin Cities. The research underlying this book is unique because it reveals the factors that support or impede Somali incorporation; moreover, the findings described herein provide the basis for specific policy recommendations that can increase incorporation in the cities under investigation and beyond. These findings can potentially help cities domestically and abroad reap information about the incorporation of new immigrant communities under different political, economic, and social conditions. Attention to the social incorporation of an immigrant community during times of suspected terrorist links is also a unique contribution of this book. As concerns about global terrorist threats increase, it is imperative that governments create policies that target terrorist groups without discriminating against a community based on ethnic group affiliations. This is a challenge for all governments, but one where American policy makers in particular have fallen short, with the treatment of Japanese Americans and German Americans during World War II serving as notable examples.

Theoretical Underpinnings: Comparative Research, the "Context of Reception," and State Culture

Employing a comparative method to understand how urban areas or nations address political challenges is not new. In the domestic literature, Rufus P. Browning, Dale Rogers Marshall, and David H. Tabb's (1984) study on racial and ethnic coalitions in ten California cities was a seminal contribution. They discovered that minority group mobilization at the local level could lead to incorporation in city governance and, ultimately, to governmental responsiveness to minority residents' concerns. In her book *Mayors and Money* (1992), Ester Fuchs explores how political and economic decisions in New York and Chicago during the 1970s led to vastly different results. In Chicago, fiscal collapse and bailout were avoided because of governance and structural factors that New York lacked. The absence of such conditions in New York resulted in a fiscal crisis in the city in the 1970s. My book *Mayors and Schools* (2006) includes a similar methodology for understanding school-reform outcomes in two different midwestern cities—Chicago and Cleveland. In this case, divergent structural factors related to school governance resulted in different outcomes for minority communities served by the schools. In *Black Atlantic Politics* (2002), William E. Nelson Jr. adopts a comparative, transatlantic approach to understand how the slave trade and contemporary policies affect blacks in today's Boston and Liverpool, England. Examining cities with some general similarities but also important differences can aid in understanding the implications of policy choices. This is important for not only scholars of urban, racial, and ethnic politics but also policy makers, who are often forced to rapidly make decisions that have an impact on the lives of urban residents.

On the international front, one of the most important scholarly contributions to comparative migration research is Irene Bloemraad's *Becoming a Citizen* (2006). By examining the citizenship process for labor migrants and refugees in the United States and Canada, Bloemraad demonstrates that government policies affect immigrant incorporation. Canada's immigrant incorporation outcomes are significantly better than those of the United States as a result of the former's multicultural and interventionist immigrant policies. More specifically, Canada's active support of the naturalization process contributes to higher rates of citizenship and retention of cultural identity. A government-led effort to increase naturalization is not a major priority of the U.S. system; rather, the cultural assimilation of newcomers is encouraged. Bloemraad also finds that the Canadian system is more conducive to formal immigrant political representation, something much less prevalent in the United States. These findings are particularly relevant to this book in terms of electoral opportunities for new immigrant communities in the two regions under investigation. Although each city is part of the same nation, differences in local political structures lead to a range of political outcomes. Examining these differences is important, but it is also critical to consider national factors in the United States that create challenges for new Americans.

Like the studies highlighted above, this book identifies factors that contribute to different incorporation levels in an effort to offer specific policy recommendations. Both regions have histories of relative homogeneity and roots in European immigration. Columbus and St. Paul are also state capitals. In both cities, Somalis are concentrated in low-wage and low-skill jobs. Both areas appear to have high levels of residential and economic segregation, such as Somali businesses and shopping being isolated in certain areas of the city. In assessing these differences, the "most similar design" or "Mill's method of difference" is used, which consists of comparing very similar cases that differ only in the dependent variable (Etzioni and DuBow 1970).

Beyond the comparative approach, another important concept applied in this book is the "context of reception" developed by Alejandro Portes and Rubén Rumbaut (2006). Migrants arrive in new destinations with human capital that influences their experiences as they assimilate. Human capital is just one of the factors that is important in the context of reception, or the conditions under which assimilation takes place. This context is determined by the policies of the receiving government, labor-market factors, and the character of the new ethnic community (139). In many respects, these conditions parallel the analysis of Somali political, economic, and social incorporation used in this book. More specifically, the policies of the receiving government align with political incorporation, labor-market factors reflect economic incorporation, and social incorporation can be evaluated through the lens of the human capital of the Somali community. Such political, economic, and social conditions shape this examination of the context of reception in Columbus and the Twin Cities.

Finally, this study takes advantage of the research on state culture to better position the two cases in a national context. The classic works of Daniel Elazar on state culture and Robert Putnam's state social capital analysis, for example, contextualize Ohio and Minnesota in useful ways. Elazar's *Exploring Federalism* (1987) offers a detailed analysis of state culture across the United States. In his book, Elazar distinguishes between three types of political cultures: moralistic, traditionalistic, and individualistic. Each of the three typologies differs in terms of the conceptions about the role of government and the individual in society.

According to Elazar, moralistic states include government structures that support the public good and where citizen participation is of paramount importance. Traditionalistic states view the relationship between the government and citizens hierarchically, with the government in the preeminent position. The government is tasked with providing stability, and citizens are expected to abide by established rules. Finally, the individualistic state falls somewhere between the moralistic and traditionalistic. Under the individualistic model, the government's role is to support the marketplace and advance individual and private interests. Citizens are neither expected to be active participants in the political sphere (moralistic), nor are they seen as subordinate to the government (traditionalistic). Rather, the individual has the freedom to be active or not in the political process. As Chapters 2 and 3 discuss, Elazar classifies Ohio as an individualistic state, whereas Minnesota is considered moralistic.

Putnam is best known for his research on social capital. In *Bowling Alone* (2000), his classic text on the subject, he argues that the United

States has experienced a dramatic decline in social capital since the 1960s and 1970s. Putnam defines social capital as "connections among individuals—social networks and the norms of reciprocity and trustworthiness that arise from them" (19). He finds the decline in social capital troubling and observable through such measures as a decline in union participation, a drop in PTO meeting attendance, and an erosion of membership in political parties, among other indicators. For the purposes of this book, his findings on social capital in the fifty states are more important. Putnam creates a comprehensive Social Capital Index based on a fourteen-point analysis of community networks and social trust, including such measures as volunteering for activities, attending public meetings, and serving as a leader in an organization. In this index, Minnesota is designated as "very high" in social capital, while Ohio falls in the middle. Interestingly, Putnam then examines a range of policy areas across the states to illustrate that the results of his Social Capital Index align with the results from other national studies. The policy areas he discusses include, for example, children's welfare, education, public safety, general health, and fewer violations of tax law. For the purposes of this project, and in line with Putnam's findings, Minnesota consistently outperforms Ohio in all the policy areas he explores.

Midwestern Migration

To appreciate the difficulty of the journey from the northeastern coast of Africa to the midwestern United States, one must first understand the political, economic, and social situations of the Somali refugees. In 1960, Somalia was carved out of former Italian and British colonies. During the Cold War, it served as a proxy for the United States and for the Soviet Union in the bitter battle to control the strategic Horn of Africa (International Crisis Group 2008). While he was in power from 1969 to 1991, long-time leader Mohamed Siad Barre's kinship group benefitted from widespread corruption fueled by foreign aid, which inspired frustration and envy among rival groups. Siad Barre's brutal suppression of uprisings in turn led to his eventual ouster in January 1991 (International Crisis Group 2008). The ensuing vacuum was rapidly filled by rival "political faction leaders-turned-warlords" (International Crisis Group 2008).

By 1992, the combination of drought and the political, economic, and social collapse in Somalia resulted in the death of twenty-five thousand Somalis (Healy and Bradbury 2010). In 1992, the United States led an attempt to protect food provisions for famine victims and to eventually oust the dominant faction leader, Mohamed Farah Aidid. Yet the United States withdrew in late 1993 after a botched military operation resulted in the deaths of eighteen U.S. service members—a tragedy that horrified the American people, haunted American military forces, and inspired the film *Black Hawk Down* (2001).

In 1991, thousands of Somalis fled their home country to seek refuge. Many traveled to refugee camps in Kenya and were later assigned to new refugee resettlement locations in the United States and other nations by the United Nations High Commissioner for Refugees (UNHCR). For those assigned to the United States, the State Department coordinates with UNHCR to connect refugees with the Office of Refugee Resettlement (ORR) within the U.S. Department of Health and Human Services. From there, ORR works with voluntary agencies in different geographical areas in the United States to resettle refugees. Many voluntary agencies are religious-based organizations, including Jewish Family Service, Lutheran Social Services, Catholic Charities USA, or Arrive Ministries, in the case of the Twin Cities. These organizations assist with an array of services, including English-language education, housing, health care, and general acclimation for the first ninety days a refugee is in the country (DeRusha 2011). Voluntary agencies have played an important role in immigrant resettlement since the late 1800s (Forrest and Brown 2014).

In the early 1990s, cities commonly associated with the relocation of Somalis included Minneapolis, Minnesota; Norfolk, Virginia; and Seattle, Washington. By 1994, Columbus, Ohio, was another popular destination city. As time passed, some refugees migrated to secondary locations as they learned of new opportunities in other American cities. The process of secondary migration has been, and remains, very common among Somalis. What are easy to overlook are the costs associated with leaving their initial placement cities. Beyond the fact that moving can be costly, federal benefits do not follow refugees if they leave their assigned homes in the United States. In other words, for poor refugees, such as Somalis, mobility comes at a considerable price.

When Somali refugees first started to migrate to the United States, the majority settled in Minnesota and Virginia. The Twin Cities have a particularly positive track record with refugee resettlement as a result of the Hmong refugee establishment in the region beginning in the late 1970s (Yusuf 2012), but Somalis in Virginia found the cost of living high and had trouble finding jobs. Similarly, other Somalis who had originally settled in San Diego later migrated to the Twin Cities in search of jobs, a lower cost of living, and a vibrant Somali community. Columbus's abundance of factory and warehouse jobs, coupled with low rental rates, made the city an attractive secondary relocation destination for Somalis who were not assigned there by the ORR. Somalis who initially settled in Columbus shared news of job opportunities and housing affordability. Later, waves of secondary migrants told friends and relatives in other American cities of their improved living situations in Columbus, and the region became a popular new destination. Before long, Columbus was one of the foremost secondary destinations for Somalis in the United States.

Today, Columbus ranks second in the United States in the size of its Somali population, behind Minneapolis and ahead of such cities as the District of Columbia, Seattle, Norfolk, and Lewiston. Figure 1.1 illustrates the concentration of Somalis in the United States. The data are derived from the county-level data available through the American Community Survey estimates from 2006 to 2010. Estimates vary regarding how many Somalis have made a home in Franklin County, where Columbus is located. On the low end, the U.S. Census reports that fewer than ten thousand Somalis reside in Columbus. By contrast, the book *The Somali Diaspora* reports that roughly forty-five thousand Somalis call Columbus home (Roble and Rutledge 2008). The precise number of Somalis matters less for the purposes of this research than does the fact that a sizable population exists. The population of Somalis in the Twin Cities is significantly larger than the population in Columbus, although the exact population is again

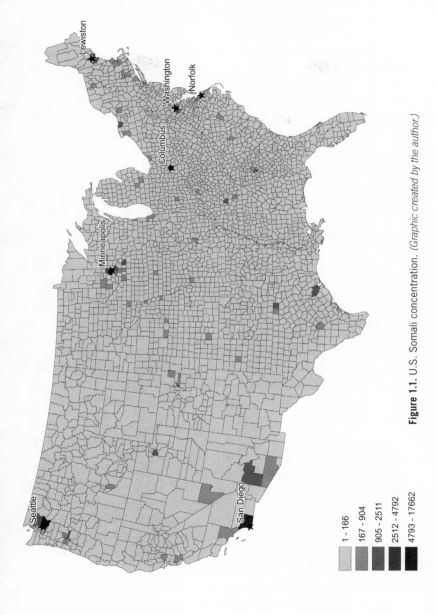

Figure 1.1. U.S. Somali concentration. *(Graphic created by the author.)*

1 - 166
167 - 904
905 - 2511
2512 - 4792
4793 - 17662

difficult to estimate. In describing the complication associated with Somali population estimates, Cindy Horst writes:

> It is likely that official census figures greatly underestimate actual numbers, as many Somali extended families live in one house with larger numbers than allowed, so they underreport their numbers. Public school enrollment and welfare statistics suggest a range of fifteen thousand to thirty thousand Somalis in Minnesota, a number that is still growing. (2006, 8)

Tracking Somali secondary migration complicates population estimates further. Not surprisingly, many of the individuals included as respondents in this study were originally sent to a different city in the United States and migrated to Columbus or Minneapolis after hearing reports about opportunities in these destinations.

Refugees or Immigrants?

Characterizing Somalis as either refugees or immigrants is complicated. On the one hand, the majority of Somalis with roots in the Twin Cities and Columbus arrived in the United States as refugees in the 1990s. There are also many native-born Somali Americans since the population has had time to grow since the 1990s. The majority of Somalis migrated to their new American destinations as refugees but have since become citizens of the United States. The Somali scholar Ahmed Samatar writes:

> A *refugee* . . . is an individual who is unable to find a modicum of shelter and safety in his/her homeland or decides that what is available is so unappealing and unappetizing that becoming a brittle, and at times unwanted foreigner is a preferable fate. (2008, 5; emphasis original)

For decades, thousands of Somalis have lived in squalid conditions in Kenyan refugee camps after being forced from their homes in Somalia. For those who are willing and able to build a new life outside their homeland, immigration is an option. As Samatar explains:

The category of *immigrant* is designated to describe one who has made an autonomous and personal choice of "creative destruction" to seek membership in another society—an act that can be either temporary or could culminate in new citizenship. (2008, 5; emphasis original)

Somalis in this study are characterized as immigrants, because most made the courageous decision to become residents and/or American citizens. For many, this decision was difficult because of their love for their country of origin. At the same time, a majority of the respondents in this study identify as Somali Americans and place a very high value on civic engagement in their adopted country. Even among those firmly rooted in the United States, there is a contingent of Somalis in both cities who return to areas in Somalia to pursue humanitarian work or visit family. For Somali youth, many of whom have spent most of their lives in the United States or who are native-born U.S. citizens, ties to Somalia are often weaker. In this sense, there are generational effects within the community, which are discussed in later chapters.

General Social Services for Refugees

The social service benefits available to refugees include a combination of federal benefits and a range of state, local, and nonprofit benefits, depending on the state and locality where a refugee establishes roots. Several key national events have influenced refugee resettlement in the United States. The overarching pattern involves a relatively open process in the mid–twentieth century, with major changes beginning in the 1980s that have restricted social service benefits for refugees, particularly as a result of welfare reform and changing attitudes in the wake of the terrorist attacks of 2001.

After World War II, the 1949 guidelines established by the United Nations (UN) Geneva Conventions created general humanitarian standards for working with refugees. The United States accepted these guidelines and started receiving refugees through an ad hoc process. In 1980, during President Jimmy Carter's administration, the Refugee Act created a clearer and more comprehensive system of benefits for refugees. Together with the Hart-Celler Immigration Act of 1965, which abolished a quota system and significantly broadened immigration from Asia and Africa, the Refugee Act established a new and more humanitarian system of refugee resettlement (Ali 2011, 88).

The mid-1980s marked the beginning of the erosion of refugee support and social service benefits (Ali 2011, 88). The nation's welfare policies came under attack during President Ronald Reagan's administration, and refugees did not escape the misperception that they too were abusing the public assistance program, much like the infamous "welfare queens" Reagan bashed. The conservative assault on publically financed social services continued and was ultimately embraced by Democrats, who supported the passage of the Personal Responsibility and Work Opportunity Reconciliation Act (PRWORA) in 1996 (Fennelly 2006a, 31). This law shifted the administration of welfare benefits from the federal government to the states. Reductions in federal funds to the states created a situation in which states were incentivized to reduce benefits for different categories of immigrants (31). The PRWORA also established a five-year lifetime limit on welfare benefits for all recipients (Ali 2011, 91). Another provision stated that noncitizens, including refugees, were eligible for welfare benefits only during their first five years in the United States—regardless of whether they received those benefits for the entirety of that duration (91). This seemingly small provision created a two-tiered system of benefits that would negatively affect new refugees.

In 1997, refugees experienced another blow. Most refugees are deeply committed to helping family members left behind in their homeland. Beyond remittances that provide some financial support to loved ones, there is often the hope of family reunification in the United States. After a year in the United States, refugees become permanent residents and are eligible for citizenship. Among the provisions of the 1996 Illegal Immigration Reform and Immigrant Responsibility Act was the new rule that nonrefugee immigrants could remain in the United States only if they were "sponsored" by a family member, friend, or employer (Ali 2011, 93). Sponsors would be responsible for all financial needs, and the newcomer would forfeit access to welfare benefits for their first five years in the country (93). For former refugees who could get a family member into the United

States, their desperation for their loved ones' safety prompted them to sign virtually any document that would keep their relatives in the country legally, regardless of whether they had the means to support another person (Twin Cities community member interview, May 31, 2014). The economic strain this has placed on already financially strapped families is considerable.

The terrorist attacks of September 11, 2001, also negatively affected refugee policies in the United States. A new federal program, the National Security Entry-Exit Registration System (NSEERS), required men from Arab and Muslim countries to register with the federal government and agree to annual government interviews (Ali 2011, 95). Somalis were categorized within this system, and the new guidelines created tremendous stress and anxiety in their community, particularly for those who had experienced horrific governmental abuse in their homeland (Twin Cities community member interview, June 1, 2014). NSEERS was implemented at the same time that the number of refugees admitted to the United States was being curtailed. To make matters worse, the federal government cut cash benefits for refugees from thirty-six months to eight months of coverage (Ali 2011, 97; Fennelly 2006b). Today, responsibility falls on state and local governments, voluntary agencies, and individual families to provide adequate economic safeguards for new arrivals. Depending on the state and nonprofit community, a range of benefits are available to the small number of new refugees who arrive in the United States today. Even a state like Minnesota, known for its progressive social service benefits, had imposed significant benefit reductions since 2000. Between state and federal cuts, the United States has entered a new, less generous era in refugee social service benefit provisions.

Methodology

Each type of incorporation is evaluated based on a range of related indicators in each area under investigation. Based on variation between Somali communities in Columbus and the Twin Cities, comparisons and insights are offered in light of the conditions that contribute to different levels of incorporation in each geographic area based on extensive interviews and data collection. The findings gleaned from this process contribute to an understanding of the phenomenon of immigrant incorporation in American cities.

The political incorporation measure draws on the work of Browning, Marshall, and Tabb (1984). Like them, I argue that political incorporation is a measure of how well group interests are reflected in policy making and the level of a group's engagement in the political system. As Chapter 4 demonstrates, political incorporation is higher for new immigrant groups in cities with ward-based elections, where parties engage in immigrant outreach, politicians include the group in electoral and governing coalitions, city bureaucrats attempt to support the new Americans, there is a tradition of union outreach, and competition is low between ethnic community organizations.

In the case of the Twin Cities, ward-based elections, partisan outreach, inclusion in electoral and governing coalitions, strong Somali union membership, and lower levels of competition between Somali community organizations make that region more conducive to Somali political incorporation than Columbus. The findings in this regard are applicable beyond Somali Americans and can be considered relevant for other immigrants in metropolitan America. In other words, several of the positive indicators of political incorporation offer parallel benefits in cities across the country.

Immigrant economic incorporation can be measured by the extent to which a group has full access to opportunities for upward economic mobility. Economic incorporation for new immigrant communities will remain low in the absence of economic policies and specific efforts from the public sector to assist with upward mobility. Although there are slight differences in the degree of economic incorporation in both areas under investigation, with the Twin Cities being slightly better for Somalis, serious obstacles to upward mobility remain in both areas. Employment data, homeownership rates, small-business opportunities, and extended family obligations are considered to reveal evidence of the economic incorporation of Somalis in the Twin Cities and Columbus. Additionally, in both areas, the roles of nongovernmental organizations (NGOs) and nonprofits are considered as they relate to economic incorporation. Small-business loans that comply with Islamic law also receive attention, because some interpretations of Islamic teachings reject any form of interest-bearing loans—an additional hurdle for Somali entrepreneurs. Economic incorporation is also examined through the lens of Somali employment in the public and private sectors.

Finally, social incorporation for new immigrant communities is a measure of the extent to which a group is accepted by mainstream society and the group's perceptions of acceptance in the host society. Social incorporation is higher when an area has a history of welcoming previous refugee communities, where opinions included in the local media reflect favorably on immigrants, where local philanthropic organizations support the immigrant community, and where police departments pay special attention to recruiting and promoting immigrant officers. The police measure of social incorporation is important, because minority representation in law enforcement can increase levels of community trust and help nonminority officers understand traditions and customs of the minority community. Given the attention Somalis receive from federal agencies regarding terrorist connections, it is even more important that they view the local police as a force that understands and respects the Somali community.

The slightly more promising level of social incorporation for Somalis in the Twin Cities is related to the region's tradition of welcoming refugee communities, the support of Somali-based projects by the philanthropic community, and the unique strategies that have created a base of Somali police officers in that region. At the same time, even cities without a long history of welcoming refugee communities can make progress toward higher levels of social incorporation. Columbus, for example, has taken some modest, although important, steps toward social incorporation, despite the fact that the city is not a traditional refugee settlement site. Letters to newspaper editors in Columbus and in the Twin Cities reveal similar levels of Somali incorporation in these regions.

In terms of similarities in social incorporation, Somalis in both cities have experienced overt examples of discrimination. In fact, the discrimination against Somalis in the Twin Cities appears more extreme on the surface and more numerous, as documented by the local media. This tension notwithstanding, Minneapolis is still regarded as the better city for Somalis to reside in by virtually all the Somali respondents in this study. Still, residential segregation remains high in both of the communities under investigation. More importantly, the Twin Cities receive considerable national attention because of suspicion and some documented instances of recruiting by al-Shabaab and ISIS. Somalis across the country risk discrimination and assumptions about their supposed links to terrorist networks, making life difficult for the majority of the population, which has absolutely no links to any terrorist groups. Given the government's and media's attention to Somali recruitment by al-Shabaab and ISIS for terrorist purposes, Somali incorporation in contemporary times is a highly sensitive issue. Understanding how to incorporate a community socially, especially when accusations of terrorist connections are swirling, is an issue that city, state, and federal leaders must handle delicately. Striking the balance between civil rights and liberties versus national security has long been a challenge in the United States. The experiences of German Americans—and, more significantly, Japanese Americans—in the United States during World War II do not inspire confidence. During the post-9/11 era, many social and political actors have struggled to combat discrimination against Muslims. This book aims to help policy makers and scholars think through ways of incorporating groups that are in danger of mistreatment because of their national origins, religious beliefs, or race.

Somali Voices: A Contextualized Methodological Approach

An essential component of this book is the use of in-depth interviews conducted in Columbus and the Twin Cities about the political, economic, and social incorporation of Somalis in these areas of study (see the questionnaire in Appendix A). A total of fifty interviews were completed in Columbus between July 2013 and October 2015. A series of follow-up interviews were conducted in 2015 with seven previous respondents, bringing the total number of interviews to fifty-seven. The Columbus portion of this book on Somali incorporation started a year earlier, while I was conducting research for a paper on new immigrant destinations. Of the forty-nine respondents in Columbus, all but seven were Somali Americans. Approximately 80 percent of the Somalis interviewed had moved to Columbus as secondary migrants. I made five research trips to Columbus, and the majority of respondents were interviewed in person. When that was not possible, I conducted phone interviews with respondents. I started with an initial list of Somali leaders, compiled with the assistance of the Columbus mayor's office. In addition, I connected with scholars at The Ohio State University to identify a preliminary list of important Somali leaders in Columbus. As the interviews progressed, I added new names to my list of potential respondents based on suggestions I received from those I interviewed. This method allowed me to interview a broad range of political, economic, and social leaders in the Somali community and non-Somalis with expertise on their incorporation in the city. Gaining credibility in the Somali community in Columbus would not have been possible without the assistance of the city's New American Initiative Office, an office within the Columbus mayor's office. A Somali representative from that office was my initial contact and ultimately helped with outreach in his community by talking to people about the importance of this project.

Using the same strategy in the Twin Cities, I conducted sixty-five interviews between April 2014 and June 2015. During 2015, thirteen respondents participated in follow-up interviews, bringing the total number of interviews to seventy-eight. The same strategy of creating an initial list of potential respondents was employed in the Twin Cities. Much to my advantage, a Somali American graduate of Trinity College, my employer, wrote a book on Somalis in Minnesota (Yusuf 2012). Through the help of this individual, I compiled my snowball sample and had an advocate who persuaded Somali leaders to speak with me. The vast majority of interviews conducted in the Twin Cities were with residents of Minneapolis or its suburbs. Forty-four of the respondents were Somali Americans. Approximately 50 percent of the Somali American respondents who were assigned by ORR to a city settled first in Minneapolis. I made a total of five research trips to the Twin Cities during the period when interviews were conducted.

Unlike participants in my previous research, which has relied on in-depth interviews with members of marginalized communities (Chambers 2006; Chambers and Nelson 2014; Chambers and Schreiber-Stainthorp 2013), Somalis were generally unwilling to have their interviews recorded, despite my promise of anonymity. In recent years, the Somali populations in both cities have experienced significant challenges in terms of negative mainstream media publicity. Assumptions about community connections to al-Shabaab, al-Qaeda, ISIS, or other stereotypical terrorist organizations made respondents uncomfortable with recordings, although they were willing to allow me to take detailed notes during our meetings. Interviews generally lasted between forty-five minutes and an hour, with outliers lasting several hours. Direct quotations appear throughout this book, although respondents are identified only by category—for example, Somali community member, Somali bureaucrat. The only exceptions are elected or formerly elected officials, who understood that their public positions would mean their comments would be connected to their names. Much in the way Helen Marrow weaves the voices of Latino respondents in her book, *New Destination Dreaming* (2011), this book uses Somali vignettes and direct quotations to help capture the political, economic, and social incorporation of Somalis in the cities under investigation.

During an interview with a Somali American academic leader, we discussed the challenges and opportunities associated with my status as a non–Somali American scholar. Although I initially viewed this as a liability, my respondent pointed out that as an outsider with endorsements from prominent Somali community leaders, I was in a unique position to gain access to Somali respondents. My respondent explained that standards and expectations in the community are higher for members of the community under investigation—particularly for Somalis. The Somalis who excused my cultural faux pas and lack of familiarity with Somali or Islamic customs might not exercise the same patience with a Somali scholar. In this respect, I was able to begin seeing my advantage as an outsider doing research that relied heavily on the voice and trust of a community of which I was not a member (Twin Cities academic interview, July 1, 2014).

A final note on the significance of the voices of respondents in this study is necessary. In both communities under investigation, the phenomenon of "research fatigue" is evident. Because the cities in this study are each home to their state's major research institutions, the proliferation of undergraduate and graduate students interested in studying this "new immigrant group" has led to some understandable frustration in the Somali community. As an outsider myself, I was well aware of the generosity and trust extended to me over the years. I was also aware that prominent Somali leaders in both cities were in dialogue about my work, through telecommunications or when they traveled to meetings discussing the Somali diaspora. Through word of mouth, I was accepted by many and given the opportunity to conduct participant observation during my visits in both communities under investigation. I attended Somali graduation events, poetry readings, an International Women's Day event organized by a Somali women's organization at the Ohio statehouse, and community organization meetings; participated in English and cultural education training with refugees at a resettlement agency; spent five hours on patrol with Somali police officers in Minneapolis; and even broke the fast during my visits during Ramadan. In addition to the extensive literature review for this book, the numerous reports on Somalis in the cities under study, and my interviews, my acceptance at important Somali events was a reflection of the trust that developed between me and the people who opened their lives to me. It is my hope that this book will help identify ways that American policy makers can improve Somali incorporation, and the incorporation of other immigrant communities, in our cities in the years ahead.

Plan of the Book

After this introductory chapter, Chapters 2 and 3 provide an overview of the regions under investigation, Columbus and the Twin Cities. Each chapter pays particular attention to the Somali experience in that area. Understanding the political, economic, and social background of the cities, in addition to their immigration histories, union traditions, religious trends, and issues of discrimination, helps set the stage for analyzing Somali incorporation in the two areas. Each chapter opens with several Somali vignettes that illustrate how respondents in this book made their way to their current homes. These patterns reflect some of the most common among migrants and give the reader a sense of the rich interviews with Somali respondents in this study.

Chapters 4, 5, and 6 speak to the heart of this study: the political, economic, and social incorporation of Somalis in Columbus and the Twin Cities. Chapter 4 examines how Somali *political* incorporation differs between the two locations. Chapter 5 considers how Somali *economic* incorporation varies between the two locations. And Chapter 6 explores the different indicators of Somali *social* incorporation in the two locations. In all three realms, the Twin Cities have slightly higher levels of incorporation, yet it is also evident that the Twin Cities region is far from an ideal area for Somali Americans.

Chapter 7, the final chapter of this book, features a discussion of the major incorporation findings, followed by policy recommendations for increasing incorporation of new immigrant communities in the political, economic, and social realms. Although the findings are specific to Somalis, they highlight policies that might benefit other major metropolitan areas with new immigrant communities that struggle to thrive.

2 /

Columbus

Somalis in the Heartland

Although Columbus, Ohio, does not conjure up images of international diversity, nor is it known as a traditional destination for immigrants to the United States, central Ohio is now considered an important "new gateway" for immigrants (M. Waters and Jiménez 2005). Columbus was a magnet for German immigrants in the late 1800s; since the 1990s, the city has become a destination for Latino, Asian, and African immigrants (A. Waters 2012). The city is now home to the second-largest Somali diaspora in the United States, according to the U.S. Office of Refugee Resettlement (ORR). Somali migration began in earnest starting in the mid-1990s, although a small group of Somalis settled in Columbus prior to their country's civil war in 1991. These early migrants typically moved to Columbus in pursuit of postgraduate work at The Ohio State University. The remaining majority of Somalis who call Columbus home arrived in the mid-1990s as political refugees in the aftermath of civil war in Somalia. Although precise estimates vary, the secretary of state and community leaders estimate that somewhere between 30,000 and 45,000 Somalis live in Columbus,[1] a city with a population of approx-

---

1. See http://www.sos.state.oh.us/sos/ProfileOhio/diversity.aspx and http://somali can.org/yahoo_site_admin/assets/docs/Somali_Community_In_Ohio.203230447.pdf.

imately 850,000, according to 2015 U.S. Census records.[2] According to U.S. Census records, approximately 86,000 foreign-born residents live in the city of Columbus, only 12,227 of whom are Somali.[3] The discrepancy between the figures is likely due to general U.S. Census undercounts (see de la Puente 1990; Romero 1992), secondary migration, and reluctance among some Somalis to respond to requests for household information. With regard to the latter explanation, several respondents mentioned that Somalis often live in apartments with extended family. Concerns about eviction create a reluctance to disclose the number of people living in a single-family unit (Columbus city bureaucrat interview, June 17, 2013; Columbus community leader interview B, July 26, 2013; Columbus community member interview, July 24, 2013; Horst 2006). Somalis reside primarily in the northeastern and western sides of Columbus, although there are smaller enclaves throughout Franklin County, where Columbus is located. Figure 2.1 includes a map of Franklin County, highlighting the areas where Somalis are concentrated in the Columbus area.

The state of Ohio and the city of Columbus have struggled to fully incorporate the Somali population. Ihotu Ali muses that Somali refugees arrived in the United States at an inopportune time:

Since the 1990s they have arrived in the thousands, many as penniless refugees in the midst of an anti-welfare movement, as *hijab*-wearing Muslims in the aftermath of September 11, 2001, and as taxi drivers and hotel staff in a period of competition over low-wage and "illegal" labor. (2011, 83)

Somali Americans who settled in Columbus have encountered numerous challenges with regard to their political, economic, and social incorporation. At the same time, word quickly spread throughout the Somali diaspora in the United States that Columbus was an attractive destination because of its job opportunities, low cost of living, and plentiful affordable housing. In this sense, chain migration occurred as a result of the growing Somali community.

---

2. See http://www.census.gov/quickfacts/table/PST045215/3918000.

3. See https://www.census.gov/programs-surveys/acs/.

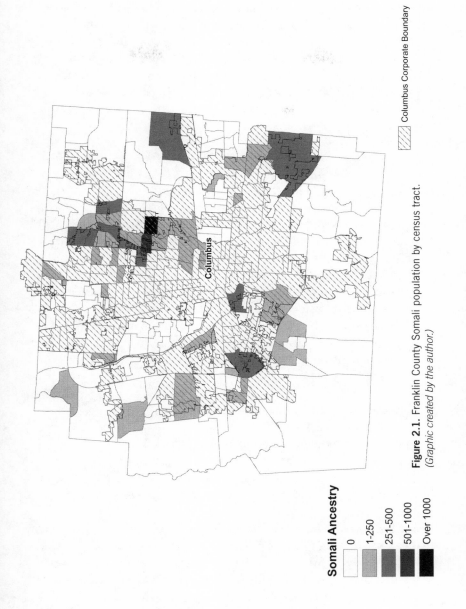

Figure 2.1. Franklin County Somali population by census tract.
(Graphic created by the author.)

Somali Ancestry

0

1-250

251-500

501-1000

Over 1000

Columbus Corporate Boundary

This chapter provides the contextual background necessary to understand why Columbus is home to the second-largest Somali population in the United States. It also provides insight into the unique Somali experience in Columbus and sets the stage for the chapters on the political, economic, and social incorporation of Somalis in the two regions under investigation. The three vignettes that follow provide background on the Somali journey to Columbus.

Somali Vignettes

Abdullahi (pseudonym) came to Columbus in 2005 through the family reunification process. He arrived in the city with a strong educational background and is well on his way to earning a Ph.D. He is the founder and executive director of one of the city's leading Somali nonprofit organizations.

Born in the city of Mogadishu in 1977, Abdullahi was one of nine siblings in a culture where large families are typical. Abdullahi was in high school in 1991 when Mohamed Siad Barre's government was overthrown in Somalia. This was a particularly dangerous period in Mogadishu as a result of the power vacuum and ensuing clan violence. Abdullahi ultimately left Somalia and spent ten years living in various refugee camps in Kenya. His journey out of Somalia was laced with hardship. He described the period leading up to his departure from Somalia in this way:

> We became under constant attack. It was becoming intolerable by the day, but the family did not have enough resources to move. My mother gave some money to the three oldest children—my sister [who now lives] in Canada, myself, and my older brother, whom we lost in the civil war, to flee the city. (Columbus community member interview, February 22, 2015)

The siblings sought refuge in the home of their maternal uncle, but they were soon in danger because of interclan warfare. They found safety in a religious compound for a few months and then traveled separately to the southern city of Kismayo. Abdullahi's vehicle broke down 170 miles from this destination. He ultimately found a group of men from his clan who together made the journey by foot to the Kenyan border. He recalled:

> It was the most difficult trip that I had to take to date. Eleven days of walking with no food. You avoid human beings, because they may be from the wrong clan, and everyone was armed to the teeth. We were eating wild fruits and leaves, but there was plenty of water, as it was the rainy season. We went through deserted villages and ghost towns along the way. As a teenager, it was a mind-boggling experience. (Columbus community member interview, February 22, 2015)

Abdullahi was ultimately reunited with his siblings and the rest of his family in Kenya, although he lost a brother and a sister during the war.

When Abdullahi arrived in Kenya, he spoke no English. He learned English, graduated from high school, and worked for a variety of relief agencies in the camps. He was also employed as a middle school teacher. In 2001, he became the first student from the Dadaab refugee camp to receive a college scholarship in Kenya from the Windle Trust. The organization was reluctant to give a scholarship to a Somali, because previous Somali scholarship awardees had not completed their studies, but Abdullahi convinced them he was dedicated to his work. Abdullahi's academic successes led the Windle Trust to extend scholarships to many more Somalis. Abdullahi shared:

> I communicated with friends at the Windle Trust, and they told me that they are currently sponsoring more than one hundred Somali students in Kenyan academic institutions. Although I did not give a scholarship to any of those kids, I feel that I paved the way for them, and I consider this as my greatest achievement to date. I graduated with honors from the school of economics at the University of Nairobi. (Columbus community member interview, February 22, 2015)

From Nairobi, Abdullahi applied for asylum in the United States. Because extended family had already relocated to Columbus, he was sent to the city in 2005 through the family reunification process. The resettlement agency, or voluntary agency, that helped Abdullahi with his transition needed skilled interpreters, given the growing number of Somalis with limited to no English-language skills. Abdullahi accepted a position that paid about $30 an hour. Through his work, he soon realized that Somalis lacked information about the resources that would help them thrive in their new homes. He set a professional goal of creating a community outreach organization aimed at providing Somalis with information to help them pursue their educational and employment goals. He explained:

> I found that people in my community had misconceptions about America. There was a flying narrative that all you need to succeed in America is to make money. Most young people did just that by driving a cab or a truck or working in menial jobs. All this was happening because there were no good role models in the community. There were people who were educated in Somalia but whose law degrees, medical licenses, and teaching licenses became obsolete upon arriving here. This served to prove [to them] that education is useless. (Columbus community member interview, February 22, 2015)

Abdullahi's personal commitment to education is a thread that runs through the priorities established by his organization. Today, the organization also provides scholarships to roughly sixty Somali undergraduates. Abdullahi set a personal goal of earning a master's degree in public policy and management and a Ph.D. in international development, both at The Ohio State University. In addition to running his organization, he also serves as a Somali-language instructor at The Ohio State University, which boasts one of the only Somali-language programs in the United States.

Suuban (pseudonym) came to the United States in 2005 at the age of eighteen with her younger brother. Prior to her arrival, Suuban had spent her youth living between Mogadishu, Somalia, and the Ifo refugee camp in Kenya. Family members had settled in Columbus earlier, so she was placed in Columbus as part of the family reunification process. When she arrived, she spoke no English, but she had a tenth-grade education. This was in large part thanks to her mother, who—deeply concerned about Suuban's education—had sent her to school in the refugee camp when other families saw no need to educate their daughters. Suuban embraced education and treasured the few books she owned. She explained:

> I fell in love with reading. For a kid not brought up with libraries, books, or newspapers, a book was the best thing. Reading helped me understand how life was outside [of the camp and Somalia]. (Columbus community member interview, March 10, 2015)

Suuban was also passionate about world events and followed international news closely via a small, battery-operated transistor radio:

> I used to hassle my mother for batteries. At the ages of ten, eleven, and twelve, I knew exactly what was going on in the world from listening to the radio. (Columbus community member interview, March 10, 2015)

When she first arrived in Columbus, Suuban watched people's children while she pursued her education. She held a variety of low-paying jobs in warehouses. While holding several jobs and working sixteen hours a day, seven days a week, she managed to get a high school diploma and is now working toward a bachelor's degree from The Ohio State University. She still works many hours a day, but she is now proficient in English and works at a translation agency.

One of the most unconventional parts of Suuban's story is that her passion for world events has led her into freelance journalism with a news organization. Suuban has navigated the education system and freelance journalism without the financial support of family members or mentors. She has been responsible for her own living expenses as well as the education and living expenses of family back in Somalia. For her, supporting her mother, who remains in Somalia, is a top priority. She sends monthly contributions that are central to her mother's survival. Suuban explained:

> Remittance is a lifeline. My mother had a very harsh life, and I
> was her only girl. She gave me a fighting chance by educating
> me. I want to give her a fighting chance. (Columbus commu-
> nity member interview, March 10, 2015)

The issue of remittance is something Somali respondents in all
cities mentioned as a vital part of their lives and family responsibilities. This issue is addressed in greater detail in Chapter 5.

I spoke with Mamahawa (pseudonym) through the assistance of a
Somali interpreter. Mamahawa was first resettled in San Diego when
she arrived in the United States with her husband and eleven children
in 1996. The couple found San Diego expensive, and after learning
about opportunities in Columbus, they made the journey to Ohio
in 1999. For nearly seven years, Mamahawa worked in a Columbus
warehouse. For about a year, her husband did warehouse work too,
but he soon became ill and was unable to work. The couple suffered
the loss of a daughter shortly after their arrival in Columbus. For
years, the couple also struggled to locate their twelfth child in Somalia and bring him to the United States through family reunification,
which eventually happened in 2005 (Columbus community member
interview, March 24, 2015).

Mamahawa was the primary breadwinner in her family once she
arrived in the United States. For many Somalis, traditional gender
roles shift when they migrate to the United States, as women take on
jobs outside the home, something less accepted in Somalia. Mamahawa's husband took responsibility for their young children while Mamahawa worked, frequently taking on overtime shifts on the weekend
to support their large family. In 2006, Mamahawa's husband passed
away, and she was left to care for herself and her children alone.

Warehouse work in Columbus paid enough for Mamahawa to
support her family. However, after September 11, 2001, her job became more difficult. She and her Somali co-workers noticed that
employers were less likely to accommodate their religious practices.
A group of Somalis started discussing the need to unionize, but this
idea was quickly put to an end by management. The warehouse start-

ed issuing layoff notices and making demands of employees that were unreasonable. She recalls that several people were asked to do jobs they could not perform, which led them to quit. In her case, working conditions became so uncomfortable that she left the warehouse and took a housekeeping position. Although this position paid much less, she was more comfortable in a job where she was treated equitably.

All but one of Mamahawa's children have graduated from college, whether community college or a four-year institution. The last is still in high school and intends to go to college soon. Countering the odds against the child of a housekeeper earning a college degree, Mamahawa always placed great emphasis on education. Her children are primarily small-business owners in the home health care, transportation, and daycare industries. Mamahawa enjoys living in Columbus and has become something of a neighborhood leader in her community.

––––––––

These stories represent several individual stories of migration but also reflect common migration trends and experiences among Somali respondents in Columbus. Economic hardship, the importance of education, personal loss, and the ongoing struggle to support relatives in Africa were mentioned by virtually all Somali respondents in Columbus. Regardless of differences in terms of social class, English-language skills, or other areas, nearly all Somalis in Columbus have endured tremendous hardship during their lives and been touched by the loss of family members in postwar fallout.

Immigration and Columbus

Columbus's immigration history is not significantly different from that of other midsize American cities in the late 1800s. Beginning in the 1840s, significant numbers of Irish and German immigrants began arriving in Columbus. Although they settled in different areas of the city, both groups came in search of economic opportunities and faced discrimination. The Know-Nothing Party, a notoriously anti-immigrant and anti-Catholic organization, had a strong presence in the city. The Irish faced high levels of hostility as a result of their immigrant status and religious traditions. Germans were predominantly Lutheran but also included Catholic and Jewish contingencies. The German influence in Columbus remains strong today, especially in the historic "German Village" on the southern end of the city. Beyond the Know-Nothings, the state of Ohio also has a historic relationship with the Ku Klux Klan, a white supremacist and anti-immigrant organization (Curnutte and Berman 2013). Ohio is one of sixteen states with organized Klan chapters. Although Columbus is not one of the chapter locations, the city's status as the state capital means that it is sometimes the target of hateful Klan messages protected by the First Amendment. Discrimination is an unfortunate part of Columbus's immigration history.

During recent decades, Mexican, Somali, and Bhutanese Nepalese populations have also made Columbus home. Whereas Mexican Americans in Columbus initially moved for job opportunities, Somalis and Bhutanese Nepalese have predominantly arrived as refugees, the latter migrating to the city in more recent years. Beyond the general federal services for refugees discussed in Chapter 1, Columbus has three voluntary agencies that provide basic resettlement services upon arrival in the city—Community Refugee and Immigration Services (CRIS), US Together, and World Relief Columbus—and work closely with new refugees during the first three months after their arrival. Each organization welcomes refugees at the airport, assists with housing and clothing, helps with application for public assistance through the county, ensures that health care needs are met, assigns eligible individuals to English-language courses necessary to pass a citizenship exam, and works to support the transition to employment.[4] Refugees are eligible for state financial and health care assistance for the first eight months after their settlement in Ohio. In contrast to the Twin Cities, where the government's attention to refugee mental health has received considerable press, specific programs for refugee mental health are less developed in Columbus. A representative from a Columbus voluntary agency explained:

> Refugees are required to complete a physical health screening within the first ninety days after arrival. This is the longest

---

4. See https://jfs.ohio.gov/refugee/resettlement_agencies.stm.

allowed time, but it usually happens within thirty, as children need to be current with vaccinations to begin school. Until last year, there was no mental health component of this screening, and there is still no standardized mental health screening that takes place for refugees nationally. Some states have adopted their own screening tools and procedures, but this has not been done in a systematic or coordinated way as of now [in Ohio]. (Columbus refugee resettlement interview, October 16, 2015)

Although precise estimates are unavailable, it is evident that Columbus is a strong secondary destination for Somalis who were initially resettled in other American cities (Forrest and Brown 2014). While ORR tracks secondary migration from state to state, it does not have data on the movement of specific groups, such as Somalis. However, 2013 ORR data reveal that Ohio receives the third-largest number of secondary migrants in the nation (737), ranking behind Minnesota (2,133 migrants) and Florida (1,046 migrants). Similarly, Latinos have migrated from such states as California to Columbus because of the abundance of jobs and the low cost of living (Cohen and Chavez 2013). A major difference between those who enter the country as refugees and those who immigrate without this special status is that refugees are eligible for the cash assistance and health benefits outlined above; refugees who move to secondary destinations forfeit their benefits once they leave their initial settlement cities. Although benefits are quite limited to begin with, the decision to move to Columbus speaks to the allure of the city for Somalis and other immigrant groups who make homes for their families there. It is also worth noting that most Columbus respondents in this study have visited the Twin Cities because family and close friends reside there. In fact, a van travels from Columbus to Minneapolis on Fridays and returns to Columbus on Sundays. One respondent explained:

Easy Ride is one large van that transports people and cargo every weekend. It is operated by a couple of Somali individuals. It departs from the Banadir Mall in Columbus every Friday evening and comes back there on Sunday evenings. (Columbus community leader interview, October 15, 2015)

This privately run transportation system between the two areas speaks to the connections between the two Somali communities in this book. In fact, many of the Somali respondents in this project became aware of my research through word of mouth between respondents in Columbus and in the Twin Cities.

Franklin County, Columbus's home, has experienced a tremendous growth in the immigrant population, with estimates for 2000–2005 indicating that immigration accounted for 82 percent of the population growth in the county (City of Columbus, 2013). Table 2.1 illustrates the population by country of origin in the Columbus metropolitan area. Although Mexico and India are the two leaders in foreign-born population contributors on the 2006–2010 American Community Survey five-year estimates, Somalis represent a sizable and growing population. More importantly, this figure does not account for the children born in the United States to Somali immigrant parents. The Somali Community Access Network (SomaliCAN), a Columbus community organization, estimates that more than 3,500 Somali Americans are enrolled in local colleges and universities in the Columbus metropolitan area (Columbus community leader interview, March 9, 2015).[5] Because Somali families include an average of four children, and because the largest segment of the Somali population is still of reproductive age, it is likely that the Somali community will grow at a rapid rate. As the Somali population grows, its effect on elections could increase considerably.

Columbus: The Land of Economic Resilience

The urban politics literature documents the rise and fall of industry in what has come to be known as the "Rust Belt" of the United States. This region consists of parts of New York State, Pennsylvania, Indiana, Ohio, Illinois, and Wisconsin. The regional economy was centered on heavy industry, manufacturing, and the transportation of raw materials during the early twentieth century. In Columbus, such firms as Buckeye

---

5. Neither of the state universities in this study (Ohio State and the University of Minnesota) collects data on Somali students. Somalis are grouped with African American students.

TABLE 2.1. FOREIGN-BORN POPULATION BY COUNTRY OF BIRTH, GREATER COLUMBUS, 2006–2010 ESTIMATES

Country	Foreign-born population by birth country	% Foreign-born population by birth country
Mexico	18,327	14.9%
India	13,150	10.7%
East Africa, including Somalia*	7,806	6.4%
China	6,516	6.3%
South Korea	3,576	2.9%
Canada	3,342	2.7%
Japan	3,274	2.7%
United Kingdom	3,158	2.6%
Ghana	2,836	2.3%
Germany	2,790	2.3%
Ethiopia	2,605	2.1%
Philippines	2,471	2.0%
Other†	52,825	42.1%
Total	122,678	100.0%

Source: Data from U.S. Census Bureau, American Community Survey 2006–2010 estimates.

*Includes Burundi, Comoros, Djibouti, Madagascar, Malawi, Mauritius, Mayotte, Mozambique, Reunion, Rwanda, Seychelles, Somalia, Tanzania, Uganda, Zambia, and Zimbabwe.

†Includes all groups constituting less than 2% of the population.

Steel Castings; Columbus Coated Fabrics, which produced oilcloth; and Jaeger Machinery, which made cement mixers, were among the many companies headquartered in the city (Hunker 1996). Columbus became a magnet for immigrants from eastern Europe beginning in the 1890s because of the availability of low-skilled manufacturing jobs and positions on assembly lines (Otiso and Smith 2005). Beginning in the 1940s, Columbus emerged as the primary destination among the Ohio cities, largely because the city was able to develop service and information employment at the same time that manufacturing jobs were booming (Otiso and Smith 2005). Table 2.2 illustrates the immigration and employment levels in Ohio's three largest cities. As evident in these illustrations, Columbus's population explosion coincided with

TABLE 2.2. OHIO CITY POPULATION AND EMPLOYMENT, 1940–2010

City	Year	Total population	Total employment	% Total employment	% Foreign born	Foreign-born population
Cincinnati	1940	455,610	169,970	37.3%	5.7%	25,970
	1950	502,010	201,702	40.2%	4.1%	20,582
	1960	502,550	189,604	37.7%	3.3%	16,584
	1970	452,376	174,900	38.7%	2.7%	12,214
	1980	385,457	159,396	41.4%	2.8%	10,793
	1990	364,040	148,881	40.9%	2.8%	10,193
	2000	330,662	150,574	45.5%	3.8%	12,565
	2010	296,943	152,350	51.3%	5.2%	15,441
Cleveland	1940	878,336	319,582	36.4%	20.5%	180,059
	1950	912,840	390,423	42.8%	14.6%	133,275
	1960	876,050	338,178	38.6%	11.0%	96,366
	1970	750,932	286,784	38.2%	7.5%	56,320
	1980	573,822	213,852	37.3%	5.8%	33,282
	1990	505,616	182,225	36.0%	4.1%	20,730
	2000	478,393	180,459	37.7%	4.5%	21,528
	2010	396,815	192,126	48.4%	4.6%	18,253
Columbus	1940	306,087	112,447	36.7%	3.9%	11,937
	1950	362,205	153,803	42.5%	2.9%	10,504
	1960	471,316	181,232	38.5%	2.3%	10,840
	1970	539,469	218,683	40.5%	2.1%	11,329
	1980	564,866	261,852	46.4%	2.9%	16,381
	1990	632,958	325,088	51.4%	3.7%	23,419
	2000	711,644	374,892	52.7%	6.7%	47,680
	2010	787,033	428,188	54.4%	10.9%	85,787

Source: Data from U.S. Census Bureau, Decennial Census; 2010 employment data from 2010 American Community Survey.

an increase in job opportunities and immigration from 1940 to 2010. The arrival of Somalis in the 1990s contributed to this growth.

Much in the way early America developed around waterways, the Great Lakes fueled the economic growth of this region, but the rise of the "Sunbelt" in the 1970s pulled industry and jobs to the southern part of the United States. The absence of strong organized labor, low taxes, a mild climate, and transportation and telecommunications advances made this southern region an attractive draw for the manufacturing industry. The moniker "Rust Belt" emerged as the heartland of industry slowly transitioned to become an economically stagnating region that existed in the shadows of its former industrial glory. However, unlike other Rust Belt cities, Columbus transitioned quite well in the face of a shifting national economy.

Despite the economic shock to the region during the postindustrial exodus to the south, Columbus was able to adapt to industrial change and modify its economy. Henry Hunker explains that despite Columbus's limited water resources and lack of attraction as a tourist destination, the city successfully moved from an industrial economy to a service economy at the same time that it capitalized on its cultural assets (2000, 27). The cultural assets of the city include the fact that Columbus is the state capital, a decision reached in 1812 because of Columbus's the location in the center of the state (50). Like other capital cities in the United States, location in the center of the state's political sector can benefit the local economy in terms of employment opportunities within state government. At the same time, state and federal office buildings reduce the amount of taxable property, an issue Columbus was able to counterbalance through the annexation of land over time. Annexation by the city in the 1950s through the 1960s increased its geographic size but also allowed the city to tap into resources beyond its geographical boundaries, such as access to water and sewers. The added taxing authority gained through annexation also helped the city avoid some of the challenges faced by other Rust Belt cities, particularly the Ohio cities of Cleveland and Cincinnati, which were unable to annex surrounding areas. Columbus is also home to the state's flagship research university, The Ohio State University, which is one of the top employers in the region. By the 1980s, the *Wall Street Journal* reported that Columbus was "recession proof" because of the mixed economy that included government jobs, service-sector jobs, trade, and manufacturing (56).

The city's service-sector emphasis falls into three main areas: wholesale and retail trade, general services (including education), and government (Hunker 2000, 58). The adaptation to the service sector was not a response to industrial shifts but something the city had nurtured as a secondary economic focus for decades. Examples of the focus on the service economy are evident when examining some of the groups that are headquartered in the city, such as Battelle, one of the world's largest private research organizations (2). The city is also seen as an international leader in information technology and is the site of the headquarters of CompuServe and many insurance and financial firms, such as Nationwide and Huntington. JCPenney and the fashion brand The Limited, among others, have taken advantage of Columbus's interstate highway system, which facilitates the efficiency of warehouses. Many of the low-skilled jobs in these warehouses are held by Somali and other immigrants who migrated, in part, because of the plentiful supply of those very jobs. However, these are not unionized positions, which limits the collective political and economic power of Somalis and other immigrants who dominate the industry (Columbus city bureaucrat interview, June 17, 2013).

The ties between Columbus's public and private sector are a key factor in the city's ability to weather economic storms. Several key families have guided economic development in the city. Although there has never been a comprehensive study of the impact of local business on Columbus's political decisions, it is clear that political elites have maintained conditions in the city that have remained attractive to local and national businesses. Among the family dynasties in the area that have played a role in civic development, the Wolfe family built a local empire based on their ownership of the city's newspaper (Hunker 2000, 77). The Dave Thomas family (of the Wendy's fast-food chain), Cheryl Krueger (of Cheryl's Cookies), and the leaders of various banks, insurance companies, and research institutions are largely viewed as civic elites who significantly influence local political and economic affairs (Hunker 2000). Today, Leslie Wexner, owner of The Limited and its many affiliates, is ubiquitous in Columbus's local economy and culture.

Overall, Columbus is an attractive area to business interests, because it has gained a reputation as an area that is an ideal test market for new products, supports business innovation, offers a strong labor pool, and maintains a low cost of living. Columbus's rich corporate and service-sector history helps paint a picture of why the city has been economically successful and why it was viewed as an attractive location for Somali refugees in search of a new home with affordable housing options and job opportunities.

In addition to the many Somalis who hold low-skilled jobs, some are small-business owners. Somali women own many of the shops in the Somali strip malls in the city. The capital for starting up businesses is derived primarily through informal networks of friends and family who pool money and make arrangements for repayment. On the one hand, this creative form of financing has allowed many small businesses to emerge that cater specifically to the Somali community. On the other hand, the reluctance of Somalis to work with U.S. financial institutions as a result of Islamic law considerations means that Somali-owned businesses tend to be undercapitalized (Golden, Garad, and Boyle 2011). It is estimated that there are more than four hundred Somali-owned small businesses in Columbus, primarily small shops that cater to Somali buyers, home health care establishments, and local transportation businesses. A few Somalis hold state, municipal, or federal jobs.

Political Culture in Columbus

In Daniel Elazar's classic book (1987) on political culture in the United States, Ohio is classified as an "individualistic" state. According to his model, individualistic states limit the government's obligations to support the marketplace and advance individual and private interests. Although Elazar's typology is criticized by some scholars for being flawed (Erikson, McIver, and Wright 1987; Nardulli 1990), it has some utility when considering the political culture in Columbus, particularly as it relates to the collaboration between the public and private sectors. Ohio also falls in the center of Robert Putnam's Social Capital Index, which measures social capital across the United States to contextualize the decline in community networks and social trust he claims has occurred in recent decades. Compared to what Putnam found in Minnesota, a state at the top of his Social Capital Index, Ohio's lower ranking has relevant implications. Putnam goes beyond the Social Capital Index to examine a range of studies that compared states across such policy areas as child welfare, education, health care benefits, and levels of tolerance. In all of these studies, Putnam illustrates that Ohio is consistently in the middle of the states, while Minnesota is at the top.

TABLE 2.3. AFRICAN AMERICAN MEMBERS OF COLUMBUS CITY COUNCIL	
Name	Term
James Poindexter	1880–1884
James Roseboro	1972–1974
Jerry Hammond	1974–1990
Ben Espy	1982–1992
Les Wright*	1990–1999
Jeanette B. Bradley	1992–2003
Michael B. Coleman*	1992–1999
Charleta Tavares*	1999–2010
Frederick L. Ransier III	January 2000–September 2000
Kevin Boyce*	2000–2009
Patsy Thomas*	2003–2007
Priscilla Tyson*	2007–present
Hearcel F. Craig*	2007–present
A. Troy Miller*	2009–present
Michelle M. Mills*	2011–present
*Indicates council members who were initially appointed to their positions	

Ohio also receives considerable national attention during presidential elections because of its status as a swing state with eighteen electoral votes. Although the state itself is heavily conservative, Columbus is far more Democratic. As of 2015, Republicans control the entire Ohio congressional delegation and both chambers of the state legislature. The Columbus City Council and mayor, in contrast, are all Democrats. President Barack Obama received Ohio's electoral votes in both 2008 and 2012, largely thanks to the cities. Obama carried Columbus in both elections.

The city's recently departed mayor, Democrat Michael Coleman, served from 1999 through January 2016. Coleman was the first Democrat to serve as mayor since 1972, and he was the city's first African American mayor. Interestingly, the city council has become increasingly diverse since the 1990s. In fact, the current council includes a slight majority of African American council members despite the racial composition of the city, which is 61 percent white and 28 percent African American.[6] The diversity in the mayor's office and on the city council reflects trends elsewhere in urban America, where African Americans—and in other areas, Latinos—have increasingly made gains in elective office. However, this diversity does not necessarily correlate with progressive policies. Like previous mayors, Coleman had an agenda that emphasized economic development, particularly attracting white-collar jobs to the city. This agenda helped secure campaign contributions and four consecutive election victories (Chambers and Schreiber-Stainthorp 2013). Although Coleman has considered running for governor, he has never run statewide. This is likely due to the fact that although his politics and racial background are an advantage in a politically moderate city like Columbus, the same may not hold true at the state level, where successful candidates tend to be white and Republican.

As documented by Yvette Alex-Assensoh (2004), Columbus's African Americans have faced decades of political, economic, and social neglect. The at-large election system for the city council, coupled with the significant racial segregation in the city, limited the opportunity of African Americans to win in citywide elections until the 1990s. Beginning in the early 1990s, there was an uptick in the number of African Americans elected to serve on city council. Table 2.3 lists the African American members of the Columbus City Council between 1880 and the present. Interestingly, vacancies on the city council have allowed that body to select replacements who ultimately run for office in their own right. Of the sixteen African American members, nine were initially appointed to fill vacancies and went on to win election to the Columbus City Council. This somewhat unconventional way of diversifying the Columbus City Council has worked in favor of African American candidates, despite the problems posed by the at-large electoral system.

New Somali residents settled in the same neighborhoods where African Americans had lived for decades. As in other urban areas, there have been moments of tension in Columbus between the African American and Somali communities, both of which dispro-

---

6. See http://www.census.gov/quickfacts/table/PST045215/3918000.

portionately compose the poor segment of the city. This tension is reminiscent of other struggles that have emerged between different racial and ethnic minorities in such cities as Los Angeles, where relations between Latinos and African Americans have been strained because of a perception that one marginalized group is receiving more than another (Sonenshein 1997). When marginalized groups have overlapping residential patterns but distinctly different cultural traditions, conflict may occur. Only three respondents in this study referenced tensions between African Americans and Somalis (Columbus community leader interview C, July 26, 2013; Columbus community member interview, June 19, 2013; Columbus community member interview, March 6, 2014), mentioning previous conflicts between African American and Somali students in school (Columbus community leader interview C, July 26, 2013) and a 2003 dispute between members of the communities living in a residential area (Columbus community member interview, June 19, 2013). The third respondent mentioned specific concerns about the consequences of Somali and African American youth relations:

> They [African Americans] walk around with their saggy pants, selling drugs, drinking alcohol, skipping school, taking part in crime. Our [Somali] kids see this in our neighborhoods, and some are influenced by this. . . . We have more in common with the whites who live in the suburbs. Our beliefs and culture fit better. (Columbus community member interview, March 6, 2014)

This negative comment about African Americans stands in stark contrast to what other Somali respondents said about African Americans. However, the statement is also reminiscent of the issues addressed by scholars who examine assimilation of second-generation immigrants (see Portes and Zhou 1993; M. Waters 1999). Because Somalis often live in poor neighborhoods in Columbus, alongside poor African Americans, a different group that also struggles to succeed, this negative sentiment is not terribly surprising.

Like African Americans in years past, Somali Americans struggle to have a voice in local politics because of the electoral system and because they are largely neglected by the two major parties. According to the vast majority of Somali respondents in this study, only during elections do candidates and parties court Somali voters, who are an incredibly reliable bloc. One respondent noted:

> We [Somalis] take the right to vote seriously. Politicians and candidates attend our events and visit with our community at strategic times, right around elections. People recognize that this is pandering for votes—we're savvy people. (Columbus community member interview, July 24, 2013)

Aside from appeals for their votes, Somalis are generally taken for granted by the political establishment. Although estimates vary, one study suggests that about 30 percent of Somalis in central Ohio— about fourteen thousand individuals—are U.S. citizens and vote regularly (Borgerding 2008). They overwhelmingly support Democratic candidates, the only candidates who make efforts to attract Somali votes. Respondents in this study were unified in their view that the statistics for Somali voting are higher than official numbers indicate. Because the secretary of state does not collect data on the ethnicity of voters, and because heavily Somali precincts are also heavily African American, precise numbers are difficult to estimate.

Even if the figures for Somali voter turnout are higher than those officially reported, the community has not forged coalitions with other groups in the city. However, there is some discussion among Somali community leaders about how coalitions could be created (Columbus community member interview, January 15, 2015). The idea of an African American and Somali or East African coalition is unrealistic and overlooks the cultural, linguistic, and ideological divisions within the African diaspora communities. Somalis, as many conservative Somali leaders report, have more in common with conservative whites in Ohio, who have "similar family values, oppose gay marriage, and do not believe sex education should happen in schools" (Columbus community member interview, July 25, 2013). This comparison is interesting but overlooks the fact that conservative whites in Ohio are far more likely to see similarities between Somalis and African Americans in Columbus who happen to live in the same neighborhoods and ignore them. The degree of racial, cultural, religious, ideological, and often linguistic isolation among Somalis in Columbus makes coalitional politics unlikely without significant changes in the political culture of the region.

Unions

Ohio is one of organized labor's most important states and has been called one of "the strongest bastions of unionism in the nation" (Burstein 2012, 36). The American Federation of Labor (AFL) was headquartered in Columbus in 1886,[7] and the United Mine Workers of America (UMWA) established its headquarters in the city in 1890.[8] Even with these noteworthy union headquarters in Columbus, the political and economic influence of unions was modified by the strong relationship between business and political leaders, who shared a focus on making Columbus a region that would attract business. Today, roughly 13.4 percent of Ohio's workforce is unionized, although this figure includes 43.1 percent of all public-sector employees (36). Ohio is not a "right-to-work" state, which means that only union members are allowed to benefit under collective-bargaining agreements reached with employers. Like many other midwestern states, Ohio has recently witnessed several attempts by Republican legislators to end the collective-bargaining rights of public-sector employees in an attempt to transition to a right-to-work state. In fact, a poll in 2012 revealed that Ohio voters favor right-to-work 54 to 40 percent (37). Yet despite attempts to weaken unions in Ohio, they remain an important part of Columbus's economy.

Somalis, however, are underrepresented in Columbus's unions. This stands in stark contrast to Somalis in the Twin Cities, who have a significant affiliation with Service Employees International Union (SEIU) Local 26. Union membership can promote the mobilization of underrepresented groups around such issues as wages, working conditions, and job protection while also creating leadership opportunities for members. Some unions are also politically active, thus

---

7. See http://ohiohistorycentral.org/w/American_Federation_of_Labor?rec=835.
8. See http://www.coal-miners-in-kentucky.com/UnitedMineWorkers.html.

increasing the likelihood that members will participate in politics, at least around labor issues. However, because of the low rates of Somali unionization in Columbus, this type of activity is absent in the area.

Community Organizations

There are a number of Somali community organizations in Columbus. In 1996, Somali Community Association of Ohio (SCAO), the first Somali community organization, was created. However, pinpointing the precise number of groups in existence today is somewhat difficult, because not all are registered as 501(c)(3) organizations, and some that were formerly active no longer exist. The city currently has ten registered organizations and informal Somali groups. One scholar who has researched Somalis in Columbus explained:

> Several of the Somali community organizations emerged and fell apart. This was partly due to competition and partly due to inadequate funding opportunities. (Columbus academic interview, February 27, 2014)

The Columbus mayor's New American Initiative Office continues to try to find solutions to the organizational saturation in an attempt to support a stronger and more unified Somali group. One New American Initiative bureaucrat noted:

> We've tried to talk to all of them to convince them to unite in one center, to create one umbrella to help all people. We don't want the community to be divisive and chaotic. The leaders have not been willing to compromise. We try to get them to work together. We use Minneapolis's community center as an example of what could happen in Columbus, but it hasn't worked. We explain that if there are ten groups, the funds from the county and state will be too small to help anyone. (Columbus city bureaucrat interview, July 26, 2013)

Since the late 1990s, several Somali women's organizations have emerged to empower women socially and economically, although they have encountered challenges. One Somali woman who runs one of the strongest women's groups explained that first and foremost, funding remains a major challenge to running a successful nonprofit. As a result of such challenges, a number of the Somali women's groups have failed. One non-Somali scholar who has researched the Somali community explained:

> There have been at least three different Somali women's organizations that have dissolved or have been significantly reorganized due to ideological differences between the founding members. Disagreements included disputes over the purpose/mission of the NGO and the populations that the NGO should serve. (Columbus academic interview, February 27, 2014)

These factors, combined with general tensions between interethnic organizations, have caused serious difficulties for Somali women's groups.

Even without a central organization, several important Somali community organizations exist and provide important services to members, including English-language instruction, employment assistance, educational training, translation services, health assistance, housing support, and sensitivity training for public-sector employees. At the same time, there is room for more collaboration among these organizations to maximize returns. Some Somali community leaders interviewed for this study were open to the idea of collaboration, while others remained highly skeptical of the motivation for doing so.[9]

Religion

Ohio's strong Christian roots make the Islamic traditions of Somalis stand out more prominently. Historically, midwestern states like Ohio have reflected the religious traditions of nineteenth-century immi-

---

9. Although some might assume that the inability to collaborate stems from interclan conflict (Chemelecki 2003), the research I conducted for this project suggests otherwise. Many of the organizations are led by members of the same clan, in some cases cousins (Columbus community leader interview, October 15, 2015); community leaders identified a lack of resources as the root of the tensions.

grants who came from Germany, Ireland, Scandinavia, and eastern and southern European countries (Silk and Walsh 2008, 182). Catholics and Protestants remain the largest religious groups in Ohio and in the city of Columbus.[10] More recent immigration has resulted in what Mark Silk and Andrew Walsh call "global" religions, including Islam, Hinduism, and Buddhism (2008, 182). This is especially relevant when considering the Bhutanese Nepali refugee community, which is largely Buddhist, and Somalis, who are predominately Sunni Muslim.

There are seven Somali mosques in Columbus, each with its own imam, or religious leader. Services in these mosques are conducted in Somali. The other mosques in Columbus hold services in English, according to the Council on American-Islamic Relations (CAIR). For Somalis with limited English-language skills, these services are impractical. One non-Somali Muslim explained:

> Language barriers set Somalis apart from the American Muslim community. It limits their ability to collaborate with others who share many of the same beliefs. (Columbus CAIR representative interview, March 11, 2015)

Beyond the separation Somalis experience from other Muslims in Columbus, the Somali imams are seen as powerful within the community, but they are not very involved in helping mobilize the community beyond religious issues (Columbus community member interview, March 9, 2015).

Education

Respondents in this study routinely mentioned that the public education system is failing the youth of Columbus, claims that are reflected in test results for the 2013–2014 academic year. Columbus's schools lag significantly behind state averages in all areas, including graduation rates, general achievement, literacy, and progress.[11] As in cities across the United States, charter schools have emerged in Ohio as

10. See http//ssrs.com.
11. See http://reportcard.education.ohio.gov/.

an alternative to the traditional public schools. Although they are publicly funded, charter schools have greater autonomy in terms of curriculum, employees, and overall governance. Approximately seventy charter schools are operating in Franklin County, although several have recently closed, and new charters are being issued by the state regularly. Of these, several have Islamic themes that appeal to some Somali families. Although the charters are nondenominational in accordance with the First Amendment, the schools often include Islamic-sensitive curricula, making it easier for Muslim students to attend schools that simultaneously support their religious traditions. For example, these schools often restrict pork products from the lunch menu and might go out of their way to create a space for students to pray during the school day. Arabic- or Somali-language instruction is also offered in some of these schools. Finally, several have after-school programs with Islamic themes.

Although the exact number of Somali children attending charter schools is unavailable, a few schools enroll a significant number of students. These include Sunrise Academy, Westside Academy, International Academy of Columbus, Focus Learning Academy of Northern Columbus, Horizon Science Academy, Midnimo Cross Cultural Community School, and Zenith Academy. Of these schools, only Sunrise Academy is located in a suburb of Columbus (in Hilliard). During interviews, I spoke with parents who send their children to traditional public schools and to charter schools. While the focus of this study is not educational options for Somalis, it was clear that some families appreciated having these choices for their children.

Somalia to Columbus: Adaptation and Discrimination

When Somalis first started to migrate in large numbers to the United States, the majority of refugees settled in Minnesota and Virginia. The former destination remains a Somali stronghold and a major focus of this book. But Somalis in Virginia found the area's cost of living high and had trouble finding jobs. In contrast, Columbus had available factory and warehouse jobs, coupled with lower rates for rental housing. A small number of Somalis moved to Columbus and shared news of their improved living situations with friends and family. One of the first Somalis to move to Columbus noted:

> I left Virginia in the early 1990s, because it was so expensive. Columbus had warehouse jobs. I didn't want any handouts, so I took a job immediately and told my brothers this was a good place to live. There were apartments large enough for Somali families. They are large, sometimes [big enough for] six to eight people. We could get these apartments for under $500 a month. Some Somalis were here earlier, because they went to university at OSU [The Ohio State University]. They also told people that this was a good place. (Columbus community leader interview A, July 26, 2013)

Before long, Columbus was one of the foremost destinations for Somali refugees.

Yet even with employment opportunities, affordable housing, and a reasonable cost of living, life in Ohio has not been easy for Somalis. Somalis have registered many complaints of anti-Muslim discrimination with CAIR (A. Waters 2012, 55). Allegations of abuse have also been directed toward the Columbus Division of Police and the Franklin County Sheriff's Office. In 2005, an unarmed Somali man was shot to death by sheriff's deputies after they entered the apartment where he lived (55). Although the man suffered from mental illness, the event was viewed within the Somali community as an excessive use of force by law enforcement. Police in Columbus continue to look for Somali men and women to serve on the force, but none have passed the necessary exams as of this writing.

Beyond accusations of police brutality, a very real concern for Somali parents is the education and safety of their children. The graduation rate for Somalis is low, although the true number is impossible to specify because Somalis are lumped into the "African American" category. Respondents in this study expressed uniform concern about providing educational and employment options for young people, who might otherwise turn to illegal activities, gang affiliation, or other negative behaviors. A Columbus respondent explained:

Somali kids don't see a lot of options. A good number don't graduate [high school], and then they are left without options. They have the same problems we see among other kids from poor areas of Columbus, only they have the added challenge of feeling as though people in the community don't care about them because they're Somali. (Columbus community member interview, March 12, 2015)

A Twin Cities respondent echoed a similar position but was more explicit about the scrutiny Somali youth face as a result of perceptions about terrorist connections:

Our children are assumed to have a propensity toward terrorism or extremism. When the schools fail them, and the public perceives them in this way, they internalize this negativity. We desperately need opportunities for Somali youth so they can be successful, feel confident in society, and achieve their goals. (Twin Cities community member interview A, June 4, 2014)

Anxiety is also high because of the increasing attention of law enforcement officials, who are concerned about terrorist recruitment of Somali youth. Beyond the concern parents feel about this possibility, there is fear that their children will be discriminated against because of their Somali heritage (Columbus community leader interview, June 26, 2014).

Summary

Today, Columbus's Somali population ranks second in size behind that of Minneapolis and ahead of such cities as the District of Columbia, Seattle, Norfolk, and Lewiston. As noted earlier, estimates vary regarding how many Somalis have made Franklin County, Ohio, their home, but the precise number matters less for the purposes of this research than the fact that a sizable population exists.

The city is economically resilient and has nurtured the transition to a service-sector economy in a way that many other Rust Belt cities did not. For this reason, employment opportunities in the Columbus metro community have been attractive to Somali immigrants, although these jobs are largely nonunionized.

The community votes in high numbers and primarily supports Democratic candidates. Realizing the value of the Somali vote, in recent years, some candidates have made appearances at events to woo Somali voters, although these efforts are largely limited to the election season. Even with these appeals, there are few Somali appointed officials and no elected officials. The at-large elections system for the city council significantly limits the chances for Somalis to win seats.

Although several influential community organizations operate within the city, they share very limited collaboration and experience very little outreach from the non-Somali community. Together with the other factors that separate Somalis from the majority population, such as religious traditions, dress, and language, the population remains relatively isolated, especially when compared to that of a region like the Twin Cities.

3 /

The Twin Cities

Somalis in the North Star State

The Twin Cities of Minneapolis and St. Paul, Minnesota, are thriving metropolitan communities in the Upper Midwest. Together, they constitute the fourteenth-largest metropolitan area in the United States and the largest economic hub in the area between Milwaukee, Wisconsin, and the Pacific Coast (Dahl 1988, 111). Each of the cities is an independent municipality, yet their close proximity muddles the distinctions between the two. Minneapolis has a population of 410,000, and St. Paul around 300,000.[1] The metropolitan area of the Twin Cities boasts a population of around three million.[2] St. Paul serves as the state's capital, while Minneapolis is the most populous city in the state and home to the state's flagship educational institution, the University of Minnesota. The Twin Cities area is the most economically resilient region in the Upper Midwest, a region that includes Minnesota, Wisconsin, Michigan, North Dakota, and South Dakota. Because of its strong economy, the Twin Cities area has become an important new destination for immigrants. Although Minnesota's population is largely white, the Twin Cities have a strong

---

1. See https://www.census.gov/quickfacts/table/PST045215/2743000,2758000,00.
2. See http://stats.metc.state.mn.us/profile/detail.aspx?c=R11000.

record of refugee resettlement. The arrival of Somalis in the Twin Cities beginning in the early 1990s has enhanced the area's reputation as one that welcomes newcomers. Today, the Twin Cities are home to the largest Somali population in the nation.

Minnesota is not a major immigration hub, nor is it a very diverse state. With the exception of various American Indian tribes, the region has remained relatively homogenous, with descendants of Scandinavian and German immigrants forming the largest ethnic groups (Fennelly 2006a). Eighty-six percent of the population of Minnesota is white, compared to about 74 percent of the entire U.S. population.[3] Five-year estimates of the state's population in 2014 included only 7.5 percent of residents who were foreign-born,[4] a number significantly below the 13 percent national average.[5] However, these figures are somewhat misleading. Although the state is not among the most diverse in the nation, since 1990, Minnesota's foreign-born population has tripled, while the nation's foreign-born population has increased only twofold.[6] This statistic is especially relevant for the Twin Cities, since the Minneapolis and St. Paul metropolitan region is home to nearly 80 percent of the state's foreign-born population and therefore is the most diverse area of the state.[7] Figure 3.1 includes a map of Hennepin and Ramsey Counties, the area where Minneapolis and St. Paul are located. The map is broken down by census tracts and illustrates where Somalis are concentrated in the Twin Cities. The Twin Cities metro area has the greatest concentration, although Somalis have also settled in other areas in the state because of employment opportunities, particularly in meat-packing facilities. In addition, the region includes a significant percentage of suburban immigrants, a trend primarily related to the lack of affordable housing options, particularly within Minneapolis proper (Fennelly 2006b).

Similar to the trends observed in Columbus, the Twin Cities attracted Somali refugees because of factors that included low-skilled job opportunities in a thriving economy, a low cost of living, and affordable

---

3. See https://www.census.gov/programs-surveys/acs/.
4. See http://www.census.gov/quickfacts/table/PST045215/27.
5. See http://www.census.gov/quickfacts/table/PST045215/00.
6. See MNcompass.org.
7. Ibid.

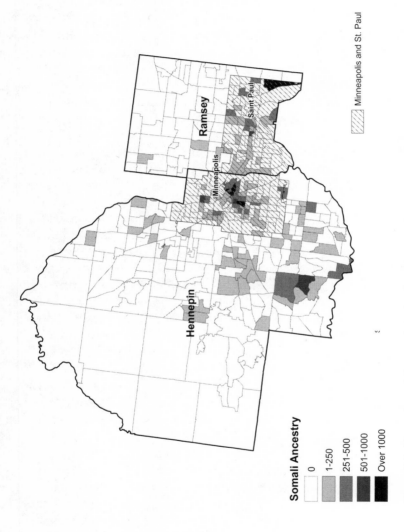

Somali Ancestry
- 0
- 1-250
- 251-500
- 501-1000
- Over 1000

Minneapolis and St. Paul

Figure 3.1. Hennepin and Ramsey Counties Somali population by census tract. *(Graphic created by the author.)*

rental housing options.[8] In addition to these economic attributes, the state has historically provided generous social welfare benefits, offers a strong public education system, contends with little crime, and boasts a reputation for being "Minnesota nice." Moreover, the region has a long history of welcoming other refugee populations, as detailed later in this chapter. Many of the Somalis who moved to Minneapolis in the very early 1990s migrated from California, Virginia, or Texas, some of the major Office of Refugee Resettlement (ORR) relocation sites for Somalis (Fennelly 2006a, 119). The high cost of living and the limited employment options in several of these sites forced many Somalis to look for better options outside their first American cities. Minnesota became a magnet for many Somalis who were willing to endure the dramatic change in climate and frigid winters in exchange for economic opportunity in an area with a rapidly increasing Somali population.

This chapter provides an overview of the Twin Cities and the Somali experience in the region. It offers a foundational backdrop for the analysis in Chapters 4, 5, and 6 on the political, economic, and social incorporation of Somalis in the two cities. In this chapter, several key aspects of the Twin Cities are presented as they relate to the Somali experience. Whereas the literature on Somalis in Columbus is limited, there is a rich scholarly literature on Somalis in the Twin Cities (Abdi 2014; Ali 2011; Allen 2011; Fennelly 2006a; Fennelly and Orfield 2008; H. Samatar 2005; Yusuf 2012). Drawing on this literature and the fieldwork associated with this book project, the Somali experience is presented and serves as the basis for the discussion of political, economic, and social incorporation in Chapters 4, 5, and 6. Like the previous chapter on Columbus, this chapter begins with three vignettes to illustrate trends in the journeys of Somalis who call the Twin Cities home today.

Somali Vignettes

Liban (pseudonym) left Somalia in the early 1980s in search of educational opportunities in the United States. Even though the civil war

---

8. Many of those affordable housing options have since disappeared as a result of gentrification and near-capacity affordable housing stock (Fennelly 2006b).

had not yet started, Liban sensed that political upheaval was inevitable in Somalia. He explained the situation he left behind in these terms:

> I knew it and could feel the raging lava of discontent roaring beneath us. What I did not know, however, was its destructive nature and how much of my country it was going to consume. But I definitely had the feeling that it was going to explode, and I did not want be a victim. (Twin Cities community member interview, February 10, 2015)

Liban did not enter the United States as a refugee, as so many other Somalis would in the 1990s. Rather, he received a student visa and attended university in St. Louis for a year before running out of money. He connected with Somali friends in Atlanta, moved there, and found a job as a cashier, which he hated. He explained:

> When I did not find what I was looking for in Atlanta, I went on to chase the mirage for greener grass—a typical Somali trait. I next tried my luck with New Orleans, then New York, and ended up in Hartford in 1989. (Twin Cities community member interview, February 10, 2015)

He struggled for several years in Hartford, working as a parking attendant, before enrolling at Trinity College, where he received the necessary financial assistance to flourish. In search of a career after graduating in 1997, and knowing that Minnesota was the state of the progressive politician Hubert Humphrey and the largest home to Somalis in the country, he decided to make the move to Minneapolis:

> I took the first employment opportunity that availed itself to me: a part-time cashier in a downtown Minneapolis parking lot. Soon thereafter, I got a job with the University of Minnesota but kept the part-time [job] for almost ten more years. Through it, I went to graduate school, published some writing, and got married. Now, as we speak, I am teaching in a high school in Minneapolis and still doing some writing. (Twin Cities community member interview, February 10, 2015)

Liban's wife is also a Somali immigrant. They have one son, who is part of a rapidly growing population of first-generation Somali American children who "see the advantage of life here, compared to the experiences of their parents who were raised in Somalia" (Twin Cities community member interview, April 24, 2014). Beyond his social service day job, Liban is a prominent Minnesota author, poet, and playwright today.

————

Nadia left Somalia at the age of eight after the outbreak of civil war. Prior to the war, she lived with her father in Mogadishu. When Nadia was young, her mother passed away, and her father worked as an educator in Somalia. Just before her ninth birthday, she witnessed Somalia erupt in civil war. Nadia moved with her father and extended family to the Utango refugee camp in Kenya, where she spent several years. As in nearly all refugee camps, life was difficult, and death from malaria was rampant. But Nadia continued her studies, and when she was twelve, she and her father moved to Arlington, Virginia, through the refugee resettlement process.

When she arrived in Virginia, she knew only the most basic English phrases. Despite this inexperience with the language, Nadia was placed in a sixth-grade classroom, where she quickly exceled academically and in terms of her English-language skills. She recalled how one of her teachers signed her yearbook each year in a way that tracked her English-language progress:

> My middle school teacher signed my yearbook with phrases that summarized my progress in English and my life trajectory. First, in 1995, he inscribed, "Nadia '95—'Hello and shut up.'" In 1997, he wrote, "Nadia in 1997—'Hi, my name is Nadia, and I want to be your friend.'" In my last middle school yearbook, he wrote, "Nadia 2022—'Hi, my name is Nadia, and I want to be president.'" (Twin Cities community member interview, June 11, 2015)

Nadia's academic progress was positive, but life at home was a challenge financially. Her father, a highly educated man, first worked at the airport in a low-wage position for twelve-hour shifts each day. He later changed jobs and started driving a taxi to make more money to support Nadia and his extended family back home. Eventually, he decided to join other family members in Minneapolis, where he found work in a tech company and later with the U.S. Postal Service. Nadia, too, worked shifts at the post office as a seasonal worker. Eventually, she managed to work occasional night shifts at the post office and hold a job at the Mall of America, all while completing her high school courses in three years. During summers, her father was able to send her to stay with relatives in England, although he insisted that she first take summer-school classes at the high school. His emphasis on education was a critical factor in shaping Nadia's desire and ability to earn an associate degree and then a bachelor's degree.

Today, Nadia holds a prominent position in public service. She is deeply committed to supporting the Somali community, but she also strives to help the non-Somali population understand Somali culture and how Somali American Minnesotans enrich the state's culture. She is politically engaged and regularly participates in Democratic-Farmer-Labor (DFL) Party caucuses and elections. She plans to run for a seat in the Minnesota State Legislature.

Hassan was born in Mogadishu in 1986, the second of four children. When the civil war broke out, Hassan was five years old and left the city with his mother and two younger siblings, but his father stayed behind. The family traveled for the next several years, spending time in several refugee areas, including the Liboye, Dadaab, and Utanka camps. In 1996, he and his family returned by boat to a town in Somalia where conditions were reportedly safe, but the family's sense of safety eroded during the four-year period that followed their return. Believing that their country was too dangerous, they applied for resettlement in the United States. Hassan's older brother had left Somalia years earlier and was settled in Minneapolis, working as a taxi driver. When the family of four arrived, none had any formal education, as they had grown up constantly moving between refugee camps with very few options for schooling. Hassan spoke no English and started school in eighth grade at the age of fourteen. He explained:

I went to school at Sanford Middle School. There were a lot of Somalis at the school, and we received ESL [English as a second language] instruction. This was my first experience with formal education. (Twin Cities union interview, April 16, 2015)

Hassan graduated from high school on time, at age eighteen. Minnesota's mandatory high school exams, particularly the writing component, posed a major challenge, but he ultimately passed and received his diploma. He enrolled in community college but soon dropped out. With his two jobs as an airport dispatcher and security guard, the time and cost of education were unmanageable. Through his security position, he joined Service Employees International Union (SEIU) Local 26 and soon started organizing other Somali security officers. The union leaders recognized his talent, and in 2011 they hired him as an SEIU union organizer. Today, he works with a range of SEIU members, but he plays a particularly important role for Somali members. Hassan explained:

I can relate to them, and they can talk to me about what is wrong. Rather than telling a Caucasian person, they feel comfortable with me. I speak their language, I'm in the community, and I can help them. (Twin Cities union interview, April 16, 2015)

Beyond Hassan's labor work, he assists SEIU members with organizing in response to policy issues that matter in the community, such as remittances and the desire for Islamic-compliant mortgage loans.

These vignettes highlight the mobility of many Somalis in the United States, along with the successes that some have achieved in Minnesota. Virtually every Somali respondent in this study has experienced significant uprooting, many having spent time in multiple American cities. The challenges Liban, Nadia's father, and Hassan faced in finding living-wage jobs are another common thread in the lives of so many Somali Americans, not just those in Minnesota. The other themes that come through in these Twin Cities vignettes are the significance of unions and the ways in which Minnesota's culture has opened doors that remain closed in Ohio. What is also noteworthy about Liban, Nadia, Hassan, and the many other respondents in this study is that they are passionate about sharing their stories with a non-Somali like me, because they want their collective experiences to be understood.

Immigration, Refugee History, and the Twin Cities

Although southern and coastal states have larger immigrant populations and received more immigrants between 1990 and 2010, some important midwestern outliers, such as Minnesota, also attract a notable number of settlers (Fennelly 2012). The state as a whole experienced a 235 percent increase in the number of foreign-born residents from 1990 to 2010 (1). One noteworthy characteristic of the state's foreign-born population is that it includes one of the highest proportions of refugees in the nation (Fennelly and Orfield 2008). Like Ohio, these population changes can be seen in the number of English-language learners (ELLs) in the public schools: Minnesota experienced a 350 percent increase in ELL students between 1990 and 2000 (7).

The state's refugee relocation tradition started after the federal Displaced Persons Act of 1948 (Fennelly 2006a, 118). Minnesota has seven voluntary organizations that help refugees transition to life in the state (11), including Lutheran Social Services, Catholic Charities USA, Minnesota Council of Churches, International Institute of Minnesota, Arrive Ministries, Jewish Family Service, and Jewish Family and Children's Service of Minneapolis (11). Voluntary agencies—operating with a budget of $425 per person (Ali 2011,88)—help refugees secure English-language courses, housing, and health care for the first ninety days they are in the country (DeRusha 2011). Once the 90 days are up, refugees rely on public services and nonprofits as well as on family and friends (Ali 2011, 90).

Since the end of World War II, Minnesota has accepted large numbers of refugees. The state was among the first to accept Jewish refugees from Europe in 1948, in the aftermath of the Holocaust (Ali 2011, 90). Although the Jewish experience in Minnesota was not always easy (Berman and Schloff 2014; Weber 1991), the state has a rich Jewish tradition today. In the late 1980s, Russian refugees established roots in the Twin Cities as the Soviet Union began to collapse (Fennelly 2006a, 120). More significant non-European immigration in Minnesota happened in the 1970s, when many Southeast Asians—many belonging to the Hmong ethnic group, which comprises Asian ethnic groups from China, Vietnam, Laos, Myanmar and Thailand[9]—began to find refuge in Minnesota, and specifically in St. Paul. The Hmong American population explosion after the end of the Vietnam War occurred thanks to government, nonprofit, and religious outreach to struggling Hmong groups in Asia (Fennelly 2006a, 120). Secondary migration of Hmong from other regions, such as Fresno, California, to the Twin Cities has made the area home to one of the largest Hmong communities in the nation (120). By 2000, the Hmong population had reached 42,863, a 225 percent jump since 1990 (120). Hmong political involvement in St. Paul has resulted in high levels of political incorporation and election to local and state offices (Lor 2009).

Latinos are also an increasingly influential group in the Twin Cities. Although the largest proportion of the Latino population is Mexican American, other Central and South Americans are represented in the region. In the 1980s, refugees from countries including El Salvador and Guatemala arrived in the Twin Cities as a consequence of civil war in their native lands. Others from more peaceful areas came in search of economic opportunities. As noted in the economic overview earlier in this chapter, the availability of jobs in the meat-processing plants in the state has been a major draw for immigrants searching for a life where jobs, quality education, and a reasonable cost of living are within reach.

Similar to the story of Somalis in Columbus, a large number of Somalis arrived in the Twin Cities after civil war erupted in their homeland around 1991. Minnesota's history with refugee resettlement was an important precursor to the arrival of Somalis. The networks and voluntary agencies that aided Hmong refugees a decade earlier were well established (Yusuf 2012, 42). In Minnesota, as in

---

9. See http://education.mnhs.org/immigration/communities/hmong.

other parts of the nation, refugees receive federal, state, and local support for a period of time to help with their economic and social transition (Singer and Wilson 2006), but Minnesota is an outlier in terms of its social service benefits: 28 percent of state revenues go to social welfare programs (Ali 2011, 90). Minnesota's generous social service benefits, strong public school and university systems, employment options, and reasonable cost of living played comparatively positive roles for Somalis who settled in the state. The area also boasts a large number of nonprofits, homeless shelters, and food banks (90). As a result, Somalis and other East Africans, including Ethiopians and Kenyans, began arriving in increasing numbers in the 1990s. Table 3.1 reflects the changes in St. Paul's foreign-born population from 1980 to 2010. After the Hmong population, East Africans are the largest foreign-born population in that city, a figure that includes Somalis. Table 3.2 illustrates the population by country of origin in Minneapolis, where East Africans, including Somalis, constitute the largest percentage of the foreign-born population.

TABLE 3.1. FOREIGN-BORN POPULATION BY COUNTRY OF BIRTH, ST. PAUL, 2009–2013 ESTIMATES

Country	Foreign-born population by birth country	% Foreign-born population by birth country
Laos	8,935	17.3%
East Africa, including Somalia*	8,222	15.9%
Mexico	7,041	13.6%
Thailand	6,997	13.6%
Burma	3,254	6.3%
Vietnam	1,970	3.8%
El Salvador	1,681	3.3%
China	1,360	2.6%
Other (including all populations < 2%)	12,149	23.5%
Total	51,609	100.0%

Source: Data from U.S. Census Bureau, 2009–2013 American Community Survey.

*Includes Burundi, Comoros, Djibouti, Madagascar, Malawi, Mauritius, Mayotte, Mozambique, Reunion, Rwanda, Seychelles, Somalia, Tanzania, Uganda, Zabia, and Zimbabwe.

TABLE 3.2. FOREIGN-BORN POPULATION BY COUNTRY OF BIRTH, MINNEAPOLIS, 2009–2013 ESTIMATES

Country	Foreign-born population by birth country	% Foreign-born population by birth country
East Africa, including Somalia*	13,876	23.5%
Mexico	12,156	20.5%
Ecuador	4,444	7.5%
Laos	2,955	5.0%
China	2,505	4.2%
India	2,102	3.6%
Korea	2,023	3.4%
Thailand	1,667	2.8%
Other (including all population < 2%)	17,438	29.5%
Total	59,166	100.0%

Source: Data from U.S. Census Bureau, 2009–2013 American Community Survey.

*Includes Burundi, Comoros, Djibouti, Madagascar, Malawi, Mauritius, Mayotte, Mozambique, Reunion, Rwanda, Seychelles, Somalia, Tanzania, Uganda, Zabia, and Zimbabwe.

Although the rich diversity of refugees-turned-Minnesotans offers the state many benefits, the receiving community has also faced some important challenges. Mental health problems are an issue for many Somalis in the United States who came to the country as refugees. The majority have experienced some level of trauma, and for some, the experiences were extreme. For this reason, the Twin Cities region has developed a mental health infrastructure to serve this population. The same issues exist in Columbus, but the mental health infrastructure specifically for refugees there is not as comprehensive as that found in the Twin Cities, or in Minnesota more broadly. The Amherst H. Wilder Foundation in St. Paul has researched the implications of the mental health of refugees (Thao 2009). Unmet mental health needs, coupled with economic hardship, can make life very challenging for refugees, who also face the stigma associated with asking for help. Therefore, many vulnerable Somalis have resorted to living in homeless shelters in increasing numbers, according to several Somali community leaders queried in this study (Twin Cities community leader interview, June 3, 2014; Twin Cities community leader interview B, June 3, 2014).

The Twin Cities: A Strong Economy

A combination of geographic, agricultural, and transportation innovations in the 1800s contributed to the early economic power of the Twin Cities. Railroad expansion in the late 1800s facilitated the movement of agricultural products and livestock westward from Minnesota. Minneapolis would come to be known as the "Mill City," because wheat from the Upper Midwest was sent to mills in Minneapolis for conversion to flour (Dahl 1988). The city's strategic location on the Mississippi River and the waterpower it derived from St. Anthony Falls gave Minneapolis the advantage of being able to operate mills and the ability to transport products downriver to gulf ports (Dahl 1988). Where Minneapolis had the advantage of St. Anthony Falls, St. Paul's location on the Mississippi was easier to navigate and gave St. Paul a trade advantage (Kane 1961). The desire of Minneapolis's leaders to dominate manufacturing and trade created conflict between the two cities. Much like the early "urban wars" between such cities as Wheeling, West Virginia, and Cincinnati, Ohio, a rivalry existed between the Twin Cities over control of portions of the Mississippi (Wade 1959): St. Paul desired waterpower, and Minneapolis coveted navigable parts of the Mississippi. However, both cities were ultimately able to develop independently into major commercial industrial metropolises. Lucile Kane notes:

> Both [cities] were the commercial industrial cities they had dreamed of becoming, and together in relative peace, they formed the double-headed metropolis supreme in the northwest. (1961, 323)

By the mid-1900s, the Twin Cities region was attracting European immigrants for work in agriculture, food processing, and the countless industrial jobs needed to support the agribusiness industry. Such companies as the Minnesota Grain Exchange, Cargill, General Mills

(Pillsbury), and Land O'Lakes were major employers in the region for many years (Dahl 1988).

The financial services industry developed in Minneapolis to meet the needs of the farming industry (Dahl 1988). Even as the United States experienced shifts in industrial capacity, the Twin Cities area remained economically strong because of its twentieth-century expansion into service, health care, and banking. Companies including 3M, Target, Best Buy, SuperValu, UnitedHealth Group, and US Bancorp are some of the leading employers in the region. Owing in part to government jobs in St. Paul and the state capital and the many employment opportunities created by the University of Minnesota, the region has remained the powerhouse of the Upper Midwest. Table 3.3 illustrates the employment levels by decade, alongside the foreign-born population from 1940 through 2010. Like Table 2.3, Table 3.3 demonstrates a steady increase in employment as the foreign-born population increases, particularly in Minneapolis.

City	Year	Total population	Total employment	% Total employment	% Foreign born	Foreign-born population
ST. PAUL	1940	287,736	104,216	36.2%	11.7%	33,716
	1950	311,349	128,010	41.1%	7.8%	24,344
	1960	313,411	123,233	39.3%	5.6%	17,414
	1970	309,866	125,357	40.5%	3.9%	12,085
	1980	270,230	125,331	46.4%	4.9%	13,135
	1990	272,235	131,022	48.1%	7.3%	19,873
	2000	287,151	139,067	48.4%	14.3%	41,138
	2010	285,068	140,451	49.3%	17.9%	51,027
MINNEAPOLIS	1940	492,370	186,386	37.9%	13.1%	64,364
	1950	521,718	231,300	44.3%	9.4%	48,862
	1960	482,872	207,831	43.0%	7.1%	34,448
	1970	434,400	190,528	43.9%	4.8%	20,851
	1980	370,951	183,033	49.3%	4.9%	18,260
	1990	368,383	188,558	51.2%	6.1%	22,471
	2000	382,618	203,951	53.3%	14.5%	55,475
	2010	382,578	207,045	54.1%	15.2%	58,152

TABLE 3.3. TWIN CITY POPULATION AND EMPLOYMENT, 1940–2010

Source: Data from U.S. Census Bureau, 2010 Decennial Census; 2010 employment data from 2010 American Community Survey five-year estimates.

Another important factor in Minnesota's economic history is the progressive policy making in the 1970s that led to an innovative tax-sharing program known as the "Minnesota Miracle." Under this program, 40 percent of the business tax base is shared and distributed regionally to create greater fiscal equity. Essentially, this funding formula gives poorer communities the ability to fund important public services, including firefighting and policing. Along similar policy lines, the Twin Cities have made a concerted effort to integrate low-income housing. For a fifteen-year period, 70 percent of all public housing was located in predominately white, suburban communities. This housing policy is no longer in place, but the region has done better than many others in terms of programs that fight poverty and help with integration (Newshour 2015).

A diversified economy has been a key element to economic success in the Twin Cities. Even during the Great Recession of 2008–2009, the unemployment rate in the Twin Cities reached only 8.9 percent, compared to national averages that hit 10 percent in October 2009, according to the U.S. Bureau of Labor Statistics. In the eighteen years prior to the recession, the region was thriving in terms of employment and gross domestic product (Senf 2003 quoted in Fennelly 2006a, 117). Current unemployment rates from the Department of Labor hover around 3 percent, still below the national average of around 5.5 percent.[10] Agricultural production also remains an important industry in the Twin Cities, as are blue-collar jobs in the service sector. The Twin Cities have attracted a large number of immigrants and refugees in search of a better life for themselves and their families.

Somalis in particular hold many jobs in the meat-processing plants as well as many blue-collar janitorial, industrial, and service positions in the Twin Cities. A small but important cohort of Somalis hold highly skilled white-collar jobs in medicine, politics, and academia. Others have become businesspeople; some are highly successful, but far more operate without much economic security (Golden, Garad, and Boyle 2011; H. Samatar 2005). It is estimated that at least 375 Somali small businesses operate in the Twin Cities (Golden, Boyle, and Jama 2010, 44). As in Columbus, some of these

---

10. See http://data.bls.gov/pdq/SurveyOutputServlet.

small businesses are undercapitalized and exist in a saturated market—specifically, small shops that operate in Somali malls (Golden, Garad, and Boyle 2011; H. Samatar 2005).

Political Culture in the Twin Cities

Daniel Elazar's classic book on political culture in the states, *Exploring Federalism* (1987), classifies Minnesota as a "moralistic" state. According to Elazar's model, moralistic states build government structures that promote the public good, where the bureaucracy is viewed as potentially advancing common goals, and where collaboration with nongovernmental entities is seen as a way to advance communal interests. Elazar, Virginia Gray, and Wyman Spano would later write a book about Minnesota's political culture that characterizes it as "the archetypical example" of a state with a moralistic culture (1999, 19). According to Robert Putnam's Social Capital Index, Minnesota consistently ranks among the top states in terms of community networks and social trust (2000, 293). The state is considered to be wholesome, as evident in the 1973 *Time* magazine cover with the state's governor pictured fishing in one of the state's ten thousand lakes with the caption, "Minnesota: A State That Works" (Risjord 2005, 224). The National Public Radio celebrity Garrison Keillor and his iconic Lake Wobegon have reinforced this image for much of the country. Befitting its image of an involved and caring place, Minnesota also ranks first in the nation for voter turnout (Fennelly 2008, 1).

When it comes to Minnesota politics, progressive politicians, including Hubert Humphrey, Walter Mondale, Paul Wellstone, and Al Franken, who represent the state at the national level, come to mind. However, the state's liberal reputation is not entirely accurate. One scholar commented that "in a few generations government in Minnesota has gone from conservative to radical to liberal to cautious to receiving leadership from a wrestler who says he stunned the world" (Brandl 2000, 191). The wrestler referenced is Jesse "The Body" Ventura, who served one term as the state's governor under the Reform Party label from 1999 to 2003. Former Tea Party leader Michele Bachmann also served in the U.S. House of Representatives from 2007 to 2014. Minnesota is a state more appropriately seen as a "maverick" in terms of independent-minded politicians (Risjord 2005), but its progressive spirit *can* be seen through Minnesota's cutting-edge social service benefits, particularly in terms of health care for children and the poor (227). However, these liberal social service offerings are shrinking as the state moves in a conservative direction with a Republican governor and a Republican-controlled State House of Representatives, although the State Senate remains in DFL hands.

Minnesota as a whole may be veering toward the right, but progressive traditions still continue to shape the state. Senator Wellstone (1991–2002) was a leader in this regard. Even though civil rights advocates, such as Humphrey and Mondale, were household names in national politics, there was very little coalitional politics between the DFL and the small percentage of racial and ethnic minorities in the state prior to Wellstone's rise to power (Twin Cities academic interview, June 2, 2014). In fact, outreach to African Americans by the DFL was almost nonexistent before Wellstone's Senate victory (Twin Cities academic interview, June 2, 2014). He was known as the politician who tried to organize marginalized groups, such as the Hmong and later the Somalis (Twin Cities academic interview, June 2, 2014). Although African Americans made noteworthy efforts to influence politics in the Twin Cities (Delton 2001), as did American Indians who organized the American Indian Movement (AIM) in Minneapolis in 1968 (Wilkins and Stark 2010), DFL party members did not focus much of their attention on mobilizing racial and ethnic minorities. Wellstone was a professor-turned-progressive-politician who engaged in grassroots mobilization throughout the state in the late 1980s. Just as Somalis were making a home in the Twin Cities, Wellstone was making a name for himself in the U.S. Senate. One respondent noted:

> We were becoming Americans as he was becoming a senator. He met with us, listened to us, and tried to help us. This was important, because he didn't need us. We couldn't vote when we arrived, so he didn't need us in the electoral sense. (Twin Cities community member interview B, April 13, 2015)

Wellstone's outreach to Somalis was uniformly mentioned by Somali respondents in this study as an example of Minnesota's welcoming climate. His untimely death in a plane crash in 2002 left large shoes to fill. Fortunately, the leadership of DFL politicians, including Mayor R. T. Rybak and Congressman Keith Ellison, renewed the optimism among many Somalis, who viewed these individuals as vital political allies. Rybak ran for office in 2001 and served as Minneapolis's mayor from 2002 to 2014. He not only courted Somali voters but also took their interests to heart as a leader. He commented:

> I was mesmerized by how much [Somali] people knew about politics. . . . It was great that there was this core group of very knowledgeable Somalis. I came to learn that this was not unique. Somalis in Minneapolis are the most politically aware group of any group, including longtime-established Anglos. (Rybak interview, July 11, 2014)

Congressman Ellison is the state's first African American member of Congress and the first Muslim to ever serve in the House of Representatives. For Somalis, almost all of whom are Muslim, their faith connection to Ellison is important. He has been one of the foremost supporters of maintaining opportunities for family remittances, a major concern for Somalis in the United States, who often support multiple family members who remain in Africa. The practice has been under fire politically because of claims that some of these funds are being diverted to terrorist organizations.

The elections of Mayor Rybak and Congressman Ellison coincided with Somalis' gaining their citizenship and voting rights and thus becoming an important political force. As seen in Columbus, Somalis in Minnesota vote in high numbers. The precise number of voters is impossible to determine, but many scholars estimate that about 80 percent of eligible Somali Americans vote in presidential elections (Greenblatt 2013). Among those interviewed for this study, many insisted that Somalis are keenly interested in politics because of their personal experiences in their homeland (Twin Cities community member interview, May 24, 2014) and that they take civic responsibility very seriously. As a result of the political engagement of Somalis in Minnesota, today's successful DFL candidates must consider their interests when campaigning and leading.

The Minneapolis City Council is composed of thirteen wards with members who serve a four-year term. Since 2009, the city council has been elected using a single-transferrable vote system, which essentially allows voters to rank their choices and can lead to an instant runoff. Some argue that this system helps underrepresented groups win elections, because they can strongly back candidates who reflect their interests or demographics (McClain and Stewart 2010, 62). The diversity of the city council, which reflects demographic patterns in the city, indicates that this contention is correct. The 2013 council election was especially significant, because the first Hmong, Somali, and Latino representatives were elected. Important organizing by Somalis and Latinos during the 2010 redistricting process, discussed in Chapter 2 and later in this chapter, has opened political doors for both groups.

Abdi Warsami, a Somali American, was elected to the Minneapolis City Council in 2013 and is the first elected Somali state representative in the nation. Prior to Warsami's election, Hussein Samatar, who was elected in 2010 to the Minneapolis School Board, became the first Somali American ever voted into public office in the country. His untimely death from leukemia in 2013 was a tremendous loss for the Somali community. Today, in addition to Representative Warsami, other prominent Somalis have served in elected offices, including Mohamud Noor, who was elected to the school board but then failed by a significant margin to unseat a twenty-two-year incumbent in the state legislature in 2014. As I discuss in the next chapter, there are a number of viable and exciting Somali candidates in the Twin Cities, including some women.

As of this writing (in 2015), the Minneapolis City Council is controlled by the DFL, with one Green Party member in the minority. Since Humphrey's election as mayor in 1945, only one non-DFL candidate has served a four-year term as the mayor of Minneapolis. Since 1966, DFL mayors have also controlled St. Paul, with the exception of Mayor Norm Coleman, who changed his party affiliation from DFL to Republican in 1996. The St. Paul City Council also uses a ward system of elections and is fully controlled by the DFL.

Unions

The state of Minnesota, like Ohio, is not a "right-to-work" state, which means that only union members are allowed to benefit under collective-bargaining agreements reached with employers. According to U.S. Bureau of Labor Statistics data from 2012 to 2013, both Minnesota and Ohio rank among the top eleven states in terms of union membership. As discussed in Chapter 2, Ohio's unions withstood an attempt by Republican legislators to end collective-bargaining rights for public-sector workers. Minnesota has not been immune from these challenges, but it has not passed legislation that limits unionization, as has happened in its neighboring state of Wisconsin.

Minneapolis gained a reputation as an anti-union area in the early 1900s because of the actions of a business group called the Citizens Alliance that fought against unionization. As time passed and as labor frustrations grew, labor protests began to be held in Minneapolis. In 1934, packinghouse workers attempted to unionize under the Teamsters. A strike ensued for several months, until President Franklin Roosevelt ultimately intervened to end the conflict. This action marked the end of the "open-shop" or anti-union period in Minneapolis, and it contributed to the passage of the National Labor Relations Act in 1935, a law that created many safeguards for private-sector employees attempting to unionize (Gilman 2000, 7–10). This New Deal–era law would change the role of unions in Minnesota and nationally (Delton 2001). Jennifer Delton (2001) argues that unionized positions opened doors to African American Minnesotans who previously faced barriers to entering certain jobs. Along the same lines, she contends that involvement in unions increased African Americans' political influence and contributed to the success of a number of African American leaders in the city, who would be important in the development of Minnesota's DFL Party.

Another important aspect of Minnesota's labor history is the union between farmers and urban laborers that led to the creation of the state's Farmer-Labor Party in the 1920s. Progressive values, including a commitment to workers' rights, Social Security, and public ownership of resources, encompassed their focus. In 1944, a merger between the Farmer-Labor Party and the Democratic Party was negotiated by Hubert Humphrey, the Minnesota politician who, as a result of this feat, became known as the father of Minnesota's DFL.[11] The DFL Party represents the progressive wing of the national Democratic Party and has succeeded in winning seats at all levels of government.

For the purpose of this study, the most important labor union in the Twin Cities is the Service Employees International Union (SEIU), which represents the industries of property, public services, and health care.[12] In other words, SEIU represents security workers, janitorial and housekeeping staff, and health care employees. This union boasts the largest immigrant membership and is remarkably diverse. Recent literature on unions indicates that many do not often engage in organizing efforts that speak to the racial, ethnic, class, and gender injustices workers face today (Bronfenbrenner and Warren 2007, 145), yet SEIU Local 26 is an exception. Somalis in the Twin Cities make up a large and influential portion of SEIU's membership, specifically Local 26 in Minneapolis, which represents about six thousand workers.[13] Although the specific numbers are difficult to estimate, this union includes many Somali members and has become an important stepping-stone for Somali leaders in the Twin Cities, as is discussed in Chapter 4. The SEIU counts Somalis among its leadership, and the ties between the union and the DFL Party are strong (Twin Cities union interview, July 11, 2014). Research also demonstrates that union participation is correlated with political participation (Lee, Ramakrishnan, and Ramírez 2007; Ramakrishnan and Bloemraad 2008). In addition to the SEIU's clear interest in mobilizing Somalis in the labor movement, SEIU members have made an effort to increase voter turnout (Twin Cities union interview, July 11, 2014). According to one Somali leader in the SEIU, there is an inter-

---

11. See DFL.org.
12. See SEIU.org.
13. Ibid.

est in nurturing Somalis who might run for political office someday (Twin Cities union interview, April 16, 2015). When one enters the SEIU offices in Minneapolis, multiple political banners and connections to DFL leaders, such as the city's current mayor, are apparent everywhere. Speaking to the diversity within the union, its T-shirt includes an organizing slogan in the five most common languages of its members. Although SEIU's work is noteworthy in the Twin Cities, it is important to emphasize that many Somalis in low-skilled jobs, particularly those in the food-processing sector, hold nonunion jobs (Fennelly 2006a, 123).

Community Organizations

A wide variety of Somali community organizations operate within the Twin Cities. The majority are in Minneapolis, with many housed at the Brian Coyle Center in the heart of the Cedar-Riverside neighborhood. Not only is this area Minneapolis's primary Somali residential community; Cedar-Riverside has the densest concentration of Somalis in the nation (Ali 2011, 103). The organizations found in this community range from youth antiviolence groups, to social service organizations, to groups dedicated to helping Somali women. Several of these organizations play a critical role in mobilizing the Somali community to participate in the political process beyond merely voting. Research on ethnic organizations suggests that these groups do not compete with unions and other organizations for ethnic members, because the linguistic and cultural benefits associated with these groups trump what others can offer (Aptekar 2009, 6). The vibrancy of many of the Somali organizations in Minneapolis generally aligns with this finding. Although this project finds that SEIU Local 26 does indeed play a pivotal role in the mobilization of Somalis, Somali community groups are also politically significant in the lives of many Somalis in the Twin Cities. More importantly, these organizations do not require any particular occupational status for entry.

As noted above, the Brian Coyle Center is the hub for Somali community organizations. The center is funded through Pillsbury United Communities, a major philanthropic organization in Minneapolis that was founded in the nineteenth-century tradition of settlement houses (Ali 2011, 103). Its mission statement reads:

> Brian Coyle Center brings people together. We promote social and economic equality for the residents of our community through programming that builds strength and the entrepreneurial spirit in youth, seniors, adults, and families and, through learning, creates connections that help our community thrive.[14]

Minnesota is a state with a strong philanthropic spirit, which is reflected in the support that Somali community organizations receive from such groups as Pillsbury. But in recent years, the funding available through these types of foundations for Somali community groups has shrunk. Of course, this situation is not unique to the Twin Cities but is the result of broader market forces related to economic downturns. Despite this decrease in funding, many Somali community organizations remain influential and, increasingly, act in cooperation with one another to form coalitions. One community leader said:

> We have meetings together to discuss common interests and concerns in our community. Being here at Brian Coyle together is an advantage, because we work together, in a sense. (Twin Cities community member interview B, June 4, 2014)

Many of the Somali organizations in the Twin Cities are Mutual Assistance Associations. The Minnesota Department of Human Services provides technical and capacity-building support to refugee-led groups that are dedicated to supporting their community (Ali 2011, 89). These types of organizations, combined with voluntary agencies and public-sector support, have helped create a "resettlement infrastructure" for refugee communities (89). Yet despite the vibrancy of Somali organizations, their reach does not extend far beyond Somalis and the broader East African community (Twin Cities community leader interview, April 15, 2015), although there are signs that this

---

14. See http://puc-mn.org/brian-coyle-center.

is changing. While conducting research for this project, I attended several meetings involving Somali and non-Somali community leaders to discuss such issues as educational outreach to Somali parents. There is also evidence that some Somali organizations are actively engaged in forging alliances with other marginalized groups in the city (Twin Cities community leader interview, June 5, 2014). Still, Somali membership in organizations that serve the broader Twin Cities population remains limited (Twin Cities community leader interview, June 5, 2014; Twin Cities community member interview D, June 4, 2014). Because of their figurative and literal concentration in the Twin Cities, Somalis remain relatively isolated, which has implications for their political, economic, and social power, as discussed in Chapters 4, 5, and 6.

One noteworthy community organization in Minneapolis is the African Development Center (ADC), a social-profit community developer and commercial lender.[15] The ADC operates three offices in areas of Minnesota with Somali communities: Minneapolis, Rochester, and Willmar. It specializes in business development, homebuyer workshops, and financial literacy training. Many of the small-business loans offered by the ADC have helped Somali business owners through the use of "culturally sensitive lending" (African Development Center interview A, April 15, 2015). Meanwhile, the organization's homebuyer workshops, which are intended to introduce newcomers to the financial benefits of homeownership in the United States, have offered practical and much-needed advice. Although the ADC is open to all Minnesotans, it specifically targets Somalis, who are especially in need of its services (African Development Center interview A, April 15, 2015).

The Twin Cities region is also known for having a strong community organizing tradition that is aligned with Somali interest in politics. Several Somali leaders have been trained by an organization called Voices for Racial Justice through the group's Organizing Apprenticeship Program (OAP). Employing Saul Alinsky–style strategies and tactics, the group has collaborated with Somali community organizations in the Twin Cities and has even played a role in train-

---

15. See http://www.adcminnesota.org/about/mission.

ing the founder of one of the community's most influential Somali political nonprofits, Somali Action Alliance (SAA). One non-Somali community organizer noted:

> The Organizing Apprenticeship Program (OAP) in Minneapolis has provided years of training in racial and social justice organizing the area. They adapted training for the Somali community in a way that allowed apprentices to maintain their cultural integrity while learning about collaboration with other organizations and communities. (Twin Cities community member interview A, June 2, 2014)

One Somali who went through the training explained:

> I trained as an organizer for six months through the OAP apprenticeship program. The first month, I learned about how to network and get thinking like an American, to get away from the suitcase mentality—basically, to unpack the figurative suitcase and participate here. I learned to organize our people, too, and help them vote and participate in politics. (Twin Cities community leader interview, June 5, 2014)

This training has clear ties to the work of SAA, the only Somali community organization dedicated to civic engagement, leadership training, and democratic participation (Twin Cities community member interview, June 5, 2014). Today, SAA is part of OAP, and many Somalis have received community organizing training under its purview.

Religion

Like Ohio, Minnesota is a state where religion plays a significant role in the daily lives of residents. A 2009 study by Gallup found that both states are at the median in terms of the daily importance of religion in the lives of residents (Newport 2009). Minnesota's widespread Scandinavian and German roots have led to the denominational concentration of Christians in the state. Lutherans constitute

25 percent of the population of the Twin Cities, with Catholics being the second-largest denomination after Lutherans, at 23 percent.[16] St. Paul has a larger concentration of Catholics as a result of its early French Canadian settlers and its strong contemporary German and Irish communities (Gilman 2000). Minneapolis is more heavily Scandinavian and Protestant, with Lutherans being especially prominent (Gilman 2000). The arrival of Polish and Russian Jews in the 1920s (Gilman 2000) resulted in years of religious discrimination, especially in terms of employment opportunities (Weber 1991). Consequently, Jewish immigrants were forced to rely heavily on self-employment and entrepreneurial ventures for their livelihood (Weber 1991).

Religion is very important for new immigrant communities (Allen 2010). Religious diversification often goes hand in hand with the arrival of new immigrant groups. Just as the arrival of Polish and Russian Jews in the 1920 increased the religious diversity in Minneapolis, so, too, has the Somali diaspora. As noted in Chapter 2, Somalis are predominantly Sunni Muslims, and many of their social customs and gender roles are derived from Islamic customs. While Somalis found it difficult at first to practice their faith in an area that was not predominantly Islamic, they have opened businesses and organizations that align with their religious preferences (Carlson 2007; H. Samatar 2005). For example, the importance of daily time for prayer and the acceptance of women's distinctive dress contributed to the emergence of Somali small-business development in the Twin Cities. Like Jews years earlier, a number of Somalis opted to open businesses as a way to make a living while remaining in adherence with Islamic religious practice.

Education

Minnesota is the state where charter schools got their start. In 1991, the Minnesota State Legislature passed the nation's first charter school law, and the following year the first charters opened in the Twin Cities.[17] Like Columbus, the Twin Cities area is home to a

---

16. See http//ssrs.com and http://publicreligion.org.
17. See http://www.leg.state.mn.us/lrl/issues/issues?issue=charterLike.

number of charter schools with Islamic themes that attract a range of students, including Somalis. The precise number of Somali students in charter schools is unknown, because Somalis are generally categorized under the African American subgroup. In other words, specific data on Somalis are not collected by the school systems or the Minnesota Department of Education. Somalis run at least ten charter schools (Yusuf 2012), and other charter schools operating in the Twin Cities incorporate Islamic-friendly themes. During my visit to a charter elementary school in St. Paul in 2014, I was able to observe a Somali-language class. The students in the class were in the first grade and spoke little to no Somali. Their instructor, who is also a prominent imam in Minneapolis, patiently led the students in a Somali song and shared pictures from Somalia. This short course offered a glimpse of the cultural richness in these schools, something some Somali parents clearly value in charter schools.

Some Somalis who have started charter schools in the Twin Cities did so because of conflicts that emerged between Somali and African American students (Twin Cities community member interview, June 1, 2014). In his book about Somalis in Minnesota, Ahmed Yusuf writes:

> With Somalis' arrival in Minnesota, cultural collisions soon surfaced in the schools. . . . Conflict arose as African American students and Somali students, often in competition for the same limited resources, began fighting with each other. These schoolyard challenges reflected what was happening in the adult communities, where families living in economically disadvantaged neighborhoods vied for inexpensive and subsidized housing, welfare and medical benefits, and other meager resources. (2012, 48)

Other Somalis were interested in finding schools where their children could more easily balance their education with their religious and cultural beliefs (Twin Cities community member interview, June 1, 2014). Whether these objectives have been met cannot be determined based on this study, but the topic is certainly worthy of additional scholarly attention.

Somalis in the Twin Cities: Adaptation and Challenges

Like Somalis in Columbus, Somalis in the Twin Cities have faced a number of challenges. Their hardship became more pronounced post-9/11, when Muslims in the United States faced increased scrutiny and discrimination. To complicate matters, twenty-seven young Somali men left Minneapolis from 2006 to 2011 to join al-Shabaab in Somalia (Temple-Raston 2015). More recently, eleven men and one woman left the Twin Cities to fight alongside ISIS in Syria (Temple-Raston 2015). Although the number of Somalis leaving to join terrorist organizations is small compared to the overall Somali population, the Twin Cities region is viewed as an important recruiting location in the United States by law enforcement officials (Temple-Raston 2015).

During the fieldwork for this study, participant observation was used as a research strategy during a meeting at the Brian Coyle Center with community leaders and two Federal Bureau of Investigation (FBI) representatives who were sharing information about their investigation of Somali terrorist recruitment efforts in their community. In February 2015, a preliminary blueprint was unveiled by the U.S. Attorney for the District of Minnesota in Minneapolis, who hopes to receive federal funds to counter radicalization in the Twin Cities, primarily through the expansion of social services for youth and more career opportunities (Yuen 2015). The Somali community is very interested in finding a way to stop ISIS's recruitment of their youth, but the proposal is viewed by some with skepticism, since the leading federal prosecutor in the state is behind the plan (Yuen 2015).

Many Somalis are hesitant to work with government agencies, a distrust fueled during the post-9/11 era, as several incidents of police brutality and harassment have since occurred in the Somali community. Shortly after the 9/11 attacks, a Somali elder was assaulted and killed by a white male attacker while waiting for a bus (Ali 2011, 96). In another high-profile case, a mentally ill Somali man was shot multiple times by Minneapolis police while he charged them while brandishing a machete and a crowbar (96). Soon after, several money-wiring businesses were investigated for allegedly funneling money to terrorist organizations (96). Chapter 6 discusses the restrictions on remittances to Somali in greater detail, but in brief, these restrictions have been extraordinarily difficult for Somalis, who often provide the only source of financial support for relatives in Somalia. In early 2015, it was revealed that in 2009, the FBI advised agents in several cities, including the Twin Cities, to use community outreach as a cover for gathering information on terrorist recruitment efforts (McEnroe 2015). Agents in the Twin Cities claim to have ignored the directive for fear it would undermine community trust. Trust building between law enforcement agencies and Somalis in the Twin Cities has been tenuous as a result of claims of police brutality and accusations of profiling by various federal law enforcement agencies (Twin Cities community member interview, May 31, 2014). The issue of immigrant incorporation during times of foreign intervention is addressed in more detail in Chapter 6, which focuses on social incorporation.

Summary

The Twin Cities region is home to the largest Somali population in the United States. The region's experience with refugee resettlement is noteworthy, especially in terms of the number of Somali, Hmong, and Russian refugees who have made a home in the area. Since the 1990s, the foreign-born population has grown dramatically, despite the fact that the state has never been a major immigration hub and is relatively homogenous.

Somalis in the Twin Cities vote in high numbers and have also won positions in elective office. Somali community organizations in the city are well organized in comparison to those in Columbus. Some Somalis work in unionized industries, which has increased their propensity for politicization and their development of leadership skills. Economically, the strength of the Twin Cities has benefited Somalis, who have found employment, although the majority hold low-skilled and fairly low-paying jobs. Still others are self-employed, although many of these businesses are undercapitalized.

Although one could make the case that Somalis in the Twin Cities fare better than those in Columbus, there are some noteworthy exceptions. The high cost of housing and increasing gentrification have increased the cost of living and driven Somalis, as well as other new immigrants, to poorer suburbs of the Twin Cities (Fennelly and Orfield 2008). Educational achievement remains a concern for Somali youth, and the added anxiety regarding terrorist recruitment is a major concern among Somali parents. Chapters 4, 5, and 6 discuss these issues and more, as they provide an analysis of the political, economic, and social incorporation of Somalis in Columbus and the Twin Cities.

4 /

Political Incorporation

> Entry into the political arena can be slow, uneven, and
> truncated, or it can be rapid, effective, and complete. The
> characteristics of individuals, groups, political practices,
> and institutional structures all affect that trajectory.
>
> —JENNIFER L. HOCHSCHILD AND JOHN H. MOLLENKOPF,
> *BRINGING OUTSIDERS IN*

The incorporation of newcomers into the American political system has received considerable attention from migration scholars in recent years (Bloemraad 2006; Chambers et al., forthcoming; Hochschild and Mollenkopf 2009; Hopkins, Tran, and Williamson 2014; Ramakrishnan and Bloemraad 2008). While some have focused on the challenges of incorporating undocumented immigrants, others have examined the experiences of refugees turned permanent residents or the political experiences of new Americans. In this chapter, the experiences of Somalis in Columbus and in the Twin Cities are examined in an effort to understand why the latter area shows higher levels of political incorporation. Emphasis is placed on political incorporation in Minneapolis over St. Paul, because the former is the city where more Somalis live, vote, and serve in elective office.

The work of Rufus P. Browning, Dale Rogers Marshall, and David H. Tabb (1984) serves as the foundation for measuring Somali political incorporation. These authors operationalize political incorporation by evaluating a marginalized group's level of engagement with the political system (25). Building on this definition, political incorporation in this book is defined as the level of engagement with the political system combined with how well group interests are reflected in policy making. This two-stage measure is important, because it includes involvement and policy outcomes. On the one hand, we want to know that groups participate in the democratic process. At the same time, we also want to know that their participation shapes the policy outcomes. Using this definition, it is possible to see engagement with the political system and subsequent responsiveness to— or neglect of—group interests. Incorporation and non-incorporation are best conceptualized as opposite ends of a continuum. The process of immigrant political incorporation begins with entry into the host country and ideally progresses toward influence over political actions and institutions (Hochschild and Mollenkopf 2009, 16). However, Jennifer L. Hochschild and John H. Mollenkopf wisely caution against seeing incorporation as a linear process (2009, 22). For example, even if an immigrant group succeeds in electing a member of the group to office, that individual could be blamed for policies outside his or her control, thus leading to non-incorporation (26). Somali political incorporation in Columbus and the Twin Cities is currently on a linear trajectory, but Hochschild and Mollenkopf's suggestions speak to the need for ongoing attention to immigrant political incorporation, especially because progress can recede.

Although this study considers the traditional idea of political incorporation through voting, I use a concept of political incorporation that reaches beyond this measure of democratic incorporation in an effort to include the other important ways a group can engage with the political system. The traditional mode of investigating political incorporation is especially weak in this case: depending on the stage of a Somali's citizenship status, he or she may not even be eligible to vote. Several key indicators of political incorporation are examined in this chapter to help understand the reasons for the divergent levels of political incorporation in the areas under investigation. Electoral structure, partisan outreach to Somalis, the Somali role in electoral and governing coalitions, bureaucratic outreach to Somalis, the Somali community's levels of union engagement, and the political influence of Somali community organizations are all examined to measure Somali political incorporation. The key finding in this chapter is that, relative to Columbus, several of these measures indicate higher Somali political incorporation in Minneapolis, with St. Paul following in the path of its twin.

Electoral Structures

Electoral structures have consequences. Political scientists have developed a range of theories concerning the effect of electoral structures on outcomes. Beyond the scholarship on this subject, policy makers also recognize that certain electoral structures encourage or depress voting. For example, African American voters, particularly in the U.S. South, experienced decades of limited electoral influence because of the manipulation of district lines by state legislators and other attempts to limit their electoral power. Cracking, stacking, and packing—essentially, the manipulation of district lines by state legislators—were just a few of the techniques intended to reduce the influence of African American voters, especially in terms of electing African Americans to public office. These electoral manipulations have also been used elsewhere in the United States, although they are most commonly associated with the South.

In addition, scholars of American urban, racial, and ethnic politics have written extensively on how at-large electoral structures limit the opportunities for racial and ethnic minorities to win local elections (Barker, Jones, and Tate 1999; Browning, Marshall, and Tabb 1984; Groffmann and Davidson 1992; Parker 1990). Under the at-large system, candidates must run citywide. Because racial and ethnic groups tend to be the minority of voters, and because of racially polarized voting, candidates of color have historically found it hard to capture enough white votes to win elections. In contrast, ward-based elections allow groups that live in racially or ethnically concentrated areas the opportunity to compete in districts where they can influence outcomes. Concentrating minority groups in districts can diminish their electoral power in other districts, but ward systems offer more opportunities for racial and ethnic diversity in elective office. In the Twin Cities, these more-inclusive ward or district elections exist and, therefore, allow Somalis a political voice. In Columbus, the at-large system negatively affects Somalis' political incorporation by reducing their ability to elect politicians that will best represent their interests.

Columbus

Columbus and the Twin Cities use very different electoral structures, which dramatically affects political outcomes. Columbus's at-large system of electing city council and school board members significantly limits opportunities for underrepresented groups to win elections (Alex-Assensoh 2004). Scholars of racial and ethnic politics have long argued that when minorities run in citywide contests, they have a limited chance of victory (Browning, Marshall, and Tabb 1984; Eisinger 1973; Judd and Swanstrom 2015). In contrast, when elections are held at the district or ward level, minorities have a better chance of electing a member of their own racial or ethnic group, because their vote is not diluted by the city's majority racial group. In other words, the majority group is consciously or unconsciously reluctant to vote for someone from a racial or ethnic minority group. Residential segregation of racial and ethnic minorities increases the chance that a minority can be elected in a district-level race. In an ideal situation, this elected official can substantively (through policy making) and descriptively (demographically) represent their constituents.

Until the 1990s, Columbus's African American community remained underrepresented on the city council. After the election of Mayor Michael Coleman in 1999, the number of African Americans elected to the council increased substantially. As of 2015, African Americans hold four of the seven seats on the city council, despite the fact that they constitute only 28 percent of the city's population. The electoral success of African Americans in Columbus did not happen quickly or easily—it was the result of years of hard work and grassroots organizing within the city's African American community. More symbolically, the election of the city's first African American mayor, a former council member himself, provided the community with a role model who inspired other African Americans to run for elective office. Interestingly, a pattern emerged in the 1990s whereby vacancies on the council were sometimes filled with African American council members. These council members often later ran for election and won their seats (see Table 2.3 for details). In contrast to Columbus's African American community, the city has never had a Somali elected official, and only two Somalis have ever been appointed to serve on a city commission.

The elevation of African Americans to the Columbus City Council should not lead one to underestimate the hurdles to electoral success that racial and ethnic minorities face. It took African Americans decades to achieve consistent political success. Even if we assume that the election of African Americans to the city council is evidence that Columbus's voters are open to diversity in that body, Somali residential and social isolation in the city, the absence of party outreach to potential Somali candidates, and a sparse pool of interested Somali political candidates all limit the political prospects of the Somali community. Moreover, African American electoral success was the result of decades of community organizing and the steady rise of business leaders and clergy who collaborated to increase the visibility of the African American community (Alex-Assensoh 2004)—actions that simply have not yet taken place for Somalis (Columbus city bureaucrat interview, June 17, 2013; Columbus city bureaucrat interview, July 24, 2013).

In contrast to the long-term presence of African Americans in Columbus—which, as noted above, was critical for their electoral victories—Somalis are still relatively new to the city. Beyond the challenge of being newcomers to Columbus, the Somali experience differs from the native black experience in other important ways. Somalis face economic challenges, language barriers, residential isolation, and informal discrimination. These factors, combined with the electoral structure of Columbus, make the prospect of Somalis winning elective office without substantial changes to the electoral system unlikely. Court challenges to the at-large system hold little promise of changing it. Even if Somalis mounted a challenge, they would need allies to support their case. Because African Americans have now achieved significant levels of representation on the council, their interest in building a coalition is likely weak. Moreover, the fact that African Americans are now overrepresented on the city council could weaken a case against the at-large electoral structure. Coalitions with other "New Americans," such as the Nepalese or Mexican community, are possible, although neither group has much political capital (Columbus city bureaucrat interview, June 17, 2013; Columbus city bureaucrat interview, July 24, 2013; Columbus community member interview, June 19, 2013). Under present circumstances, the best hope for Somalis interested in electoral representation is to support candidates who reflect their political interests, encourage elected officials to appoint Somalis to visible posts in the city, and nurture potential candidates who might someday run citywide.

Unlike the hurdle posed by Columbus's local electoral structure, the Ohio State Legislature's district elections hold promise for Somali electoral inroads. Because Somalis are concentrated in House District 25 of the city, and because they are rumored to vote in high numbers,[1] some Somali community leaders are hopeful that a strong Somali candidate will run for that seat in the near future. According to data from the American Community Survey's 2013 five-year estimates, of the 14,039 foreign-born in Ohio's House District 25, 59 percent are East African. Although this figure does not specify respondents of Somali origin, it is safe to assume that Somalis compose a majority of this figure, given their population and concentration in the city.[2] The seat is currently held by an African American, Kevin Boyce. Boyce is the former state treasurer and a Columbus City Council member who was appointed to fill the seat vacated by a legislator indicted on bribery charges; he won his election bid for the seat in 2016. To some observers, Boyce is considered vulnerable. One respondent said:

Somalis have little chance of winning a seat on the school board or the city council. However, there is a group of young Somalis at OSU [The Ohio State University] who have been closely evaluating the chances of winning a state legislative seat. This is really our best hope, and we have a real chance. After all, Hussein Samatar [Minneapolis School Board mem-

1. Although no governmental entity compiles the number of eligible Somali voters who regularly cast a vote, this project's respondents noted the high level of Somali voter turnout in Columbus, routinely citing 80 percent (or more) as the figure.

2. See https://www.census.gov/programs-surveys/acs/.

ber] won his seat due, in part, to the Somali vote. (Columbus community member interview, June 19, 2013)

Few Somali respondents interviewed in Columbus reported aspirations of holding elective office. Reversing this trend is a task that would ideally be shared between government leaders and the community itself. Somalis play an important role in the Ohio electorate and are actively courted by candidates during election cycles (Columbus city bureaucrat interview, June 17, 2013; Columbus state bureaucrat interview, December 26, 2013; Federal bureaucrat interview, June 28, 2014). They are reliable Democratic voters, yet Somali social views of marriage, family values, business, and abortion rights align more with those of the Republican Party. According to one Somali community leader, electoral outreach to Somalis is done not by a political party but by individual Democratic candidates (Columbus community leader interview, March 9, 2015). Republicans virtually ignore the community (Columbus community leader interview A, July 26, 2013). Ohio's status as a swing state and the process of Somali political socialization make the Somali vote particularly valuable in national elections. Voters in Ohio's cities have the power to influence the direction of the state's eighteen electoral votes. Unlike other racial and ethnic groups in Columbus, voter turnout is reportedly high among Somalis: precise numbers are impossible to confirm, but several respondents suggested that 80 to 90 percent of eligible Somalis vote. This high level of Somali voter turnout stands in contrast to research indicating that most immigrant groups have low levels of voter turnout (Tam Cho 1999). According to the Somali Community Access Network (SomaliCAN), a community outreach organization based in Columbus, David Robinson, an unsuccessful candidate for the Twelfth Congressional seat in Ohio, relied heavily on the support of Somalis in the area in his 2008 bid for election. He explained:

It's an important number of votes. We figure there's probably going to be somewhere between 350,000 and 400,000 votes cast totally for the 12th Congressional Seat, so 10,000 votes or so is an important constituency. (Robinson quoted in J. Hirsi 2009)

W. Carlton Weddington, the former District 25 representative in the Ohio House of Representatives, campaigned in the Somali community during his 2008 campaign, citing his recognition of the size and political influence of this community. Weddington was responsible for raising the Somali flag outside the Ohio State House to commemorate the forty-ninth anniversary of Somali independence (J. Hirsi 2009). For what SomaliCAN describes as the "first time," Somalis actively participated in the 2008 presidential election. The candidacy of Barack Obama was a significant mobilizing force for the community (Columbus community leader interview, June 27, 2014). Although approximately half of all respondents in this study registered concerns about politicians showing up in the community only when courting the Somali vote, these respondents still remain deeply committed to electoral participation.

During participant observation for this project, I attended a Somali high school graduation event in June 2014 that several Democratic political candidates also attended. One, who was running for a judgeship, was asked to deliver a few remarks to the graduates. The candidate was also a former one-term member of the U.S. House of Representatives, representing Columbus. Her comments quickly shifted from words of congratulations to an appeal for votes. A respondent in this study who also attended the event said:

> The appeal she made reflects the general trend. Democratic candidates want our votes, but they are unwilling to help us once they're in office. When she was in the House of Representatives, we tried to persuade her to appoint a Somali to her staff, and she refused. Now she's pandering for votes. (Columbus community member interview A, June 28, 2014)

This example is relevant, because the limitations of the electoral structure essentially reduce Somali political power. They are pursued during elections but are restricted from participation on governing coalitions.

A related issue is the absence of Somali appointed officials. Appointed officials increase the visibility of an individual and, therefore, that person's community. For this reason, minority politics scholars have long considered the presence or absence of minority appointments as an important component in political incorporation (Browning, Marshall, and Tabb 1984, 146). Currently in Columbus, no Somalis hold appointed positions within the formal government structure or on boards and commissions affiliated with government. However, Mayor Coleman previously appointed two Somalis to serve on the appointed Commission of Community Relations: Hassan Omar (2000–2009) and Musa Farah (2010–2012). The same is true in Franklin County and in Ohio more broadly: there is a total absence of Somali representation on appointed boards and commissions at the county and state levels.

Beyond appointed positions, examining the situation of Somali staffers offers another measure of representation. Aside from the symbolic nature of having a Somali on staff, the professional experience gained through working in a political office can open doors within the political system. There is currently one prominent Somali employee in the mayor's Office of Community Relations—specifically, in the Office of New American Initiative. Since its creation in 2005, two Somali men have held bureaucratic positions in the office. The first man to hold this position is now employed with the Department of Homeland Security, signifying the important stepping-stone this office can provide. However, aside from the Columbus mayor, no other local elected official employs Somali staffers. Somali respondents in this project consistently expressed disappointment that more Somalis are not serving in prominent positions within the city's government. Despite Somali power at the polls, Columbus's politicians have been slow to hire Somalis. Somali community leaders and the current Somali bureaucrat in the New American Initiative office continue to make appeals (Columbus city bureaucrat interview, July 26, 2013; Columbus community leader interview, March 9, 2015).

At the state level, one very prominent Somali man serves within the Department of Education in the Office of Curriculum and Assessment. This individual plays an important role in policies regarding Limited English Proficiency (LEP) programs. In both cases, the Somali bureaucrats at the city and state levels represent issues that are specifically connected to their communities. Although this representation is of vital importance, Somali interests are as broad as the interests of other Ohio residents. For this reason, it is important that Somalis be placed in appointed and elected positions in a variety of policy areas. In addition to the symbolic benefits of such inclusion, it sends a clear message that Somalis are part of the fabric of the political community.

The Twin Cities

The high level of Somali political participation is also evident in the Twin Cities, where it is estimated that voter turnout is often above 80 percent (Greenblatt 2013). Although these figures are unsubstantiated, they remain a commonly referenced statistic among virtually all respondents in this study. Assuming we accept this high level of participation as accurate, it suggests that political candidates likely take Somali views into consideration, at least during campaigns. More importantly, the electoral structure in Minneapolis has created opportunities for Somalis to win city council and school board elections. Both Minneapolis and St. Paul use ward-based electoral systems. Under this structure, minority candidates have a much better chance to win than they do under an at-large system. Both cities also use the single-transferrable vote system, thus allowing voters to rank their choices, a method that gives underrepresented groups a better chance of winning elections (McClain and Stewart 2010, 62). Minneapolis has seen two Somalis serve on the school board: Hussein Samatar was elected in 2010, and Mohamud Noor was appointed after Samatar's unexpected death in 2013. Noor also ran unsuccessfully for the state senate in 2011 and for a state house seat in Minneapolis in 2014. That same year, Abdi Warsami unseated an incumbent to become the first Somali city council representative in the nation. These electoral advances have stemmed, in part, from the electoral structure in the area.

Hussein Samatar, the first Somali elected to the school board, was a business leader in the Somali community who "dedicated his life to helping new Americans acclimate and thrive in America" (Twin Cities community member interview B, June 2, 2014). Samatar's untimely death in 2013 ended the trajectory of what appeared to be a very promising political career. In addition to a well-established career as a banker in the Twin Cities, he started the African Development Center (ADC) in 2003, an organization dedicated to culturally sensitive financial services for African Muslims in Minnesota. Samatar's leadership and innovative perspective on the community caught the attention of then–Minneapolis mayor R. T. Rybak, who appointed Samatar to the Minneapolis Library Board of Trustees in 2006.[3] Samatar's political appointment served as a springboard to his winning a seat on the school board. One respondent noted:

> Samatar was young when he died. He had tremendous political potential and was just starting on his path in public service. Many Somalis and non-Somalis were hopeful that he would become one of the area's rising stars. He already was one. (Twin Cities community leader interview, June 5, 2014)

Their relationship also benefited Mayor Rybak, who learned about Islamic legal restrictions on interest-bearing loans from Samatar (Rybak interview, July 11, 2014). Together, the two men worked on strategies to help the ADC create new programs for Somali small-business owners who needed culturally sensitive loans (Rybak interview, July 11, 2014).

Upon Samatar's 2013 death from complications due to leukemia, and in accordance with Columbus law on filling vacancies, school board members appointed Noor to fill the position. Noor had previously run unsuccessfully for elective office to fill a vacancy in Minneapolis's State Senate District 59 in 2011. In 2014, he announced his intention of running against Phyllis Kahn, a forty-two-year incumbent, in Minneapolis's House District 60B, a district that includes the University of Minnesota; the Cedar-Riverside neighborhood, which is the heart of the Somali community; and areas of eastern Minneapolis. The two candidates faced off at the Democratic-Farmer-Labor (DFL) caucus in April 2014, where Noor proved a formidable challenger. The two were forced into an August 2014 primary, which Kahn ultimately won with 55 percent of the vote (Becker 2014). In the gen-

---

3. See http://www.adcminnesota.org/about/staff/hussein-samatar.

eral election, she was challenged by Abdimalik Askar, a Republican Somali American candidate, who lost the race by an overwhelming majority, with Kahn receiving 77 percent of the vote (Becker 2014).

But Noor's political journey does not represent a failure; rather, it demonstrates resiliency. Particularly in a house race, unseating a long-term incumbent is a nearly insurmountable obstacle. Noor's showing at the DFL caucus was a victory in the sense that his support forced Kahn into a primary battle. Noor explained:

> When immigrants talk about running for office, it makes some people nervous. When you have someone new saying they will challenge an incumbent in a metro area, it is not always comfortable. But it's the only way to challenge the status quo. (Noor interview, June 24, 2014)

As shown later in this chapter, Noor's presence also contributed to high levels of Somali turnout for the nominating convention, something that points to a level of political incorporation. The other interesting aspect of this house district is the emergence of Askar as the Republican candidate, which speaks to the interest among Somalis in elective office and their willingness to consider Republican affiliations.

The story that made headlines in November 2013 was Warsami's election as the first Somali city council member in the nation. Warsami is the executive director of the Riverside Tenants Association and represents many Somalis who live in the city's famous Riverside high-rise apartments (Williams 2013). He defeated an incumbent who was also a member of the Ojibwe tribe and the only American Indian to serve on the city council. As noted earlier, the ward system and the single-transferrable vote allow voters the opportunity to rank candidates. "Warsami won nearly 64 percent of the first-choice votes and more than 40 percent of second-choice votes and 20 percent of third-choice votes" (Williams 2013). He was a passionate advocate of ward redistricting to increase the voting power of the Somali and East African community and led the coalition that succeeded in convincing the Minneapolis Charter Commission to create more racially equitable districts.

The politics behind redrawing district lines is a very important part of the Twin Cities' political incorporation narrative. Warsami and a prominent Minneapolis political consultant collaborated with a state demographer to examine all thirteen wards in the city to determine whether data supported the creation of a minority opportunity ward (Twin Cities political strategist interview, March 21, 2015). For at least a century, the redistricting process had begun at the more homogenous outer edges of the city and worked inward (Twin Cities political strategist interview, March 21, 2015). Warsami created the Citizens Committee for Fair Redistricting and argued that the process be reversed so that concentrated communities of color at the heart of the city would be drawn first. This, his organization argued, would allow for the creation of a minority opportunity ward. In a letter to the Minneapolis Charter Commission, the group wrote:

> According to the last federal decennial census, the City of Minneapolis has a minority population of 40%. Yet minorities are extremely underrepresented on the Minneapolis City Council. Currently, of the thirteen wards, there is only one elected official from the minority community. . . . If there was proportional representation on the Minneapolis City Council, five of the thirteen wards would be represented by people from the minority community. (Citizens Committee for Fair Redistricting 2012)

Warsami was well aware of the legal history and potential opportunities for Somalis if the lines of Ward Six were shifted to include a majority of Somalis (Warsami interview, June 5, 2014). Most remarkably, the Minneapolis Charter Commission accepted virtually all components of the new Minneapolis ward map proposed by the Citizens Committee for Fair Redistricting. It is unclear whether Warsami intended to run for office before his successful redistricting experience, but his success in the process contributed to his 2013 electoral victory.

Other vital aspects of the 2013 election, beyond the new East African voting power, were the elections of the first Hmong and Mexican candidates to the Minneapolis City Council. However, it is worth noting that neither of these candidates secured the percentage of first-choice votes that Warsami garnered (Rao 2013). According to two respondents familiar with the ward revision process, the Citizens Committee for Fair Redistricting considered the importance of creating a majority Latino ward, although Latinos were not part of the committee (Twin Cities political strategist interview, March 21, 2015; Warsami interview, June 5, 2014).

Warsami facilitated the coalition building between different ethnic groups, although some respondents also mentioned the role played by a powerful Minneapolis political consultant, whom one respondent viewed as an "old-style machine boss" (Twin Cities community member interview, July 11, 2014) and another described as an "enlightened strategist who has elevated the position of Somalis in elections and elective office" (Twin Cities community member interview B, June 3, 2014). These different perspectives highlight the politicization of redistricting. The story also suggests that even with the benefits associated with ward-based city council elections, there are still political challenges and dynamics that must be navigated.

Beyond electoral victories in Minneapolis, the appointments of Somalis to public positions and the hiring of Somalis to serve on the staffs of elected officials are becoming more common. As noted earlier, Mayor Rybak was the first to appoint a Somali, Samatar, to the Minneapolis Library Board. Samatar used that position as a springboard to election to the Minneapolis School Board. Had he not died unexpectedly, his political potential might have taken him to even higher office. Betsy Hodges, the current Minneapolis mayor, recently appointed Abdi Phenomenal, a Somali spoken word artist, to the Minneapolis Arts Commission. Evidence of Somali incorporation is also beginning to happen at the state level. In March 2015, Minnesota's DFL Governor Mark Dayton appointed Ibrahim Mohamed, a Somali minimum-wage cart driver, to serve on the Minneapolis St. Paul Metropolitan Airports Commission. The appointment was encouraged by Service Employees International Union (SEIU) Local 26 and community leaders—two groups that are interested in drawing attention to the low wages of many airport workers, particularly Somalis.

Many elected officials in the Twin Cities, including Norm Coleman, a former Republican member of the U.S. House of Representatives, have Somali staffers. As of this writing, Congressman Keith Ellison, the first Muslim in the U.S. House, also has a Somali staffer. Ellison is viewed across the country as one of the most important Somali allies because of his dedication to maintaining paths for remittances from Somalis in the United States to their relatives in Africa. Two Minneapolis City Council members also have Somali staffers. In the mayor's office, a Somali man serves as the mayor's policy aide on labor and housing and as the mayor's liaison to the Somali community. In comparison to the position held by the lone Somali staffer in Columbus, the Minneapolis mayor's Somali aide is in a more prominent position that extends beyond working with immigrants. He has broad connections throughout the city as a result of his professional responsibilities in labor and housing policy. Many Somalis also hold city jobs. Identifying the precise number of Somali municipal employees in either city is difficult, because Somalis are grouped with African Americans in city and state data. However, the presence of Somalis can be—and is—felt. As one respondent explained:

> Over time, we have seen an increased presence of Somalis in government. Some are elected, but others are appointed and hired in political offices. These are the people who are becoming some of the most influential in helping the Somali people. (Twin Cities community member interview A, April 13, 2015)

The Somali community in St. Paul is smaller and less powerful than in Minneapolis. Nevertheless, several recent events suggest that the city is following a similar path as that taken by Minneapolis. Most notably, as of this writing, two Somali men are challenging a Hmong incumbent for representation of St. Paul's First Ward. Although Somalis from St. Paul constitute only eight of the respondents in this study, all St. Paul respondents agreed that their city lacks Somali political incorporation compared to Minneapolis, in terms of Somali appointments and inclusion in the governing coalition. However, Somalis active in Minneapolis also played a role in supporting Somali candidates in the St. Paul City Council election, indicating an important connection between the cities.

Party Outreach

Political parties have played an important role in American urban politics. Although the heyday of the urban machines is past, both regions in this project have one-party dominance at the local level. In Columbus, the Democrats control the city council, although they do not exercise the same power at the state level. In Minneapolis, the DFL Party maintains a strong hold at the local level, with higher-level offices being held by a mix of DFL members and Republicans. Columbus and Minneapolis are similar in that both are dominated by one party at the local level, although in Minneapolis the dominant party is actively engaged in all aspects of Somali incorporation, and in Columbus it is not.

Columbus

Outreach to Somalis by the Democratic Party in Ohio is virtually nonexistent; rather, appeals for support of Somali voters are left to individual candidates. This was most apparent during the presidential elections of 2008 and 2012, when an overwhelming majority of Somalis cast their votes for Obama. Somali respondents in this project referenced uniform disappointment with the lack of attention that they receive from the state's Democratic Party. However, one Somali community leader in Columbus explained:

> The Ohio Democratic Party is not doing anything to bring Somalis on board. This is not entirely their sole responsibility; Somalis in Ohio are also not reaching out to the political party. There are many factors that led to the lack of political engagement in Ohio—a relatively newer community, a relatively more conservative state, a lack of formidable [Somali] contenders to bring forward, barriers such as the need to seek votes citywide for a council seat, etc. (Columbus community member interview, March 4, 2014)

Even when the Somali community's lack of engagement is viewed as resulting from party neglect and Somali apathy, the fact remains that without inclusion in party activities, Somalis are further isolated politically.

Republican candidates in Ohio make no attempts to mobilize Somali voters, much less recruit them as political candidates. Some Somalis express views that align with Republican social positions, particularly in terms of opposition to same-sex marriage (Columbus community member interview, March 6, 2014). Given the ideological similarities between conservative Republicans and socially conservative Somalis, one could argue that a lack of outreach hurts Republicans. However, alignment on social issues is not enough, for the positions taken by Republicans on immigration and the government's social safety net for newcomers place Somalis at odds with the party (Columbus city bureaucrat interview, June 17, 2013). The situation of Somalis in Minneapolis, where members of the DFL Party and Republicans engage in much more extensive outreach, presents a very different model of political incorporation.

The Twin Cities

The previous chapter provides a brief history of the progressive politics of Minnesota's DFL Party. The legacy of such political giants as Vice President Hubert Humphrey, Vice President Walter Mondale, U.S. Senator Paul Wellstone, and Minneapolis Mayor R. T. Rybak were regularly mentioned by Somali respondents in this project as important contributors to the political culture in Minnesota, specifically as it related to Somali incorporation. Whether DFL attention to the Somali community is a consequence of the ward structure of elections or reflects a general commitment to welcoming immigrants, the fact remains that the party courts Somali votes and interests and is actively working to recruit candidates.

Every Somali elected official in Minneapolis is a member of the DFL Party. According to one non-Somali respondent who is active in the DFL Party:

Party leaders are committed to social justice and inclusion. With the changing composition of the city [of Minneapolis] in the 1990s, there were more attempts to work with new citizens. (Twin Cities academic interview, June 2, 2014)

A DFL party leader described the excitement around Somali candidates:

> I would say to some degree the [nominating convention] delegates are "suckers" for candidates who in our eyes exemplify the American dream. We were the first to endorse a Somali candidate in 2010 and subsequently had the first Somali elected official [Samatar to the school board]. So I would say we do our best to welcome them with open arms. (Twin Cities DFL representative interview, September 9, 2014)

Somalis who have run under the DFL Party label report positive experiences working with the party and its leaders (Noor interview, June 24, 2014; Warsami interview, June 5, 2014). One Somali DFL candidate said:

> I've always had a good relationship with top DFL leaders. I challenged a sitting DFL incumbent, so it was like a civil war within the party. Still, the leaders told me that if I won the endorsement, I'd have their full support. I had to earn it, and it took a long time, but it worked. (Warsami interview, June 5, 2014)

Nominating conventions in Minneapolis provide another example of growing Somali political incorporation. Delegates to the conventions are elected at precinct caucuses. Conventions are held in even years for school board and state elections. Municipal races are in odd years quadrennially. Minnesota has an open primary and caucus structure, meaning that voters are not required to register with a party in advance of elections. For this reason, the DFL Party does not have lists of registered party members, but it does maintain lists of convention delegates. A DFL Party leader provided Minneapolis delegate lists from 2011 through 2014, the years when Somalis participated in the conventions. From lists of delegates, Somali names were identified

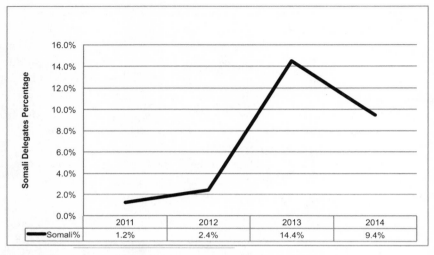

Figure 4.1. Somali representation. *(Graphic created by the author from Minnesota Democratic-Farmer-Labor Party data.)*

and confirmed with the help of a Somali research assistant. In each of these elections, a Somali was on the ballot. Hussein Samatar ran for school board in 2012; in 2013, Abdi Warsami ran for city council; and in 2014, Mohamud Noor ran for the state house. Figure 4.1 illustrates Somali delegate participation at each convention in Minneapolis. The narrative the figure tells is one involving a consistent increase in Somali participation. The 2013 spike centers on Warsami's election to the city council. Both his candidacy and, ultimately, his ability to unseat an incumbent were somewhat extraordinary and served to mobilize the Somali community. Participation in 2014 appears low in comparison to the 2013 surge; however, one can also argue that the decline had more to do with participation returning to normal levels. In 2014, Noor's attempt to unseat a forty-two-year state house incumbent stimulated participation, but the odds against his victory probably depressed participation relative to 2013 levels.

The increase in Somali delegate participation tells the story of a community that has become more involved in electoral politics over time, especially as more Somali candidates have run for office. In 2011, Noor ran for state senate; Samatar was already serving on the school board at that time. In 2012, Samatar was reelected to the school board. During the 2011 and 2012 nominating conventions, Somalis constituted 2 and 1 percent of convention delegates, respectively. The 2013 race for city council resulted in Warsami's election to the city council. The excitement around his candidacy can be seen in the jump (from 1 to 14 percent) in the percentage of convention delegates who were Somali. Although the Somali convention delegate participation rate dipped to 9 percent in 2014, when Noor ran for the state house, the figure still points to sustained Somali engagement in electoral politics. In discussing the increase in Somali convention participation to corroborate my analysis, a DFL Party leader said:

> I'd like to be able to take credit for the increased [Somali] participation. My opinion is that it has been driven by participation by Somali candidates. (Twin Cities DFL representative interview, September 9, 2014)

Another key aspect of party politics in Minneapolis is the collaboration between the DFL Party and community organizations. These connections were regularly mentioned by community leaders in this project as important factors in the political incorporation of Somalis. One community leader explained:

> Although we don't specifically coordinate our voter drives with the DFL, they are very supportive of our work. (Twin Cities community leader interview, April 15, 2015)

Another community leader said:

> DFL leaders work with us and members of our community. . . . [C]andidates will sometimes meet with our members, and we always have information on voting provided by the DFL. (Twin Cities community leader interview, August 5, 2014)

In practical terms, party outreach to existing ethnic organizations, regardless of whether they are overtly political, is strategically smart—especially since Somalis vote in high numbers.

Overall, partisan politics in the Twin Cities provides a conducive environment for Somali political incorporation. In contrast to Columbus, where party involvement is virtually absent, the situation in the Twin Cities is instructive and illustrates how party outreach can be integral for political incorporation.

Electoral and Governing Coalitions

Electoral coalitions include groups of individuals and organizations that coalesce around a particular candidate to influence electoral outcomes. Sometimes the coalition includes groups with different policy concerns, which can create challenges as a victorious candidate transitions from an electoral coalition to one that is responsible for policy making, also known as a governing coalition. Raphael Sonenshein (1997) argues that racial and ethnic minorities are often the weaker coalition partners when the electoral coalitions comprise liberal whites and minorities. In this way, minorities sometimes occupy lower-status positions in the elected official's governing coalition.

Governing coalitions are responsible for overseeing and implementing policy commitments made during an electoral campaign. Unfortunately, when it comes to racial and ethnic minorities, being a part of the electoral coalition is no guarantee that meaningful inclusion in the governing coalition will follow. Elected officials sometimes find that representing powerful interests in the city, such as dominant electoral coalition partners or business interests, is more tempting than fulfilling campaign promises made to underrepresented groups.

Examining electoral and governing coalitions in Columbus and Minneapolis helps measure Somali political incorporation. Being part of the electoral coalition is important, and given the claims of high levels of Somali voter turnout in both areas under investigation, one would expect Somalis to be electoral coalition members in both cities.[4] However, the more significant indicator of political incorpora-

---

4. The high rates of Somali voter turnout cannot be confirmed. However, this study's respondents routinely cited 80 to 90 percent as the number of eligible Somalis who vote. For the only known reference to this percentage range in print, see Greenblatt 2013.

tion is inclusion in the governing coalition. Here, Somalis have the best chance of achieving substantive policy responsiveness if they have a seat at the policy-making table.

Columbus

In Columbus, Somalis play a role in elections, but it is more difficult to argue they are part of an electoral coalition. Moreover, while they get some, albeit minimal, attention during an election, they are essentially neglected in its aftermath. The Democratic Party dedicates no staff or resources to engagement with the Somali community. Individual Democratic candidates solicit Somali votes and attend Somali community events, particularly when an election is near. But beyond these appeals, and the votes that follow, Somalis do not play a significant role in campaigns in Columbus. To make a case that they are part of an electoral coalition, there should be evidence beyond candidate appeals for votes. In other words, Somalis would need a role in a candidate's election organization, and this has not happened.

Mayor Coleman, who has campaigned heavily in the Somali community, did fulfill the promise of creating a more inclusive municipal government through the creation of the New American Initiative in 2005. On the one hand, this suggests that Somalis play a role in Coleman's governing coalition. However, this is the only concrete example of policy responsiveness in Columbus mentioned by any Somali respondent in this project. To many, this office plays an important role in the city, while others perceive it as severely understaffed and underfunded. At least one Somali community leader claimed the office is merely symbolic (Columbus community member interview A, July 26, 2013).

In November 2014, Mayor Coleman announced he would not run for a fifth term. This announcement led to a flurry of candidates who announced their intention to participate in the nonpartisan primary in May 2015. One of these candidates was Franklin County Sheriff Zach Scott. Although the Democrats and Mayor Coleman endorsed the City Council President Andrew Ginther, Scott remained in the race. Notably, Scott appealed to Somali imams and recruited several Somali volunteers to work on his campaign. One Somali community leader acknowledged Scott's strategy but also registered outrage because Scott never seemed concerned about Somalis before running for office:

> I don't think he will win many Somali votes, even with Somalis working for him and trying to rally Somali votes. Those who know about his actions will not support him, even if they are promised something if he wins office. (Columbus community leader interview, March 9, 2015)

The emphasis on including Somalis in his campaign was a promising sign, even if some Somalis viewed Scott's candidacy as problematic, particularly because of complaints that Scott was a member of the SWAT team that ultimately shot to death a mentally ill Somali man in 2005. Somalis mobilized following this incident, protesting what they saw as the use of excessive force. In the end, Ginther defeated Scott with 59 percent of the vote (Sullivan and Rouan 2015).

The Twin Cities

In Minneapolis, Somalis are a highly active and pursued community by candidates and parties alike. More importantly, Somalis expect to participate as important members of electoral coalitions, to work on campaigns, and to be treated as a "valuable constituency" (Twin Cities community member interview C, June 4, 2014).

One community activist explained:

> Our significance goes beyond turning out for elections. Sure, we go to caucuses and other political events, but we have some clear concerns that we bring to the table. Many of our issues don't get the attention we want, but we keep trying. (Twin Cities community leader interview A, June 3, 2014)

What is particularly evident in the Twin Cities is that Somali political participation, local traditions of progressive political culture, and candidates with an interest in Somalis have played a role in Somali political incorporation. When Somali respondents in this study were asked which elected official had been most responsive to their interests, deceased U.S. Senator Wellstone was mentioned by all forty-four Somali respondents. Wellstone connected with Somalis as their population was increasing in the community, but before they were citizens and eligible to vote. He was a mentor to Minneapolis Mayor Rybak, an elected official thirty-six Somali respondents mentioned as being responsive to Somali interests. Although Rybak did not have Somalis on his staff, he appointed a prominent Somali businessperson, Samatar, to the Minneapolis Library Board. He also worked closely with him as the head of the ADC to find ways the city could support Islamic-compliant loans to Somalis. This is evidence that Rybak included Somali interests when creating a governing coalition. Even more importantly, Rybak opposed the George W. Bush administration's characterization of Somalis as terrorists after the attacks of September 11, 2001. Rybak explained:

> I won the primary on 9/11 and came to office at a time when our country was in a complicated state. The Bush White House called to tell me that I would be leading a city with a huge terrorism issue. I asked why. They told me, "Because there are a lot of people of the Islamic faith." I said, "Hitler was a Christian, and so am I. Does that make me a terrorist?" I did everything I could to let people of the Islamic faith know that they would be treated equally in this city. (Rybak interview, July 11, 2014)

Before Senator Wellstone's death in October 2002, he and Mayor Rybak had conversations about strategies to protect Muslims in the city (Rybak interview, July 11, 2014). When reports surfaced in 2009 that a few young Somali men in Minneapolis had traveled to Somalia to join al-Shabaab, Mayor Rybak remained a strong advocate of the Somali community, pointing to the social media–mediated radicalization of young people as a major issue on which to focus. He compared Somalis' connection to Somalia to Irish Americans' connection with Ireland; in the latter case, support of their homeland did not make Irish Americans members of the Irish Republican Army (IRA), and in the former case, support of Somalia did not make Somalis members of al-Shabaab (Rybak interview, July 11, 2014). For Rybak, the incident was an unfortunate and extreme example of a few young men who made their way to a terrorist organization. Rybak stressed the importance of finding alternative programs to help young people pursue employment, education, and peace. Although Rybak did not have Somalis on staff, his attempts to create policies that responded to their financial and safety interests reflected a level of governing coalition inclusion.

Minneapolis's Mayor Hodges (2014–) has also included Somalis in her electoral coalition. Mayor Hodges campaigned heavily in the Somali community, even wearing a hijab at certain points during the campaign, a tactic that caused mixed reactions, according to Somali respondents in this study. Some viewed the hijab as an insincere attempt to win Somali votes (Twin Cities community member interview A, April 13, 2015); others saw it as a sign of respect and appreciation for Muslim women's dress. In fact, the mayor herself explained that she was given a scarf by a Somali campaign adviser and was deeply touched by the gesture (Hodges interview, July 31, 2014). Regardless of the dialogue the hijab created, fifteen of forty-four Somali respondents in this study believed Somalis were a valued part of Mayor Hodges's electoral coalition. Her governing coalition includes several informal advisory groups that offer suggestions on policy, including the Somali Advisory Group. As noted earlier, Mayor Hodges also has a Somali staffer who serves as her Somali community liaison in addition to his role as a labor and housing expert. These examples demonstrate evidence of Somali inclusion in the mayor's governing coalition.

Congressman Keith Ellison was elected to represent Minnesota's Fifth Congressional District in the U.S. House of Representatives in 2007. Congressman Ellison is one of only two Muslims in the U.S. Congress. He was elected through the support of a broad coalition of racial and ethnic minorities as well as progressive Anglos (Ellison representative interview, June 11, 2014). Once elected, Congressman Ellison's governing coalition included Somalis not just in his district, but from around the country (Twin Cities community member interview, June 1, 2014). With the small number of Muslim leaders in the U.S. government, Congressman Ellison's election was an especially important step forward. More importantly, Ellison has been a staunch advocate for the continuation of remittances, one of the main concerns among Somalis in this study who support families back in Africa. In this respect, Congressman Ellison's consideration of Somali issues, and the fact that he has a Somali on his staff, makes him a celebrated elected official not only in the Twin Cities region but also in places with considerable Somali populations like Columbus. Many Somali respondents in Columbus mentioned Congressman Ellison as a collaborator on Somali issues.

Overall, Somalis in the Twin Cities are part of DFL candidate electoral coalitions. There are even claims that Somalis have been courted by Republican candidates, such as former U.S. Senator Norm Coleman, who hired a Somali staffer and campaigned in the Somali community (Twin Cities community leader interview, June 5, 2014). In governing coalitions, it appears that Somalis also have a seat at the table. Somali concerns about remittance rules, disproportionate targeting by law enforcement, and Islamic-compliant banking are concrete examples of issues politicians have addressed in ways that respond to Somali concerns. In this respect, Somalis in the Twin Cities have been part of electoral coalitions and have had some of their primary policy concerns responded to by politicians.

Bureaucratic Outreach

Minority politics scholars have focused much of their attention on the role of elected officials in the incorporation of racial and ethnic groups in the United States (Browning, Marshall, and Tabb 1984). These elected officials often advocate for policies that respond to minority group needs and interests. Though it is not as commonly met, the "gold standard" (Alba and Foner 2009, 282) for political incorporation is the election of minority or immigrant candidates as a method of achieving responsive policy making. Yet another way to examine the incorporation of racial and ethnic minorities is through an evaluation of street-level bureaucrats in this process. These street-level bureaucrats are responsible for the delivery of services to community members and often have more frequent contact with residents than elected officials. The work of several prominent scholars has shed light on the role of street-level bureaucrats in the incorporation of new immigrant communities in urban America (Jones-Correa 2005; Marrow 2009; Ramakrishnan and Lewis 2005).

Traditional political science scholarship suggests that bureaucratic incorporation "takes place only as immigrants accumulate resources and are able to mobilize (or be mobilized) effectively in the political arena" (Jones-Correa 2005, 14). After this occurs, politicians are more likely to order bureaucrats to address immigrant-specific needs. Much of the literature suggests that bureaucracies are impediments to democratic participation and politically corrosive as they "co-opt minority activists, shifting their energies away from direct mobilization" (14). The bureaucratic incorporation literature finds that bureaucrats play a critical role in minority incorporation. In other words, bureaucrats play a leading role in responding to immigrant requests. As Marrow (2009) explains:

> The novel findings suggest that traditional political incorporation theories may be misguided in seeing electoral mobilization as the primary, if not the only, way for newcomers to gain substantive representation over time, in viewing bureaucracies as mere "impediments to democratic incorporation" and in "ignoring agencies as a possible locus of incorporation." (758)

In fact, one of these studies finds that bureaucratic values and priorities play an even more important role in incorporation than political factors such as the ideology of elected officials (Meier and O'Toole 2006).

Columbus

Mayor Michael Coleman was elected in 1999, a period when Columbus was experiencing a steep increase in Somali residents. In 2005, Mayor Coleman launched "The New American Initiative" as a division of his Community Relations Commission. The division's mission statement reads:

> Mayor Coleman's New American Initiative was created to give all immigrants and refugees living in Columbus access to city

services and programs to help improve their lives. This initiative gives equal opportunity to all refugees and immigrants and allows them to become responsible, productive residents of Columbus.

The growing new American populations contribute to the cultural richness, and enhance the economic growth and development of the city. In order to ensure a smooth transition and seamless integration process, a comprehensive strategy of resource distribution needed to be established.

The growth rate of the immigrant/refugee population in Columbus has also posed certain challenges for the city infrastructure in meeting the basic living necessities in a culturally sensitive manner. Some of these challenges include language barriers and education, fair and affordable housing, healthcare and employment. (City of Columbus 2013)

Coleman hired two individuals to run this new office, one from the Somali community and the other from the Mexican community. Columbus was the first city to create a permanent division within the mayor's office to serve the needs of recent immigrants.

The findings of the bureaucratic incorporation literature are helpful in understanding the position of Somalis in Columbus. As mentioned above, while the Somali community has voting power, Columbus's at-large system of elections, combined with the discrimination that Somalis face (A. Waters 2012) has diminished their opportunities for descriptive representation. Another challenge to Somali incorporation is that few Somalis are employed by the city or state, with the exception of low-level civil servants who provide translation services and work in public service offices (Columbus community member interview, June 30, 2013). As a result, there are few Somali city and state bureaucrats dedicated to expanding opportunities for Somalis. In the absence of Somali bureaucrats, however, several respondents cited specific non-Somali service bureaucrats in specific policy areas, such as education, as being important for Somali advancement. These individuals fall into the "service bureaucrat" category discussed by Michael Jones-Correa (2005), or the "street-level bureaucrat" discussed by Marrow (2009). Notably, all four of the city and state bureaucrats interviewed for this project mentioned the importance of advocating for Somalis, and other new refugee and immigrant groups in Columbus. This attitude is fortunate given that each of these state and city level bureaucrats has been specifically tasked with dealing with issues specific to immigrants and newcomers. Each also reflected the bureaucratic culture discussed by Jones-Correa (2005) that leads service bureaucrats to respond positively to diverse communities. One Somali state bureaucrat noted:

> First, gaining trust is essential for community engagement and empowerment efforts as the community will appreciate the outreach, and understand the intention once you establish a positive relationship. . . . Helping implement the [New] American Initiative goals and advocacy for the new American community is what drives our work to achieve desirable results for inclusion. (Columbus state bureaucrat interview, December 26, 2013)

Respondents were overwhelmingly critical of the responsiveness of elected politicians at the city and state level. At the same time, they were largely pleased with the work of a small number of street-level bureaucrats. This finding is similar to Marrow's (2009) finding that service bureaucrats are often more effective than elected officials in facilitating immigrant political incorporation. One community leader offered a critique that was shared by ten other respondents:

> Elected officials come visit us when they want our vote, otherwise, we don't see them. We don't bother going to city hall because they don't care. (Columbus community leader interview A, July 26, 2013)

A similar complaint raised by a few of these respondents was that Mayor Coleman, an African American himself, and other elected officials are concerned about only the African American community in Columbus. Another respondent went further in criticizing the mayor for taking credit for the creation of The New American Initiative office:

The [New] American Initiative was pushed for by a Somali coalition who wanted access to the city. Those of us who had been here for a long time will challenge authority. Coleman knew Somalis would be an important voting bloc. It wasn't an act of kindness by Coleman that created that office. (Columbus community member interview, June 19, 2013)

However, in an interview Mayor Coleman was emphatic about his interest in helping Somalis, saying that it had been a priority of his from the moment he entered office (Coleman interview, June 26, 2012). Street-level bureaucrats in this study, including educators and New American Initiative bureaucrats, indicate that Coleman is responsive to their requests when it comes to Somali incorporation. This finding is not at odds with the bureaucratic incorporation literature. Whatever motivates Mayor Coleman, he did launch the New American Initiative and hire two street-level bureaucrats to run the office. These individuals, more than the mayor, are largely seen as important to the Somali community. The majority of respondents believe that the individuals in this position are responsive to Somali concerns about housing, job discrimination, the criminal justice system, remittances, and family reunification. This comports with the bureaucratic incorporation scholarship with regard to bureaucrats' influence on the integration of new immigrant communities. The community leaders who support the work of these service bureaucrats also described their progress in educating the broader Columbus community about Somali culture. However, the focus of their efforts has been not only citywide but also within the Somali community: these leaders have worked for several years to unify the different Somali community organizations so they can influence policy more effectively. One community leader said of a bureaucrat in the New American Initiative Office:

[He] has tried to explain that if we work together we can get more help from the city and state, but it hasn't worked. People are skeptical about others' motives and we have been unable to convince the other leaders creating a unified center or umbrella will help us all. (Columbus community leader interview A, July 26, 2013)

One New American Initiative representative explained that they have attempted to demonstrate that city, state, and foundations are more likely to support a unified community group. This has occurred in Minneapolis and the New American Initiative and Community Relations bureaucrats have offered their support to replicate that success in Columbus (Columbus city bureaucrat interview, June 23, 2013; Columbus community leader interview A, July 26, 2013). It remains unclear whether this will happen, but given the large number of Somali community groups competing for limited resources, the offer represents an opportunity for group advancement.

The New American Initiative Office is clearly the central clearinghouse for Somali advocacy within the city government. The office has a staff of two and a small annual budget that has experienced reductions during the city's economic downturn (Columbus city bureaucrat interview, July 26, 2013). Members of this office, along with the Community Relations Commission and other bureaucrats such as the school system's ESL director, are the most frequently referenced street-level bureaucrats when those in the Somali community are asked about government workers who care deeply about the upward mobility of refugees. These service bureaucrats report that the mayor is responsive to their suggestions and genuinely cares about the position of Somalis in Columbus. At the same time, some of these same bureaucrats mentioned that limited resources and budget concerns severely limit their ability to do more for Somalis.

The Twin Cities

Unlike Columbus, there is no government office in Minneapolis or St. Paul dedicated to helping new Americans. This absence may simply be due, however, to the fact that supporting new Americans is part of the cultural fabric of the Twin Cities, rendering a formal governmental division unnecessary. This welcoming attitude stems, in part, from the region's experience welcoming Hmong refugees, as well as the mix of public and private entities which have embraced the task of helping newcomers. Bureaucrats in Minneapolis are viewed by most Somali respondents in this study as "helpful" and "supportive" in areas such as education, health care, and labor issues. One respondent explained:

A lot has been done in terms of Somali city and state employment. This creates a higher level of cultural awareness in education, mental health and general social services. (Twin Cities community member interview, May 24, 2014)

The most frequently mentioned bureaucrat was a Somali policy aide, Abdi Muse, in Mayor Betsy Hodges's office, who serves as her Somali community housing and labor expert in addition to being her Somali liaison. Mayor Hodges was elected in 2013, and one of her first announcements was the selection of Abdi Muse, a Somali union organizer, as a new member of her senior staff; he was the first Somali staff member in the mayor's office. Mayor Rybak, did not have any Somalis on staff, although he made a concerted effort to have Somali interns in his office, was closely connected to the Somali community, and relied on his partnership with several Somali community leaders (Rybak interview, July 11, 2014). Thus, Somalis had already been given an informal voice in the Rybak administration, but the Hodges era gave them official representation in the form of a Somali staffer.

Mayor Hodges's Somali aide is tasked with responsibilities beyond the Somali or immigrant community. Indeed, his expertise as a labor organizer with SEIU Local 26 in Minneapolis and his passion for affordable housing has elevated his position within the mayor's administration. Although this is but one example, his position sends a clear signal that members of racial and ethnic groups must be part of the policy-making process and that they possess expertise beyond the issues of the group they represent demographically. The story of this staffer's position is also something of a parallel to the situation in Columbus, where the mayor selected a Somali to staff the New American Initiative office. In both cases, non-Somali elected officials recognized the importance of creating more inclusiveness within their offices. However, the situation in Minneapolis represents a higher level of incorporation, because the bureaucrat is a top policy aide to the mayor, as opposed to a staff member of an office that is technically lower in the hierarchy.

Another area where bureaucratic outreach can be seen is the inclusion of Somali staff in public offices. Two Somali city council staff members and a staffer in the local office of Congressman Ellison were regularly mentioned by Somali respondents as being politically engaged. In all three cases, these staffers have placed a priority on supporting the Somali community, but they also demonstrate a level of expertise in policy areas that resonate with Minneapolis residents more broadly. A unique finding in this study was that young Somali community activists in Minneapolis are particularly inspired by the presence of a female staffer on the city council and see her as a role model (Twin Cities community member interviews B, C, and D, June 2, 2014). One young female activist said:

> She fights for what she believes in and has a public presence. We admire her willingness to stand up for the things she believes are right. She's smart and knows how the system works. . . . She's our mentor. (Twin Cities community member interview D, June 2, 2014)

These comments align with the role-model hypothesis from the women and politics literature (Darcy, Welch, and Clark 1994; Elder 2004), which suggests that when young people have role models in public life, they are more likely to feel included and consider careers in public service.

The street-level bureaucrats in the Twin Cities and Columbus provide important representation to Somalis, although the Twin Cities case includes a larger number of street-level bureaucrats who have policy expertise in a variety of areas. The visibility of these individuals is important, because it demonstrates that Somalis are becoming involved in many areas of local politics. It also holds the promise that some of these high-profile positions could someday lead to positions in elective office.

Union Engagement

The difference between the role of unions in the Twin Cities and in Columbus is associated with higher Somali political incorporation in the latter. Chapters 2 and 3 provide a brief history of unionization in the two regions under investigation. Unions play a role in politics in both cities, but the union narrative in Minnesota involves a coalition between farmers and urban laborers in the 1920s that led to the creation of the Farmer-Labor Party. In 1944, Hubert Humphrey helped broaden this coalition by persuading the Farmer-Labor Party and the Democrats to unite under the DFL Party. Today Minnesota's DFL Party embodies the progressive wing of the Democratic Party, with U.S. Senator Al Franken as one of its most visible members.

Although unions in Columbus play a role in politics, the story in that city is more like the tale of contemporary unions in the United States. Unions remain a sought-after group, particularly by Democrats, but their power and membership base are weaker than they once were. More importantly for the purposes of this book, Somalis in Columbus do not hold many unionized positions. Although there has been talk of unionizing Somali warehouse workers among some community members, little progress has been made on this front. This stands in stark contrast to the Twin Cities, where Somalis constitute a substantial part of SEIU Local 26.

Columbus

While going between the two regions to conduct fieldwork, my questions became more directed toward the relationships between unions, Somalis, and the Democratic Party. What became clear was that relationships between unions, Somalis, and party organizations do not exist in Columbus. Somalis are not unionized, although they would clearly benefit from unionization. One of the major challenges for Somali employees is religious accommodation in the workplace. On this score, many Somalis seek legal recourse through the Ohio branch of the Council on American-Islamic Relations (CAIR). During an interview with a CAIR representative, it was noted that the type of assistance Somalis request is predominantly related to their employment. They often encounter opposition from employers when they request time and a space for daily prayer. Especially during Ramadan, when Muslims fast from sunrise to sunset, many warehouse employees find employers inflexible about their hours or requests for breaks at sunset. Another obstacle to accommodation is the fact that many employers are hostile toward Muslim cleaning rituals that involve washing their bodies before prayer (Columbus CAIR representative interview, March 11, 2015).

The need for Somali unionization, particularly among warehouse employees, is the primary area where Somali political incorporation could conceivably be strengthened. One Somali community leader explained, "Employers like Somali workers. They work hard and are productive. They're also seen as reliable workers" (Columbus community leader interview B, July 26, 2013). When this same leader was asked about unionization, he said:

> There has been some discussion of unionization here, but not enough. It's mainly a conversation among community leaders, but not among workers. They're occupied with challenging jobs and finding ways to maintain religious traditions. (Columbus community leader interview, March 9, 2015)

The Somali vignette in Chapter 2 features the story of Mamahawa, a woman who worked in a Columbus warehouse where Somalis talked of unionization. According to Mamahawa, those who participated in these conversations were laid off or given new responsibilities at work that they were incapable of performing to pressure them to leave their positions (Columbus community member interview, March 24, 2015).

My efforts to connect with unions in Columbus about Somali unionization were largely unsuccessful. It is somewhat understandable that unions who do not rely on Somali workers would remain unresponsive to requests for interviews regarding their unionization, yet this would be one of the most promising ways for Somalis to ensure that their religious needs were met in the workplace. Furthermore, as the Twin Cities analysis illustrates, unionization could also lead to leadership opportunities and political engagement for the Somali community broadly.

The Twin Cities

SEIU Local 26 is Minnesota's property services union and represents security workers, janitorial, housekeeping staff, and health care employees. SEIU 26 has more than 6,000 members in the Twin Cities area and about 225,000 members in North America overall.[5] Approximately 28 percent of SEIU Local 26's Twin Cities members, or around seventeen hundred individuals, are Somali (Twin Cities city bureaucrat interview, June 2, 2014). The combination of union outreach to Somalis and Somali receptivity to joining a union has resulted in a mutually beneficial relationship. SEIU Local 26 intentionally created opportunities for Somali leadership at all levels of the organization, which shows that Somalis' roles in SEIU Local 26 have been about more than merely being in the right occupation at the right time. While Somalis held jobs that fell under SEIU oversight, they could have joined the union without becoming leaders in the organization. However, the interest Somalis expressed in union leadership, together with SEIU's receptivity to the idea, made their membership a perfect opportunity. Three Somalis interviewed for this project have direct experience with leadership training and holding leadership positions in SEIU. One commented:

> Being part of the labor and progressive movement helped many of us [Somalis] acquire tremendous political expertise and connections. SEIU was also instrumental in appointing the first East African airport commissioner a couple of weeks ago; Governor Dayton appointed him though, but SEIU advocated for him. The entire community celebrated widely his appointment. (Twin Cities city bureaucrat interview, March 17, 2015)

SEIU also hired a Somali internal organizer in 2011. This individual had previously worked as a security officer, at which point he joined SEIU Local 26 and became active in the union. In an interview, he praised the union for recognizing his leadership capacity and helping him rise within the organization. A concrete example of how a Somali staff member can play an important role in the organization can be seen in the African Circle this particular union leader launched within SEIU Local 26. This group focuses on remittances and the importance of maintaining money transfer services to Afri-

---

5. See SEIU.org.

ca. Given the significance of this issue for Somalis, it is noteworthy that the organization takes a position on this issue.

SEIU Local 26, like other unions in the Twin Cities, reliably supports DFL candidates. The union's political engagement is apparent when one walks through the doors of the organization's headquarters—campaign signs and information about the DFL are present throughout the office. Another important link between Somali union involvement and political opportunities is Minneapolis Mayor Hodges's decision to hire a prominent union activist as her labor and housing policy staff expert. The experience this staffer brought to the table was the direct result of his union leadership, policy expertise, and involvement with previous DFL campaigns. One Somali observer noted:

He was not only someone recognized by Somalis as a highly qualified person; he had the same reputation in the broader community. It's just one example of how Somalis in Minneapolis are rising to leadership positions. (Twin Cities community member interview, May 31, 2014)

This notable example from Mayor Hodges's staff, along with the examples of political engagement connected to union involvement in the Twin Cities, stands out as a key factor in the Somali political incorporation story in the Twin Cities. The absence of a relationship between Somalis and unions in Ohio makes this difference even more prominent. My requests for interviews with union representatives in Columbus went unanswered. Consequently, the current lack of Somali unionization in Columbus remains an area in need of further investigation, because inclusion in a union could have a positive impact on Somali political incorporation in Columbus.

Somali Community Organizations

Ethnic community organizations can play an important role in political incorporation. Irene Bloemraad explains that although migration scholars have focused less on immigrant organizations and more on social capital, "immigrants' political incorporation rests in part on the community's capacity to organize" (2006, 162). Similarly, Els de

Graauw argues that "immigrant nonprofit organizations are important political actors that are heavy lifters of immigrants' incorporation at the local level" (2008, 334). In both Columbus and the Twin Cities, important Somali community organizations span the categories of professional groups (e.g., Somali Chamber of Commerce), advocacy groups, and social service organizations. In many cases, there is a crossover between advocacy and social service provisions. In terms of longevity, sustainability, and collaboration between organizations, the Twin Cities reflect a higher level of political incorporation through Somali community organizations.

Columbus

Along with the state and local governments and unions, community-based organizations can play an important role in Somali political incorporation. At first glance, the number of Somali community organizations is large. In fact, the mayor's website lists twenty-two Somali and African organizations in the city. Yet despite the large number of such organizations, competition between groups for scarce resources has prevented widespread community mobilization. According to some community leaders, the disunity among Columbus's Somali organizations is in contrast to the cooperation among Somali groups in Minneapolis (Columbus city bureaucrat interview, June 17, 2013; Columbus community member interview, June 19, 2013; Columbus community member interview, June 26, 2014; Columbus community member interview, June 20, 2013). Moreover, not all Somali community organizations are 501(c)(3) nonprofits. According to one respondent, the lack of nonprofit status limits the capacity and effectiveness of these organizations (Columbus city bureaucrat interview, July 26, 2013). The New American Initiative's employees, along with members of the Community Relations Commission and Somali community leaders, have made considerable efforts to reach consensus and create an umbrella Somali nonprofit organization, but it has proved impossible. Because many of the groups offer similar services, competition is exacerbated—especially for groups providing social services. Other scholars have noted similar tensions between Somali groups in Lewiston, Maine (Gilbert 2009; Williamson 2011). Respondents in this study were asked to identify the most prominent Somali community organizations in their area. There was consensus around several, including SomaliCAN,[6] the Somali Community Association of Ohio (SCAO), the Somali Bantu Youth Community of Ohio, the Somali Bantu Education Center, the Somali Education and Resource Center, and various Islamic centers. However, the fact that the groups do not collaborate reduces their potential collective power.

Funding for these organizations comes from a range of groups, including educational institutions, the city of Columbus, private individuals, and corporations. In an effort to improve the economic security of Columbus's Somalis, SCAO has implemented a job assistance program that addresses many of the shortcomings of the state's *Refugee Handbook.*[7] It is run by a trained, multilingual staff with a focus on language skills, the cultivation of workplace skills, coaching for those looking to start or expand small businesses, and other more individually tailored solutions. SomaliCAN acts as an advocate that speaks for the refugees' needs in a policy setting, something that Somalis themselves often cannot do (Columbus community leader interview A, July 26, 2013). This is an example of the sort of intermediary group referenced by S. Karthick Ramakrishnan and Paul George Lewis (2005) in their suggestions for improving political incorporation and participation. SomaliCAN plays a crucial role in helping immigrants connect with and understand civic affairs, which is crucial to this population's political incorporation and participation (Ramakrishnan and Lewis 2005). SCAO and SomaliCAN are important in the economic and political integration of Somali refugees into the broader society of Columbus, and the two organizations also serve as "watchdogs" in protecting Somali interests. However, these groups do not coordinate their efforts—a failure that reduces their potential policy power at the city and state levels (Columbus city bureaucrat interview, June 17, 2013; Columbus city bureaucrat interview, July 26, 2013; Columbus state bureaucrat interview, December 26, 2013; Federal bureaucrat interview, June 28, 2014). Along these lines, one respondent explained:

---

6. See http://somalican.org/1/25/15.

7. See http://jfs.ohio.gov/refugee/1RefugeeHandbook.pdf.

I have tried to persuade [Somali] community leaders that com-
bining forces and operating under an umbrella would benefit
everyone. I use Minneapolis as an example. It's been unsuccessful. (Columbus city bureaucrat interview, June 17, 2013)

Beyond these organizations, many other groups help Somalis with
English-language instruction, after-school care for children, and general social service delivery. The heads of these various organizations
all noted the scarcity of funding. During fieldwork for this project, I
visited many of these organizations and witnessed the powerful roles
they are playing in the lives of individuals. Particularly while sitting
in waiting rooms, I would informally converse with Somalis about
the importance of their community organizations. These conversations always left me with the sense that the family support, educational programs, and advocacy work done by these organizations was
of vital importance to their members, yet their influence is limited
by lack of coordination and an abundance of competition. Although
some of these same elements exist in the Twin Cities, the story there
is far more promising overall.

The Twin Cities

An unofficial list of Twin Cities' Somali organizations compiled for
this book reveals that roughly seventeen organizations have a presence in the city.[8] Most have limited financial resources, and many
of these organizations are housed in the Brian Coyle Center, which,
as noted in Chapter 3, was established by the Pillsbury Foundation
and serves as a hub for the Cedar-Riverside community of Minneapolis. Cedar-Riverside has the largest concentration of Somalis,
and the Brian Coyle Center functions as not only headquarters for
several organizations but also a meeting place for individuals and
groups, providing a vibrant and welcoming atmosphere. Beyond the
Brian Coyle Center, many other Somali community organizations
serve as advocates, provide social services, offer economic support,

---

8. Kadra Mohamed Strategic Consultants compiled a 2007 list based on information provided by the Office of the Secretary of State and the author's research.

and generally support Somalis in the Twin Cities—and some of these organizations collaborate to increase their influence. One of the most important differences between Somali organizations in Columbus and in the Twin Cities is that in Minnesota, the largest and most powerful groups, as identified by Somali respondents in this study, do not overlap in their primary goals. This means that competition plays a less significant—and ultimately counterproductive—role than that which we see in Columbus.

The first Somali community organization in the Twin Cities, the Confederation of Somali Community in Minnesota (CSCM), was founded in 1994. This grassroots organization was created as an ethnic community self-help organization through the U.S. Office of Refugee Resettlement with the goal of building community capacity among new refugees. The group provides assistance not only with general resettlement services but also with specific policy areas, such as education, housing, employment, and health. Mohamud Noor, the group's executive director, has served on the Minneapolis school board and has pursued other elective positions. The organization was one of the most prominent, visible, and frequently mentioned Somali community organizations among respondents in this study. However, several respondents also noted that CSCM struggles to be all things to all people. To represent this perspective, one respondent said:

> They have a small staff, and people expect them to provide extensive social services with a limited budget. This has made it difficult for them to maintain a position as a powerful Somali organization. (Twin Cities community member interview, April 14, 2014)

Another important community service organization is the Somali Action Alliance (SAA), which is primarily concerned with increasing democratic participation among Somali Americans. The group's mission is to "educate Somali individuals and other interested persons regarding civic engagement, voting rights and responsibilities and participation in democracy."[9] They claim to have registered

---

9. See http://somaliactionalliance.org/?page_id=2555.

more than nineteen thousand Somali voters (Twin Cities community leader interview, April 15, 2015). Founded in 2002, the group plays a significant role in electoral politics and community engagement in the political process. It initially emerged around the candidacy of the late DFL Senator Paul Wellstone, the incumbent from Minnesota. As noted earlier in this chapter, Senator Wellstone was beloved by Somalis. His death just eleven days before the 2002 election was a tremendous loss to those who worked so diligently on his campaign. However, the experience with voter registration, community organization, and leadership development planted a seed that would help the organization take root as a political force in Minneapolis. The group is closely aligned with Wellstone Action, a St. Paul–based progressive political organization created in Senator Wellstone's memory and committed to grassroots mobilization and equality. Wellstone Action has collaborated with SAA to train more than fifteen SAA members. The collaboration between SAA and other Somali and non-Somali community groups is viewed by some respondents as a key factor in the organization's success. One SAA leader explained:

> It's all about relationship building, so that different groups can support each other. That's the philosophy that helps me generate strong relationships with other Somalis and have learning exchanges among each other. We all do different things. SAA does social change, no [social] services at all. But we have a respected relationship with the great organizations doing service work. (Twin Cities community leader interview, April 15, 2015)

Although this leader also works diligently on fundraising and acknowledged competition for resources among groups, the quotation highlights nicely the lack of significant redundancy among the main Twin Cities' community organizations.

Education and racial justice are also at the forefront of SAA's work. The group has roughly one hundred parent members with a deep commitment to the fair and equitable education of their children. For example, they succeeded in mobilizing to prevent the closure of Minneapolis's Sanford Middle School, a predominantly Somali school, in 2005. Racial justice is also an overarching concern for SAA. The group encourages politicians to consider racial equity implications before enacting policies (Twin Cities community leader interview, April 15, 2015).

Another Somali organization mentioned by Somali respondents was Ka Joog. This organization's mission is reflected in its name, which means "stay away." Founded in 2007 in the aftermath of reports of Somali gang and drug activity, the group is focused on providing alternatives to Somali youth who are at risk for drug use, gang activity, and, more recently, Islamic radicalization. It emphasizes the importance of higher education and civic engagement for youth and reports having served twenty-five hundred Somali youth in Minneapolis, St. Paul, and Eden Prairie, Minnesota. The group received a prominent award from the local branch of the FBI in 2012 called the Director's Community Leadership Award, which led some respondents in this study to question whether Ka Joog is an FBI surveillance organization. Regardless of criticisms, the group is viewed by government officials as important in the community and is commonly included in discussions regarding Minneapolis's designation as one of three Countering Violent Extremism (CVE) program cities in 2014. Minneapolis was designated as a CVE city because of the roughly thirty individuals from that city who have engaged in terrorist activities abroad (Salhani 2015). The collaboration among many Minneapolis Somali organizations is viewed by some as a positive development, but others contend that organizational compliance is based on the hope that money will follow (Twin Cities union representative interview, April 16, 2015). Although Ka Joog is not the organization working under the new CVE program, several respondents criticized the group for its work with federal officials because of concerns about discrimination and mistreatment by the U.S. government. What many respondents articulated—and is so clearly described by the Brennan Center for Justice at the New York University School of Law—is the following:

These programs, however, are not new. CVE programs have existed for some time, often with dubious results. And while purportedly aimed to rooting out all violent extremism, they have previously focused only on Muslims, stigmatizing them

as a suspect community. These programs have further promoted flawed theories of terrorist radicalization, which leads
to unnecessary fear, discrimination, and unjustified reporting
to law enforcement.[10]

The fears described in this statement were apparent among many
Somali respondents in the Twin Cities. Because research for this project was conducted before and after the announcement of the new
CVE program, the anxiety among respondents regarding this program was very evident.

Summary

The higher level of Somali political incorporation in the Twin Cities
is related to the indicators explored in this chapter, including local
electoral structure, party outreach, Somali inclusion in electoral and
governing coalitions, bureaucratic outreach, union engagement with
Somalis, and politically engaged ethnic organizations. These measures
are important individually, but Somali political incorporation is the
result of the interaction among all of these factors. The election and
appointment of Somalis to important posts in the Twin Cities are the
most visible indicators of Somali political incorporation. However, a
complex web of factors contribute to these political successes. Table
4.1 illustrates the results of the measures of political incorporation in
each city.

Ward elections in the Twin Cities opened the door for political
incorporation, particularly after an organized group fought for the
creation of majority-minority districts. But even this organization
occurred as a result of the strength of community mobilization. More
importantly, the effort was led by a Somali community organizer,
who is currently the only Somali American city council member in
the United States. The progressive history of the dominant political
party in the region, the Democratic-Farmer-Labor Party (DFL), also
contributed to a strong relationship between it and Somalis. Somali
community leaders have also attempted to build relationships with

---

10. See https://www.brennancenter.org/analysis/cve-programs-resource-page.

			Electoral/			Engaged community organiza-
Measures	Ward elections	Party outreach	governing coalition	Bureaucratic outreach	Union engagement	tions
Columbus	low	low	low	moderate	low	moderate
Twin Cities	high	high	high	high	high	high

TABLE 4.1. POLITICAL INCORPORATION

the DFL Party and with DFL politicians, which the party and the politicians have been receptive to and interested in. Whether this is the outcome of mutual respect, the DFL Party's realization that Somalis are a powerful voting bloc, or that the DFL Party's core ideology impels it to be attentive to the needs of the disadvantaged regardless of race or national origin matters less than the fact that the dialogue among Somalis and DFL leaders is positive. Moreover, the influence of unions in the Twin Cities, combined with Somali involvement with SEIU Local 26, has contributed to Somali political power. Individual Somalis have become SEIU leaders, with some building on their labor expertise and being hired as bureaucratic experts in city hall who are then able to bring attention to Somali issues as well as other policy areas of broader importance in the Twin Cities.

Somalis in Columbus fall short on virtually every measure of political incorporation compared to the Twin Cities. The at-large electoral structure is a tremendous barrier to Somalis' ability to capitalize on their voting power—either by electing a candidate of choice to office or electing a Somali to city council or the school board. Party outreach is virtually nonexistent in Columbus, replaced with individual candidate appeals for the Somali vote. However, Somali support does not mean inclusion in the candidate's electoral coalition, much less an elected official's governing coalition.

Also contributing to low levels of Somali political incorporation in Columbus is the lack of union engagement. The potential leadership opportunities and political connections that union involvement can foster are absent here. Rather, the many Somalis working in warehouses are forced to fight for religious accommodations on an individual level (Columbus CAIR representative interview, March 11, 2015). According to one respondent in this study, Somali interest in unionization among warehouse employees resulted in retaliatory actions by management (Columbus community member interview, March 24, 2015). Another Somali community leader noted that although unionization has been a topic of discussion among Somali community leaders, it has not gone any further.

Somali community organizations play an important role in social service provision and advocacy work for the community, but the groups are generally less collaborative in Columbus compared to in the Twin Cities, with some notable exceptions. There is no central location for these organizations, like Minneapolis's Brian Coyle Center, which contributes to the fact that groups function more or less on their own. Nonprofit community organizations have been identified as important factors in improving the integration of new immigrant groups (Ramakrishnan and Lewis 2005), but the disunity among many Somali organizations limits their potential influence. Despite the efforts of some Somali community leaders and the street-level bureaucrats in the New American Initiative office, an umbrella Somali organization has not been established, even though it would be a key area for building Somali capacity. Given the many important services provided by these organizations (e.g., citizenship classes, adult ESL classes, and job training), uniting would help create a more powerful voice and increase opportunities for government and foundation grants. These organizations, along with street-level bureaucrats and political parties, could then help prepare new groups of Somalis for leadership in the community.

The one area where Somali political incorporation in Columbus shows potential is in the New American Initiative Office. The Somali bureaucrats who work there have demonstrated a commitment to pushing for the appointment of Somalis to boards and commissions, and they are deeply invested in working with community organizations to build capacity. Yet even with these important efforts, individual Somali bureaucrats with small budgets wield only limited power.

Policy responsiveness to Somali interests is the desired result of political incorporation. In general, Somali respondents in the Twin Cities believe they have some influence over policy, but in Columbus, the sentiment is the opposite. Somalis there do not believe that policy makers sufficiently take their views into consideration, leading to depressed levels of political efficacy. Still, in both cities, Somali rates of voter turnout are reportedly high. Even in Columbus, Somalis take seriously the idea of civic participation through voting.

Even with the promising signs of political incorporation in the Twin Cities, Somalis in both areas under investigation share several policy concerns. In both regions, the targeting of Somalis by law enforcement and their concerns about the future of remittances top their list of worries. Remittances are discussed in Chapter 5, which addresses Somali economic incorporation. Chapter 6 addresses the issue of Somali social incorporation. Particularly because of security threats posed by al-Shabaab and ISIS, policy makers must strike a balance between upholding civil liberties and at the same time collaborating with law enforcement. Somalis in this study registered clear and unequivocal concern about terrorist recruiting, but they were also concerned about community stereotypes that could inhibit their social incorporation.

5 /

Economic Incorporation

The economic inclusion of a new immigrant community contributes to opportunities for upward mobility. Economic inclusion benefits not only the newcomers but also the receiving communities that offer immigrants economic incorporation. The well-known story of the economic recovery in Lewiston, Maine, stands as a case in point. Prior to the Somalis' arrival, Lewiston lacked a low-skilled labor force and had an overabundance of unoccupied rental units. When Somalis arrived in the area, they resolved both of these problems. Meaningful economic contributions from the Somali population in Lewiston altered the popular perception of Somalis—and immigrants more generally—as a menace to a group of productive stakeholders (Voyer 2013).

In this chapter, I argue that economic incorporation is inextricably required for Somalis' economic advancement. In an ideal scenario, the economic opportunity structure is open to newcomers, who are able to take advantage of these conditions. Although building wealth is more challenging today compared to the experience of previous generations, one would expect immigrant communities to show progress toward economic self-sufficiency after a period of time. Somalis, like other large refugee communities, arrive in the

United States with the ability to seek legal employment almost immediately. However, the majority of Somalis who arrive in the United States as refugees do not hold advanced degrees, and many arrive with limited English-language skills. This situation inherently limits their chances of significant upward mobility, because their employment options are often restricted to low-skill and low-wage positions that typically do not offer opportunities for advancement. The challenges that this phenomenon presents for social incorporation are addressed in Chapter 6. Meanwhile, even Somalis who arrive in the United States with advanced degrees face hurdles, as their educational credentials are not always recognized. It is not unusual to meet a Somali taxi driver or warehouse worker who held a prominent position in Somalia before the civil war.

This chapter demonstrates that even in the Twin Cities, a region that offers greater Somali economic incorporation than is found in Columbus, there remains significant room for improvement. Yet in both areas, Somalis have made important contributions to the local economies that benefit their communities as well as their cities more broadly. Despite these contributions, Somalis are somewhat excluded from upward mobility. Comparing their situations in each area can help us understand why this exclusion has occurred and why Somalis in the Twin Cities see less of it. Certain structural factors in the private and public sectors have encouraged economic incorporation in the Twin Cities, factors that are explored in detail in this chapter. In places that lack these factors—such as Columbus—Somali economic incorporation is weaker, and their situation is more dire. By understanding more about the ways in which economic incorporation is facilitated, we can help shape better outcomes for Somali immigrants and the cities they call home.

The concept of economic incorporation benefits not only new immigrants individually but also society more broadly. Research on immigrant capital points to the important contributions immigrants make in urban America that contribute to societal wealth (Corrie 2008, 2). In examining the dimensions of immigrant capital, Bruce Corrie posits that immigrant consumer capital involves the purchasing of goods and services by immigrants (2008, 2). Their purchasing power also has a positive effect on tax revenue. Immigrant productive capital, meanwhile, refers to immigrant participation in the labor force (2). In addition to the low-skilled workforce that a new immigrant community can provide, those with higher-end skills can also help advance the labor force. Finally, immigrant entrepreneurial capital holds the promise of revitalizing areas where immigrants live (2).

In terms of the three dimensions of immigrant political capital, one can argue that Somalis in Columbus and in the Twin Cities add to the consumer capital, productive capital, and entrepreneurial capital in their communities. What is less clear is whether they are able to take full advantage of the economic opportunity structure, something I argue is central to their economic incorporation.

The indicators of Somali economic incorporation reflect traditional economic measures combined with some that are less conventional. This chapter's analysis begins with an examination of household income, followed by a discussion of Somali employment levels. After casting light on the economic vulnerability of Somalis via these measures, attention is given to private-public sector intervention as a factor in economic incorporation. Homeownership rates are the final measure of economic incorporation, accepting the traditional American view that equity through homeownership contributes to financial growth. The ability to buy rather than rent a home can provide a more stable and cost-effective livelihood. But given the religious constraints associated with interest-bearing loans, many Somalis are restricted from full participation in the American economy. The consequences of this phenomenon can be seen in Somali homeownership rates. Before delving into the factors that influence the economic incorporation of Somalis in Columbus and in the Twin Cities, remittances are discussed as one of the most pressing economic concerns among Somalis in the United States.

Remittances

Remittances provide those in the Somali diaspora a means to support relatives who remain in Somalia or in refugee camps in Africa. Because of the ongoing war in Somalia, the country does not have a functioning and reliable economic structure. For this reason, family members living outside the country often support multiple relatives.

Virtually all respondents in this project reported sending significant portions of their monthly earnings back to Somalia to support family members. Paying for food, medicine, and the education of young relatives were all mentioned as common reasons for remitting. These financial responsibilities place a heavy burden on Somalis in the diaspora. One respondent explained:

> Knowing that you've had the chance to start a new life and make a living increases the sense of obligation you feel for those left behind. Knowing that they are struggling leads to constant concern for their well-being. Also, the responsibility for their survival is in your hands. (Columbus community member interview, July 24, 2013)

The challenges associated with new restrictions on remittances raise significant concerns among Somalis in this study. The external pressure they face to support relatives is an issue that overshadows their economic incorporation in the United States.

Research on immigrant remittances indicates that sending money back home is often a priority for those who come to the United States in search of economic opportunity, but less work has been done on uncovering the differences between refugee and other immigrant group remittance practices and implications (Horst 2004, 2). Yet concern about the potential for remittances flowing from the Somali diaspora into the hands of terrorist organizations like al-Shabaab has resulted in major barriers for remittances to Somalia.

According to a 2013 Oxfam report, 16 percent of the $1.3 billion that flows to Somalia in the form of remittances each year comes from the United States (Orozco and Yansura 2013). The Somali form of remittances is known as the xawilaad (Horst 2004, 3). This system is largely informal and is used by individuals to remit funds to relatives as well as by nongovernmental organizations (NGOs) and humanitarian organizations to provide much-needed aid (Horst 2004; Horst and Van Hear 2002). Before the Somali civil war in 1991, remittances were primarily sent by Somali migrants to help relatives with investments, weddings, school fees, and other economic ventures. Transnational xawilaad organizations emerged in the 1980s to help create fast and reliable ways to transfer funds (Horst 2006, 5). After 1991, when Somalis began moving to the West as refugees, the xawilaad took on a more dire purpose—ensuring the survival of family members at home in Somalia or in refugee camps in other countries (Horst 2004, 2006, 2008). Ihotu Ali's (2011) work documents the complex reaction among Somalis to the devastating news that a group of money-wiring services would close. A Somali respondent in Ali's study explained:

> When Al Barakaat was closed, everybody felt that the others would be closed. Families back home were calling, [saying,] "Will I be getting this month's money, what's going to happen?" People here didn't know. Some people here even went so far as, "Should I even go to these places to send money? What if I'm accused of sending money?" Some people came to me, and said, "Can I go to this one that's open? Can they trace me back?" We tell them sending money is not a crime. (Quoted in Ali 2011, 96)

Cindy Horst's (2006) work documents the significance of remittances from Minneapolis to relatives in Kenyan refugee camps. Her extensive fieldwork in Minneapolis revealed a strong sense of responsibility among respondents for the financial stability of relatives on the African continent. Findings from the research for this book paralleled what Horst found, although mine included increased concern about terrorist connections.

Of the three main Somali remittance companies in the United States, one is headquartered in Columbus. The president of that organization explained:

> At present, remittances from abroad—from Somali expatriate communities and from international development and charitable organizations, such as the United Nations, Save the Children, the Red Cross, and CARE—are the principle source of funds in Somalia. All of these remittances, all of this charitable aid is delivered to Somalia by remittances companies like Dahabshil. (Dahabshil letter 2015)

Remittance companies, such as Dahabshil, play a vital role in monetary distribution, because Somalia has neither a banking system nor a stable government. Unemployment is rampant, and thanks to the country's political and economic instability, the World Bank and the International Monetary Fund (IMF) do not provide international aid to Somalia. Dahabshil's president wrote:

> In the absence of a banking system, even international relief organizations like the Red Cross and CARE must use remittance companies such as Dahabshil to fund their project, meet their payroll, and pay their rent. . . . If remittance companies are unable to do business because of actions of the banking community in the U.S., it affects not only private remittances between family members but also large-scale charitable efforts of the worldwide community. (Dahabshil letter 2015)

Changes in the U.S. policy toward Somali remittances stems from government concern that funds are making their way to terrorist organizations in Somalia. These concerns emerged in the post-9/11 era and intensified once evidence of money laundering to support al-Qaeda emerged. The United Nations has also identified instances when terrorist financing has occurred through Somali remittance organizations (Cockayne and Shetret 2012, 34). Because the xawilaad is primarily self-regulated, meaning that internal records are the primary way to manage transactions, concerns about terrorist financing are expressed by regulators worldwide. The process of "debanking," or the refusal of banks to do business with xawilaads, has intensified in recent years (46).

In 2011, Barclays Bank ended its work with Somali remittance organizations because of evidence that two Somali women in Minnesota had sent money intended for al-Shabaab. Since that time, the situation has worsened, as a growing number of banks have cut ties with xawilaads. By the start of 2015, only one bank in the United States—Merchants Bank in California—continued to work with Somali remittance organizations to facilitate money transfers. The bank ended these relationships on February 6, 2015, as a result of pressure from regulators (Hatcher 2015). Congressman Keith Ellison has called this decision catastrophic. He explained:

> For the past few years, I have been warning every regulator and official about the devastating effects of closing the last safe and legal pipeline to provide humanitarian remittances to Somalia. . . . There is no doubt that a decline in remittances will exacerbate the humanitarian crisis and erode the gains Somalia has made in recent years. (Ellison quoted in Hatcher 2015)

Congressman Ellison has been the primary voice for Somali remittances in the U.S. Congress. In 2014, he sponsored the Money Remittances Improvement Act (H.R. 4386), "which would make it easier for well-regulated nonbank institutions such as money service businesses to provide remittances to their customers across the globe" (Ellison 2014). The bill passed in both houses and was signed into law by President Barack Obama in August 2014. It essentially facilitates continuing remittances, but in a way that addresses security concerns. Although it has increased regulation and made the remittance process more restrictive for Somalis, the community's ability to send money remains intact. This bill represents the most concrete example of how the political incorporation of Somalis in the Twin Cities helped them accomplish their goals. As Ellison's press release about the passage notes, the bill was supported by a broad range of groups, including banking professional associations, regulatory groups, and international organizations like Oxfam. More importantly, local organizations in Minneapolis, including the Somali American Remittances association, Somali Action Alliance (SAA), and the Confederation of Somali Community in Minnesota (CSCM), also collaborated for the passage of this bill (Ellison representative interview, July 11, 2014).

Omitted from much of the discourse on resources landing in terrorist coffers is the possibility that remittance restrictions could make family members back in Somalia more vulnerable and dependent on extremist organizations. As one respondent explained:

The hostility toward the West is likely to increase if funds are completely cut off. This situation creates tremendous anxiety for Somalis outside of Somalia, who know that their support is the only way their family can survive. (Twin Cities community member interview C, June 4, 2014)

The scholarship of Horst and colleagues sheds additional light on the misconceptions associated with remittance crackdowns (Horst et al. 2014). Conducting interviews in Norway between 2000 and 2008, a group of researchers identified the normative judgments about migrants' financial and personal decisions to send money to family members abroad. They found that sending remittances made migrants more suspicious in the eyes of host country natives and led to questions about a migrant's loyalty and potential ties to terror groups. These normative assertions have had negative structural and emotional consequences for Somalis in Norway, and no doubt similar judgments have produced similar effects in the United States. As Anita Waters (2012) explains:

Many transnational migrants retain ties to their homeland through political participation, remittances, and communication. . . . This transnational character may affect the reception of Somalis by casting doubts on their commitment to remain in the United States or their ability to fulfill their duties as citizens.

The commitment to supporting family members in Somalia or other countries of the diaspora is a high priority for the majority of respondents in this project. Yet maintaining ties to relatives does not translate into rejecting an American identity, nor does it indicate support for, either directly or indirectly, terrorist activities.

Household Income

The median Somali household income level is staggeringly low, both nationally and in the cities under investigation in this project. Poverty remains a major barrier to economic incorporation for Somalis. Table

5.1 presents data at the national and city levels based on the 2010 American Community Survey five-year survey. Before delving into the numbers, it is worth noting that in 2010, the federal poverty line for families of four was below $22,050 (OASE 2010). As noted in previous chapters, Somali families tend to be large—it is not uncommon to find families of six to eight. Focusing on median household income, or midpoint household income, Table 5.1 illustrates that Somalis earn $19,061, which is far lower than the figures for whites ($54,999), African Americans ($35,194), and Latinos ($41,534). Hmong, the other major refugee population in the Twin Cities, are also included in Table 5.1 because of the significant Hmong community in St. Paul. The differences between the Hmong and Somali groups are worth noting. Although the reasons are beyond the scope of this book, the national median Hmong household income is $46,308, an amount significantly higher than the corresponding Somali figure.[1]

The story of Somali household income in the Twin Cities and in Columbus is similar: the median household income is $11,414 in Minneapolis; $13,370 in St. Paul; and $13,242 in Columbus. One issue to keep in mind is that American Community Survey data rely on U.S. Census data and follow-up surveys based on these data. If Somalis are greatly undercounted, as most scholars and community members assert, the median household income numbers could be artificially low. The numbers could also be low because they do not take into account some of the more informal Somali-run businesses that cater to their own community, such as home health care and daycare. At the same time, such businesses are regulated by the government, and it would be challenging to operate for a long period of time without procuring the necessary licensure. Despite the possible problems with these numbers, the overwhelming poverty in the Somali community is both undeniable and staggering. This level of household poverty adds to the forces already stacked against Somali economic incorporation and financial security. It also speaks to the dire need for economic opportunities.

---

1. For an assessment of the Hmong experience in American cities, see Hein 2006 and Vang 2008.

TABLE 5.1. SOMALI HOUSEHOLD INCOME

Household income	United States					Columbus, Ohio				
	White	Black	Hmong	Somali	Hispanic or Latino	White	Black	Hmong	Somali	Hispanic or Latino
Total households	89,046,111	13,619,955	43,443	27,396	12,871,609	214,239	82,717	—	2,631	11,295
Less than $10,000	6.0%	14.6%	7.0%	28.5%	8.5%	8.4%	18.1%	—	44.2%	10.7%
$10,000 to $14,999	5.1%	8.3%	5.8%	10.2%	6.5%	4.9%	7.8%	—	10.8%	8.2%
$15,000 to $24,999	10.2%	14.2%	11.6%	23.6%	14.0%	10.9%	15.3%	—	21.9%	19.5%
$25,000 to $34,999	10.2%	12.6%	12.2%	12.4%	13.3%	11.2%	13.8%	—	10.6%	14.1%
$35,000 to $49,999	14.0%	14.7%	17.7%	10.7%	16.4%	16.5%	15.5%	—	9.9%	17.9%
$50,000 to $74,999	19.0%	16.2%	21.0%	7.4%	18.6%	20.9%	16.3%	—	1.9%	14.8%
$75,000 to $99,999	13.0%	8.8%	13.1%	3.6%	10.3%	12.2%	7.0%	—	0.7%	6.6%
$100,000 to $149,999	13.1%	7.3%	8.9%	2.4%	8.4%	10.3%	4.8%	—	0.0%	5.6%
$150,000 to $200,000	4.7%	2.0%	1.6%	0.6%	2.4%	2.9%	1.0%	—	0.0%	1.6%
$200,000 or more	4.7%	1.3%	1.1%	0.6%	1.6%	1.9%	0.5%	—	0.0%	0.8%
Median household income	54,999	35,194	46,308	19,061	41,534	48,278	31,375	—	13,242	32,579
Mean household income	74,765	47,945	55,261	28,867	54,456	59,768	40,220	—	16,326	43,465

Household income	Minneapolis, Minnesota					St. Paul, Minnesota				
	White	Black	Hmong	Somali	Hispanic or Latino	White	Black	Hmong	Somali	Hispanic or Latino
Total households	124,192	27,214	1,388	4,749	9,614	81,252	15,339	4,846	1,270	7,516
Less than $10,000	7.1%	28.4%	19.0%	43.7%	9.9%	7.0%	24.2%	10.4%	41.4%	9.6%
$10,000 to $14,999	5.6%	9.3%	8.0%	14.6%	7.6%	4.9%	8.9%	7.4%	9.8%	4.5%
$15,000 to $24,999	9.3%	17.5%	16.7%	17.7%	17.6%	10.6%	19.3%	13.3%	26.7%	22.0%
$25,000 to $34,999	9.1%	12.6%	19.5%	11.2%	15.0%	10.1%	17.0%	14.2%	14.3%	15.6%
$35,000 to $49,999	14.5%	12.9%	12.8%	7.6%	17.6%	14.8%	11.8%	18.3%	5.1%	13.7%
$50,000 to $74,999	19.0%	10.6%	15.4%	3.1%	15.6%	19.7%	10.8%	18.5%	2.7%	17.9%
$75,000 to $99,999	12.7%	4.3%	4.6%	1.5%	9.2%	12.7%	3.7%	10.9%	0.0%	8.8%
$100,000 to $149,999	12.8%	3.2%	4.0%	0.6%	3.8%	11.5%	3.6%	4.9%	0.0%	4.9%
$150,000 to $200,000	4.8%	0.9%	0.0%	0.0%	2.5%	4.4%	0.3%	1.1%	0.0%	2.5%
$200,000 or more	5.1%	0.3%	0.0%	0.0%	1.1%	4.2%	0.2%	1.0%	0.0%	0.5%
Median household income	54,339	21,478	29,507	11,414	34,901	52,665	23,508	40,019	13,370	33,210
Mean household income	75,378	31,539	33,789	17,970	46,508	70,281	31,333	47,908	16,780	45,936

Source: Data from U.S. Census Bureau, 2010 American Community Survey five-year estimates (table DP03).

Note: Income and benefits in 2010-adjusted dollars.

Employment

Jobs drew many Somalis to Columbus and to the Twin Cities. Regardless of whether Somali refugees were relocated in one of these areas, many migrated there in search of better employment opportunities and a lower cost of living. Yet the vast majority of jobs are low-skilled labor positions. In Columbus, the warehouse industry dominates. In the Twin Cities, Somalis work in a range of jobs in the food production, security, and housekeeping industries. Others pursue entrepreneurial ventures and self-employment. The gendered nature of employment makes self-employment particularly appealing to Somali women, who often find that their traditional dress creates an informal challenge to gaining employment (Carlson 2007). The entrepreneurial spirit of Somalis is apparent in Columbus and in the Twin Cities. Many respondents in this study owned home health care, daycare, or transportation companies. By and large, these Somali-owned businesses serve a Somali clientele. Often these businesses represent a form of secondary employment beyond the respondent's "day job." Despite the prevalence of Somali small businesses in Columbus and in the Twin Cities, as the previous section of this chapter makes clear, Somalis remain relatively impoverished in both areas.

Several factors contribute to the challenges Somalis face with regard to employment options and upward mobility. First, especially for those who arrived in the United States with limited English-language skills, occupational options are limited. Equally challenging is the situation for highly educated Somalis with professional and educational credentials that are not recognized in the United States. For these reasons, the appeal of self-employment has drawn many Somalis to entrepreneurial ventures, but many of these businesses are unsustainable.

Table 5.2 presents employment data from the 2010 American Community Survey ten-year survey. Somali employment levels are relatively consistent with other racial/ethnic minorities at the national level and in Minneapolis. In St. Paul and in Columbus, however, Somali labor force participation is significantly below employment levels of African Americans and Latinos. Although self-employment and undercounts of the population could depress these numbers, the discrepancy in

TABLE 5.2. SOMALI EMPLOYMENT STATUS

Employment status	United States					Columbus, Ohio				
	White	Black	Hmong	Somali	Hispanic or Latino	White	Black	Hmong	Somali	Hispanic or Latino
Population 16 and over	180,797,802	28,526,840	143,389	58,505	33,108,596	407,683	154,401	—	5,670	26,088
In labor force	64.9%	63.1%	64.8%	62.4%	68.2%	71.5%	66.8%	—	54.1%	75.8%
Employed	60.1%	53.8%	56.5%	49.6%	61.3%	66.7%	56.2%	—	35.7%	70.1%
Unemployed	4.4%	8.7%	8.1%	12.8%	6.5%	4.7%	10.6%	—	18.3%	5.6%
Armed forces	0.5%	0.6%	0.2%	0.0%	0.4%	0.1%	0.1%	—	0.0%	0.1%

Employment status	Minneapolis, Minnesota					St. Paul, Minnesota				
	White	Black	Hmong	Somali	Hispanic or Latino	White	Black	Hmong	Somali	Hispanic or Latino
Population 16 and over	225,734	48,253	4,047	7,595	23,108	150,924	28,902	15,966	2,429	17,961
In labor force	75.9%	65.8%	48.5%	61.0%	77.6%	73.0%	64.5%	61.2%	52.3%	72.1%
Employed	71.2%	52.1%	36.9%	48.7%	71.4%	68.0%	53.1%	54.3%	40.8%	64.3%
Unemployed	4.6%	13.7%	11.6%	12.3%	6.2%	4.9%	11.4%	6.9%	11.4%	7.8%
Armed forces	0.0%	0.0%	0.0%	0.0%	0.0%	0.1%	0.0%	0.0%	0.0%	0.0%

Source: Data from U.S. Census Bureau, 2010 American Community Survey five-year estimates (table DP03).

Somali employment levels suggests an area in need of greater attention by policy makers.

Another employment issue in both cities is the low percentage of Somali teachers in public K–12 schools. Concrete data on the number of Somali teachers were unavailable after exchanges with school districts, municipal employees, and state officials, but five current or former Somali teachers were interviewed for this study and provided some insight into the situation for Somali educators. Many of the Somali teachers certified to teach do so at magnet schools with high percentages of Somali students. Both Somali teachers and students are grouped in the African American category, making it extremely difficult to draw conclusions about Somali-specific inclusion or student performance. However, assuming that respondents in this study are correct and that few certified Somali teachers are employed in public schools, this is an area where advances could be made. Recruitment of Somali students for teacher certification would increase the presence of the community in the fabric of society, which would benefit not only Somali students, who would see role models in their schools, but also non-Somalis, who might gain new cultural understanding. Given the extent of residential segregation in both areas under investigation, bringing a diverse pool of teachers to less diverse schools could have a tremendously positive outcome. This issue is addressed in Chapter 7.

The Twin Cities

In an article titled "Hard Workers and Daring Entrepreneurs: Impressions from the Somali Enclave in Minneapolis," Benny Carlson (2007) examines the factors that contribute to higher Somali employment and economic vibrancy in Minneapolis versus Sweden, where the situation is quite the opposite. The Twin Cities region has attracted domestic and international attention because of the Somali economic narrative that highlights Somali success, yet Carlson's study sounds an appropriately cautionary note about Somali success in the Twin Cities. Many of the jobs held by Somalis are low-wage positions with minimal opportunities for advancement. What draws many political leaders and scholars to the Twin Cities is the abundance of small businesses owned by Somalis. As Carlson notes, in 2004, there were roughly 550 Somali businesses in the state; by the end of 2005, the number had increased to about 800 (2007, 180–181). These figures are impressive, but the situation is not as promising as the figures suggest. Most importantly, the rate of Somali small-business failure is extraordinarily high.

A 2005 study of Somali small businesses by Hussein Samatar (2005) categorizes a number of problems with many Somali small businesses. He acknowledges the rapid increase in Somali small businesses from zero in 1994 to more than 550 by 2005. However, the failure rate of these businesses is high, in part because of a lack of planning. This is especially true for those with limited English-language skills and unfamiliarity with American business culture (83). Along similar lines, capital is typically generated through social networks in the absence of contractual agreements about repayments (84). Often, Somali business owners lack experience in their business areas and do not have the financial training necessary to operate profitably (84). Few Somali businesses attract customers from outside the Somali community, and there is tremendous market saturation and competition (85). Somali malls, or suuqs, exist in Columbus and in the Twin Cities. They function as important community centers, but they also provide a way for Somalis to operate small stalls with products aimed at Somali customers, although there is great redundancy among the businesses (86). Samatar also raises concerns about the investment of personal wealth in small businesses that often fail. Avoidance of financial institutions, owing to Quranic restrictions about receiving or paying interest, coupled with a frequent lack of familiarity with regulatory requirements, means that small Somali businesses frequently face insurmountable challenges (86).

In a follow-up to Samatar's insightful article, Shannon Golden, Yasin Garad, and Elizabeth Heger Boyle (2011) revisit the situation of Somali small-business owners in the Twin Cities. Through survey data, the authors find that several of the same problems identified by Samatar remain a challenge. Their most important findings indicate that few business owners have written business plans, only about 50 percent of businesses in suuqs have bank accounts, relationships with financial institutions for loans remain small, and market saturation continues to be a major problem (89).

Beyond low-wage jobs and self-employment, there is visual evidence of Somali inclusion in government jobs. Although the state, county, and city do not collect employment data on the number of Somalis employed in the public sector, their presence is evident throughout the government's infrastructure. Many respondents mentioned the increased presence of Somalis in government offices. Beyond providing translation services, their presence is a sign that Somalis are finding a seat at the table. Without formal numbers on municipal employment, it is difficult to make concrete recommendations, but examining opportunities for Somali upward mobility through the public sector would provide helpful evidence of government support of the community. Scholarship on upward mobility for minority communities points to the important role of public-sector employment in long-term economic advancement (Boyd 1994; Eisinger 1986; Guajardo 1999; Parks 2011; Rumberger 1983).

Columbus

Columbus is also host to a large number of very profitable national and international companies. Few Somalis, however, are able to obtain middle to upper-level management positions in these corporations. One respondent suggested:

> We understand that the city and state are unable to force the private sector to create jobs for Somalis. At the same time, there are probably ways that Columbus's business community could become more open and accepting of hiring Somalis for jobs that pay a living wage for a family. Warehouse jobs are not what Somalis need. They need a chance to prove their potential and climb the employment ladder. (Columbus media interview, June 27, 2013)

There are a small number of noteworthy exceptions, but beyond the private sector, few Somalis hold positions at the city, county, or state level in Columbus.[2] That being said, it is also evident that Soma-

---

2. Figures on Somali employment are not collected at the state, county, or city level for either of the areas under investigation. Because Somalis are classified as African Americans, true numbers are impossible to determine.

lis are actors in the Columbus economy, whether they own small businesses or have found other professional success. In light of the shortcomings of the local and state government policies, some community organizations have attempted to fill the gaps.

It is estimated that Columbus is home to more than four hundred Somali-owned businesses. Their size and scope vary, and the goods and services they provide are diverse (J. Hirsi 2009). These include restaurants, which range from serving traditional Somali cuisine to American fare. Somali business owners run marketplaces and grocery stores, cleaning companies, travel agencies, car dealerships, home health care agencies, barbershops, and employment service agencies, among others (J. Hirsi 2009).

To cover the costs of starting businesses, some Somalis engage in a system that pools resources, known as "Ayuuto" or "Shaloongo." This system is used in Columbus and in the Twin Cities. According to respondents in this study, women are the primary Ayuuto participants and often use the money to start small businesses or purchase essentials, such as used cars. Ayuuto networks usually consist of ten to fifteen individuals who save a portion of their incomes every month or pay period. The combined amount is given to one person who is ready to start a business or invest the money (J. Hirsi 2009). This process goes on for as many months as there are individuals in the group. For example, if the Ayuuto comprises fifteen people, it will persist for fifteen months so that each individual yields the benefit of the total contributions each month. Alternatively, the members of some Ayuutos will choose to pool all of their monthly savings together to make a common investment or start a small business together (J. Hirsi 2009).

Private-Sector/Public-Sector Programs

During fieldwork for this project, one economic factor emerged as a distinguishing feature in the Twin Cities: the African Development Center (ADC). This organization is a social-profit community developer and commercial lender.[3] ADC "is a leader in micro-lending

---

3. See http://www.adcminnesota.org/about/mission.

. . . dedicated to the economic empowerment and success of African immigrants."[4] It works primarily with Somalis, although services are offered to all Minnesotans. The organization provides business development through training and low-interest loans, homebuyer workshops, and financial literacy training.[5] All of these services are provided in a culturally sensitive way that gives clients lending options that are compliant with Muslim religious teachings that include restrictions on interest-bearing loans. Just as there is religious diversity within any large community, there is variation among Somali respondents in this study regarding the extent of the restrictions on interest-bearing loans. To some, the idea of a loan with interest was forbidden. Others had worked with culturally sensitive lenders who are willing to include interest in the principal as a way of achieving religious compliance. Others were willing to take out loans with traditional lenders while still maintaining their religious beliefs. What is unique about Minnesota is the existence of ADC and the organization's dedication to building wealth within the community.

Samatar, ADC's founder, worked as a Wells Fargo banker for more than a decade prior to creating the organization (Ali 2011, 105). As discussed in Chapter 4, Samatar's close relationship with Minneapolis Mayor R. T. Rybak resulted in a unique collaboration between ADC and the city. One of the programs that emerged from this partnership was an initiative that combined city and ADC resources to create Islamic-compliant small-business loans (Rybak interview, April 8, 2015). Mayor Rybak explained:

> We worked together to create a riba-free [interest-free] loan program. As I recall, about thirty small-business loans were distributed. I remember visiting some of these new businesses. There was a woman who opened a dress shop. Just three years earlier, she'd lived in a refugee camp. . . . It was pretty incredible. (Rybak interview, April 8, 2015)

---

4. Ibid.
5. Ibid.

Today, ADC is the largest small-business lender in the city and has issued between 350 and 400 small-business loans (African Development Center interview B, April 15, 2015). It has roughly two hundred active accounts in its portfolio and provides a range of services to its clients. Many clients need help with obtaining permits and licenses. Others need help with zoning and bookkeeping. The availability of these services through ADC have resulted in a 0.5 percent loan default rate among its clients, according to the Center's 2015 Fact Sheet.[6] The organization maintains strong connections with city officials, including Minneapolis Mayor Betsy Hodges (African Development Center interview B April 15, 2015). It is also active in state programs aimed at opportunities for home buying. One ADC representative explained:

> Although we don't provide mortgage loans, we do offer home-buyer workshops. There are many "mortgage-ready" Somalis, meaning that they make $50,000 or more, who would like to purchase a home. We play a role in the discussions about down-payment assistance programs and other opportunities that can benefit the community. (African Development Center interview A, April 15, 2015)

According to a 2012 report by the Wilder Foundation, an independent research group in St. Paul, the societal benefits associated with ADC are extensive. Approximately 76 percent of ADC's small-business loans go to businesses in the Twin Cities (Da'ar 2012, 2). ADC clients also had gross receipts of $6.4 million and paid $77,280 in sales, payroll, and other taxes (2). Beyond these quantifiable measures of ADC's performance, the report states:

> The number of people trained, number and amount of loans extended, number of businesses opened or expanded by ADC, for example, fail to capture the real social and economic benefits of its programming because they do not mention or quantify ways in which the quality of life for the clients and possibly the community in general are affected. (3)

---

6. This publication was sent to the author by ADC.

ADC's success has spread nationwide, and even internationally. The organization's executive director frequently receives inquiries about the reasons for this success and has even been asked whether ADC would consider opening a branch in a city like Columbus or Seattle. At the moment, ADC has no plans for expansion beyond Minnesota. This is wise, because part of ADC's success story is its connections with political leaders in the city of Minneapolis and at the state level. These political connections have helped ADC create strong partnerships that benefit Somalis and taxpayers at large. The absence of an ADC or any other culturally sensitive lenders in Columbus stands in contrast to the story in the Twin Cities.

Homeownership

Homeownership is a traditional means for wealth accumulation for Americans. In many ways, the desire for homeownership is a hallmark of American culture. Even federal agencies have a history of encouraging Americans to buy homes. For example, the Federal Housing Administration (FHA) was created in 1934 and has provided mortgages for more than thirty-four million properties since its creation. FHA also played a pivotal role during the post–World War II era by creating incentives for returning servicemen to buy homes. In many respects, FHA's encouragement reinforced the aspiration of acquiring real estate as an investment and as part of the American dream.

The story of American homeownership is not without its problems. Most recently, the collapse of the housing market in 2008 resulted from insufficient regulating oversight of the real estate market, particularly subprime lending practices. When the real estate bubble burst, many Americans lost their homes to foreclosure as a result of unmanageable mortgage payments. Despite this crisis, the desire to own homes remains strong. As the housing market rebounds, it is apparent that the tradition of homeownership remains a central part of American investments.

On a practical level, homeownership through participation in the mortgage market provides individuals with the option of making a stable monthly payment on a home they will eventually own. It also protects people from some of the challenges associated with renting a home, including the inability to prevent increases in monthly payments when leases are renegotiated. Somalis are largely relegated to the category of renters in both areas under investigation. Somali respondents routinely mentioned this problem, but finding verifiable data to back up these assertions presented a challenge. Somali homeownership data are not collected by any of the cities, counties, or states under investigation. For this reason, the most comprehensive database available, the Integrated Public Use Microdata Series (IPUMS), was used to estimate Somali homeownership.

The data available through IPUMS are collected from the decennial census and the American Community Survey. The information comes in the form of microdata, with each record representing an individual. Scholars must cull through millions of records using a statistical package that allows a sample to be drawn and analyzed. Rates for Somalis sampled in the American Community Survey 2008–2012 were pulled using IPUMS. The variable used to identify whether an individual owned a home was the "Ownership of a Dwelling" variable, which indicates whether the resident rents or owns his or her dwelling. Housing units acquired with a mortgage or other lending arrangements were classified as owned, even if repayment was not complete. The first person listed on the form for the household was used to represent the entire household, and IPUMS household weights were applied to the data. To limit the possibility of households where everyone was not related, and thus the respondent's ancestry and subsequent household ownership were not shared with the household owner, the "relate" variable in IPUMS was used to exclude mixed households. This was accomplished by restricting the sample to values 1–10, representing immediate family only. Because the sample size for Somalis in the Twin Cities and in Columbus was too small to be statistically significant, the search was broadened to include all of Ohio and Minnesota. At the state level, the sample was robust enough to illustrate general trends among those sampled. Ancestry was identified as the respondent's self-reported ancestry or ethnic origin. The ancestry variable was used to identify the respondent's heritage.

As illustrated in Figures 5.1 and 5.2, there is a wide gap in the rate of homeownership between the Somalis sampled over this five-year period in Ohio and in Minnesota when compared to the total population. On the one hand, renting allows for a greater degree of mobility to pursue new jobs and opportunities. However, this convenience is probably outweighed by the vulnerability renters experience in markets where rents are increasing. For this reason, the negative repercussions associated with renting outweigh any conceivable positives. If the figures drawn from the IPUMS samples in Figures 5.1 and 5.2 are an accurate representation of the situation for Somalis in the areas under investigation, this is cause for considerable concern. The inability to purchase a home is likely tied to two factors. The first is tied to household income figures presented earlier in this chapter. The poverty within the Somali community is a major cause of their inability to buy a home or qualify for a mortgage. For many Somalis, issues related to Islamic-compliant loans present a secondary barrier to homeownership.

In Minneapolis, the current and former mayors shared a desire to find creative and culturally sensitive ways to create opportunities

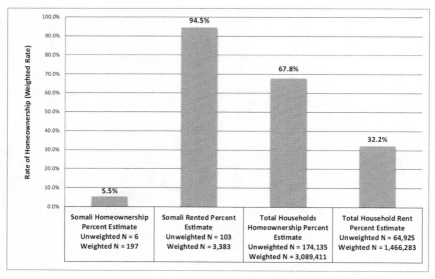

Figure 5.1. Somali household homeowners versus renters in Ohio. U.S. Census Bureau, 2008–2012 American Community Survey five-year sample.

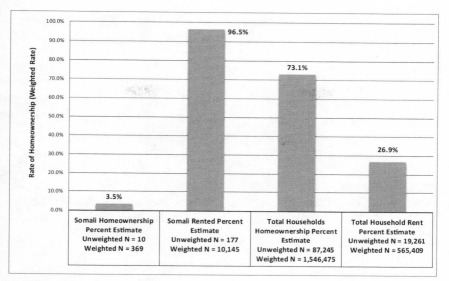

Figure 5.2. Somali household homeowners versus renters in Minnesota. U.S. Census Bureau, 2008–2012 American Community Survey five-year sample.

for homeownership for Somalis. A major concern in the Twin Cities is the rapidly increasing cost of rental units. As discussed in Chapter 4, former Mayor Rybak collaborated with ADC's executive director to identify creative financing methods for Muslims with an interest in opening a small business. There were also conversations between ADC and Mayor Rybak's office about the possibility of collaborating to provide mortgages that reflected the same culturally compliant criteria. Even with these efforts, and the ongoing efforts of Mayor Hodges and ADC, the sample of Somali homeowners in Figure 5.2 is in the same range as what we see in Columbus, where no such efforts are underway. This suggests the need for a broader dialogue at the national level on lending practices that open doors for Muslims who are left out of mainstream avenues for wealth building. It might also involve Somali leaders' challenging preconceived notions about Islam among Somali immigrants. Given the growing Muslim population in America, the conversation about Islamic-compliant loans should also include private banks and lending institutions. One method of avoiding interest is to add it to the principle and make payments based on the larger balance.

Summary

The economic incorporation of Somalis in Columbus and in the Twin Cities leaves considerable room for improvement. Although Minneapolis is commonly viewed internationally as the city where Somalis are most successful economically, a closer look tells a more nuanced story. As illustrated in Table 5.1, Somali household income is categorized as low in Columbus and in the Twin Cities. Because the number of Somalis living below the poverty line is high in both areas under investigation and ranks below what we see among other racial and ethnic groups, both regions are categorized as having low economic incorporation based on household income.

Employment levels are slightly more promising, particularly in Minneapolis, where Somali employment exceeds rates of employment among other racial and ethnic minorities. In St. Paul and in Columbus, employment figures are lower and fall behind levels seen among African Americans and Latinos. Although employment levels might be slightly depressed because of the considerable number of Somali small-business enterprises, the fact remains that employment opportunities for Somalis can be expanded, particularly in St. Paul and in Columbus. Between language barriers and the problems associated with not having their international educational credentials accepted in the United States, Somalis are often left with no options beyond low-wage jobs with little room for promotion. This fact contributes to the poverty within the Somali communities in the Twin Cities and in Columbus.

On a more promising note, the Twin Cities area is home to ADC, a private lending agency that funds hundreds of culturally compliant small-business loans to Somalis and other Africans in Minnesota. Together with leaders in city of Minneapolis, collaboration intended to provide new opportunities for Somalis is underway. These opportunities provide financing and business support that have resulted in very low default rates among borrowers. Moreover, the support and training offered by ADC play a role in lowering the turnover rates

TABLE 5.3. ECONOMIC INCORPORATION				
Measures	Household income	Employment	Public/private programs	Home-ownership
Columbus	low	moderate	low	low
Twin Cities	low	moderate/high	high	low

among Somali small businesses. Columbus has no organization similar to ADC and no visible interest among policy makers in providing opportunities to support and nurture Somali small-business owners.

Finally, Somali homeownership data presented in this chapter illustrate discouraging trends based on a sample drawn from IPUMS. These data were collected at the state level because of a statistically insignificant number of Somalis in the city samples in Columbus and in the Twin Cities. In both Minnesota and Ohio, the sample presents a 3 to 5 percent rate of homeownership among Somalis, numbers that rank far below national averages. Because homeownership is a major investment for a majority of Americans, the virtual absence of Somalis in this area is cause for concern for this and future generations. Table 5.3 illustrates the results of the measures of economic incorporation in each city.

6 /

Social Incorporation

A young Somali man from Columbus was recruited by a terrorist organization while in Minneapolis. A family [in Columbus] with a similar name complained of harassment by the police, even claiming the police told neighbors that there were terrorists living next door. . . . The family had no terrorist connections and felt helpless. This type of discrimination is common. (Columbus community member interview, June 26, 2014)

"One day, a Somali woman was caught speeding," said Mukhtar Abdulkadir, a Minneapolis police officer. "A police pulled her over. She was so nervous and fearful while she waited for the police [to] come to her window. Then she glanced at the window. Realizing the officer was a Somali, she said to him, 'Oh, you scared me. I thought you were a real police officer.'" (Abdulkadir in I. Hirsi 2014)

Alejandro Portes and Rubén Rumbaut's (2006) "context of reception" is connected to all the aspects of incorporation discussed in this book. As noted in Chapter 1, the "context of reception," or the conditions under which assimilation takes place, is influenced by a range of factors, including government treatment of the group, labor market factors, and the human capital of the migrants themselves. Thus, beyond the human capital that migrants bring to their new home, the political institutions and economic conditions they confront upon arrival have implications in terms of how effectively the migrants are able to assimilate. Assimilation is related to social incorporation, which is thus fundamentally related to the context of reception in a given area. Social ties, relationships, and general acceptance depend on the reception provided by a new community. Among the objectives of this research was to evaluate how Somalis perceive their political, economic, and social incorporation. This chapter touches on Somali perceptions of inclusion, the evolving context of reception that affects those perceptions, and the ultimate reality underlying them.

Heightened attention to recruiting by Foreign Terrorist Organizations (FTOs) in the post-9/11 era has strained the context of reception to Somalis, thus complicating all aspects of assimilation and incorporation. Somalis are an easily identifiable group as a result of religious traditions, dress, residential segregation, and skin color (Ali 2011; A. Waters 2012). Concerns about FTO recruiting, particularly in the Twin Cities but also in Columbus, have intensified the attention the Somali community receives from the mainstream media and law enforcement. What is often lost in this story is the deep sense of concern and alarm within the Somali community itself about the unfortunate actions of the several dozen individuals who have infamously joined these FTOs. Because Somalis are easily identifiable, they are vulnerable to stereotyping and discrimination as a result of the actions of a small minority. For this reason, among others, understanding Somali perceptions of inclusion in the social fabric is critical.

In this chapter, we turn to social incorporation by examining how several factors affect the Somali social experience in Columbus and in the Twin Cities. These measures of social incorporation include the region's history of welcoming refugees, an analysis of letters to the editor that concern Somalis in each area's principal newspaper, the role of Somali police, and the support of local philanthropic groups toward Somali-based projects. Each of these measures captures an aspect of the Somali social experience in the Twin Cities and in Columbus. Although social incorporation in the Twin Cities is higher, Somalis in both regions under investigation have room for growth.

Foreign Terrorist Organization Recruiting and Response

The fieldwork for this project occurred during a time when increased media and law enforcement attention was directed at a few highly publicized incidents of Somalis from the Twin Cities and Columbus joining the Islamic State (ISIS or ISIL) and al-Shabaab, Somalia's al-Qaeda affiliate (Shane 2015b). From 2006 through 2011, approximately twenty-seven Somali Americans left Minnesota to fight in Somalia with al-Shabaab (Salhani 2015). More recently, about a dozen Somalis in Minnesota have left the country to fight alongside the Islamic State (Shane 2015a). Government officials monitoring recruiting patterns found that the Twin Cities area was producing the greatest number of recruits in the country (Shane 2015a), including men and women between the ages of fourteen and forty and both converts to Islam and those born into Muslim households (Shane 2015b). On April 19, 2015, six young Somali men were arrested as they attempted to travel to Syria to join ISIS (Shane 2015b). For months preceding the arrests, an investigation into terrorist recruiting led many respondents in this study, and law enforcement officials, to believe that there was a mastermind recruiter on the ground in the Twin Cities. Contrary to these assumptions, the U.S. Attorney for Minnesota, Andrew Luger, announced that the investigation revealed no central Twin Cities recruiter and that these young men encouraged one another to join ISIS (Shane 2015b).

Radicalization via social media is something ISIS has perfected to such an extent that numerous U.S. citizens have attempted to join the group after encountering the group's online presence. The combination of social media and face-to-face recruitment by peers has proven to work well in the Twin Cities. In 2015, the Department of Homeland Security (DHS) announced Countering Violent Extremism (CVE) programs in three pilot areas: the Twin Cities, Boston, and Los Angeles (Salhani 2015). DHS will collaborate with the Department of Justice (DOJ) and state and local law enforcement agencies to implement programs that counter extremism. Minnesota's U.S. attorney is over-seeing the implementation of CVE, something several Somali respondents in this study discussed as a conflict of interest because of Luger's prosecutorial responsibilities. It remains unclear how much money will be spent on the CVE initiative, but programs aimed at youth, job training, and mentoring have been identified as central priorities. At the time of the interviews for this project, several community leaders mentioned their interest in receiving funding to run CVE programs for Somali youth. Because multiple on-the-ground Somali community organizations are already focused on countering radicalization in Minnesota, it is likely that competition among groups will intensify as funds become available. However, accepting federal funding comes at a cost for many organizations. Views toward federal organizations, particularly the Federal Bureau of Investigation (FBI), DOJ, and DHS, were generally negative among respondents in this project. Many insisted that their comments be left off any interview notes for fear of surveillance or negative consequences. The prevailing sentiment was that federal law enforcement has done a poor job of developing trusting relationships in the community. Furthermore, there is concern that if law enforcement agencies oversee programs for children, then they could also gather information for investigative purposes (Twin Cities CAIR representative interview, April 16, 2015).

During a July 2014 visit to the Twin Cities, I had the opportunity to participate during a meeting between two FBI agents and several Somali community organizations at the Brian Coyle Center. The agents made clear their interest in working with the community to understand the reasons for extremism and reinforced their commitment to increasing the dialogue between FBI agents and community leaders in the years ahead. As one community representative explained:

It's difficult for us to trust the FBI. I know they have a community relations woman working with them now, but the last time we received so much attention was when several Somalis left to join al-Shabaab. . . . We are very, very concerned about these recent reports, but trusting that [our] cooperation will result in an end to radicalization, as opposed to greater discrimination, is a challenge. (Twin Cities community member interview D, June 3, 2014)

Achieving a balance between fighting extremism while also maintaining the civil rights and liberties of thousands of innocent Somali Americans is of paramount importance. What clearly emerged during interviews for this book was the sense that Somalis feel targeted and vulnerable. Parents also registered their concerns about the discrimination and profiling of their children by law enforcement. During a time when trust building between the community and law enforcement is incredibly important, it appears that Somali social incorporation is in danger. In the next chapter, recommendations for how law enforcement officials might best incorporate Somalis while simultaneously fighting radicalization are discussed in the context of interviews with Somali Americans for this project.

History of Welcoming Refugees

The histories of refugee reception in the Twin Cities and Columbus are discussed in Chapters 2 and 3. One of the most common themes that emerged through interviews with Somali respondents is that Minnesota is a more "progressive state" and therefore a more welcoming home for Somali Americans. One Twin Cities respondent said, "Minnesota is home of [Senator Paul] Wellstone—a friend to the Somalis. It's a place with many progressive politicians and people" (Twin Cities community member interview A, June 3, 2014).

A Columbus respondent noted:

I have friends in Minneapolis, and it's a much more welcoming place for Somalis. People are friendlier, and my friends seem more connected with non-Somalis. I even know of Somalis who married non-Somalis in Minneapolis. That is very unlikely in Columbus. (Columbus community member interview B, June 28, 2014)

The political culture in Minnesota is progressive compared to that of Ohio, but it is more accurately characterized as a fluctuating progressive state. Elected officials with progressive roots, such as the late Senator Wellstone or current Senators Al Franken and Amy Klobuchar, are prime examples. On the other hand, the state has also experienced the rise of a number of very conservative elected officials, such as former governor Jesse Ventura, former House member Michele Bachmann, and former governor Tim Pawlenty.

Claims that Minnesota is a more progressive state than Ohio can be backed up with examples of elected officials, but the reception of Somalis in the Twin Cities is also tied to the fact that progressive politicians pushed for refugee policies that ultimately opened doors for Hmong refugees who settled in the area in the late 1970s. As a result, government and social service agencies were prepared for the material and social service needs of refugees by the time Somalis started arriving in the 1990s (Yusuf 2012, 42). In Columbus, refugee resettlement occurred en masse in the 1990s for the first time. The institutional infrastructure was established as Somali refugees arrived instead of being organized prior to their arrival. A long-time administrator at a refugee resettlement agency in Columbus explained it in these terms:

> Prior to the 1990s, Columbus had only limited experience with refugee resettlement—mainly with Laotians, Cambodians, Vietnamese, a few Ethiopians, and some Jews from the former Soviet Union. Catholic Charities and Jewish Family Services did this work. By the time Somalis starting arriving in the 1990s, these groups had gotten out of refugee resettlement. CRIS [Community Refugee and Immigration Services], US Together, and World Relief emerged as the new refugee resettlement agencies. (Columbus refugee resettlement interview, June 18, 2015)

In comparing refugee resettlement in Columbus and in the Twin Cities, this same representative said:

> Groups in Minnesota have a longer history with refugee resettlement. In Columbus, we have newer agencies that got involved when the Somali migration was booming. That strikes me as a big difference between what you see in Columbus and what you

see in the Twin Cities. (Columbus refugee resettlement interview, June 18, 2015)

The experience Columbus now has with refugee resettlement,
after its initial influx of Somali immigrants, will likely make it easier
for future newcomers to the city. Evidence of a growing expertise is
evident when visiting English and American culture classes offered
through a local refugee resettlement agency. There is also evidence
that the local government is becoming increasingly responsive to
the need to make official information available in the variety of languages that are spoken in the city. Finding documents and pamphlets
in Somali, Nepalese, and Spanish is now common. As opposed to
the Twin Cities, where the government added Somali to its list of
language translations in the early 1990s (Columbus city bureaucrat
interview, June 2, 2014), Columbus took significantly longer to introduce language accommodations. One Columbus bureaucrat said:

> Columbus started Somali translations nearly twenty years ago.
> For example, Columbus Public Health started translating ma-
> terials into Somali in 1997. The Municipal Court legal plead-
> ings/court papers were translated into Somali in 2003 in judges'
> court rooms, and the Community Relations Commission re-
> leased a booklet called "Opening Doors" in Somali in 2006,
> along with dozens of brochures in the Somali language. Since
> then, most of the city departments translate their vital docu-
> ments and communications into Somali regularly. (Columbus
> city bureaucrat interview, June 9, 2015)

Language inclusion through the availability of documents in Somali
provides evidence of the cause and effect of incorporation.

Media Analysis: Letters to the Editor

There are a number of problems associated with gauging the social
incorporation of Somalis through media analysis. Beyond the
numerous types of media, including social media, it is difficult to
draw direct comparisons between the two regions under investiga-

tion in a uniform way. Anita Waters (2012) conducted a study of two online social media outlets in Columbus: Topix and City Data. The purpose of evaluating these sites, where contributors post anonymously, was to understand and categorize negative attitudes toward Somalis. Her research revealed the prevalence of negative attitudes and misconceptions concerning Somalis in Columbus. Because both of the social media sites that Waters examined include Columbus, Minneapolis, and St. Paul subsections, evaluating the comments on each website initially seemed appealing, because negative attitudes toward Somalis could be compared across cities. However, this method did not turn out to be a productive endeavor. The first challenge was that City Data has had few postings about Somalis since Waters's initial study. The second problem was that the Topix site, particularly in Minneapolis, was dominated by a small group of contributors. For this reason, a search of letters to the editors in the principal newspapers in Columbus and in the Twin Cities was an appealing alternative strategy used to analyze the media coverage of Somalis in each city, which would reveal how residents of each city have responded and continue to respond to issues involving the Somali community.

Despite the shrinking circulation of newspaper readership in the United States, newspapers remain a standard source of local news coverage across the nation. For this reason, examining the context of letters to the editor in the principal newspapers of Columbus and of the Twin Cities is a valuable way to understand readers' reactions to articles covered in them. However, there are three factors to keep in mind regarding letters to the editor. First, some newspapers have ideological slants that could influence the sorts of letters to the editor that are received and printed. With this in mind, I selected newspapers that were roughly analogous in bias. Second, because letters to the editor that do not make it to print are not accessible for this project, we must simply take what is available for analysis. A final cautionary note is that newspaper readers are not a cross-section of the local population; they are people who follow the news and are perhaps more passionate about current events than the average person. Therefore, the attitudes toward Somalis revealed by letters to the editor must be interpreted with care.

Columbus

The *Columbus Dispatch* is that city's principal newspaper. It is owned by the city's prominent Wolfe family and has a reputation as a conservative newspaper (A. Waters 2012, 60). Using the database Access World News, a search of letters to the editor from January 2000 through May 2015 was conducted using the search term "Somali." Thirty-eight letters to the editor with the word "Somali" were each read and coded as being positive or negative toward the Somali community. Two letters were eliminated from consideration, because they mentioned Somalis in only a passing context; in other words, the mention of Somalis was not germane to the content. Table 6.1 categorizes the letters to the editor by content and year.

Of the thirty-six remaining letters, twenty-two were coded as "positive" about Somalis. These letters fell into a few categories. The first were letters by non-Somalis who wanted to correct misconceptions included in newspaper articles or to respond to the news of the day. Other letters were written by non-Somalis with an interest in educating readers on the experience of the Somali diaspora. For example, Russell and Patricia Wolford wrote a letter in response to a story about the columnist's depiction of Africa. In clarifying facts about the Somali diaspora, the Wolfords write:

> It may appear that the able-bodied have abandoned their families [in refugee camps]. However, every Somali refugee whom we have talked to in Nairobi and in Columbus, including teenagers working at Taco Bell, send money back to their families living in refugee camps in Somalia. (Wolford and Wolford 2000)

Another category of letters consisted of those written by Somalis interested in adding a richer context to stories on their community. A total of eight letters written by Somalis were printed in the *Columbus Dispatch*. A letter from 2000, written by Abdisalam M. Garjeex, responds to a column written by a non-Somali about the Somali community:

TABLE 6.1. LETTERS TO EDITOR						
Year	Columbus Dispatch			Star Tribune		
	Positive	Negative	Total	Positive	Negative	Total
2000	2	0	2	0	0	0
2001	2	0	2	0	0	0
2002	2	0	2	0	1	1
2003	1	0	1	0	0	0
2004	4	2	6	0	0	0
2005	2	0	2	1	0	1
2006	0	2	2	5	1	6
2007	2	5	7	2	1	3
2008	2	2	4	3	2	5
2009	3	2	5	4	3	7
2010	0	0	0	4	2	6
2011	1	0	1	4	0	4
2012	0	1	1	3	0	3
2013	1	0	1	5	1	6
2014	0	0	0	10	2	12
2015	1	0	1	4	3	7
Total	23	14	37	45	16	61
Positive: 62.2%				Positive: 73.8%		

Source: Columbus Dispatch data from Lexis Nexis; Star Tribune data from Access World News.

As a member of the community, I have noted that many Columbus residents and city officials don't know where Somalis come from and what their culture looks like. We are a nation of 10 million people, situated in the horn of Africa with a diverse and rich culture. Many Somalis immigrated to the United States, and eventually to Columbus, because of the civil strife in their home country. (Garjeex 2000)

Another category of positive letters include non-Somalis writing letters in support of diversity and refugee resettlement. One example is a letter written by Jane Gray titled "U.S. Needs to Take Care of

Refugees." Gray first discusses the role of religious organizations in the refugee resettlement process, and specifically the role of these organizations and Somalis in Columbus. She writes:

> What would our U.S. policy toward refugees be if we as American Christians, Muslims, Jews, Hindus, Buddhists, and other people of good will persuaded our elected officials to embrace the hope that all people are created in God's image, and marked with the indelible gift of dignity? (Gray 2004)

In contrast to the twenty-two positive letters printed in the *Columbus Dispatch,* fourteen negative letters were printed about Somalis from 2000 to 2015. The pattern for negative letters stemmed from specific articles about Somalis that appeared in the newspaper in response to social service benefits, terrorist threats, stories about Somali piracy, the shooting of a Somali man by the police, or in the context of Islam. For example, the negative letters in 2004 were in response to articles about refugee benefits. Anne Slifer writes:

> OK, let me get this straight: A refugee comes to this country and is entitled to eight months of public assistance, including Medicaid. Yet my son, who is born with multiple birth defects, has to wait 18 months to get a Medicaid wa[i]ver to assist us with nursing care and expensive prescriptions. Hmmm. . . . (Slifer 2004)

Steven P. Locke, responding to an editorial written by a Somali about terrorism, responds in this way:

> The problem for Muslims is the information revolution. No matter the reassurances of CAIR [Council on American-Islamic Relations], or those of our own elites, Americans and the rest of the non-Muslim world can see for themselves the nature of Islam. (Locke 2006)

Of course, Locke misses the point, which is that a growing number of Americans are actually Muslims and that the religion itself is not violent. These sorts of statements speak to the generalizations made about Somalis and Muslims in several letters to the editor. Another example of a negative letter was written in opposition to the flying of the Somali flag over the Ohio Statehouse to commemorate Somali Independence Day. Chris D. Callen writes:

> The picture of a Somali flag being flown over the Statehouse is both unpatriotic and offensive to all Ohioans. Brave men and women died so that the American and Ohio flags can fly proudly over that building. Assuming the Somalis pictured are legal residents, we can appreciate their desire to honor their own independence as an African Nation, but once they set foot on American soil and took the oath as citizens to uphold and respect the American flag and all that it represents, they should assume the proper allegiance to both flag and country. (Callen 2009)

This quotation speaks to the misconceptions held by some about Somalis. First, there is a general misunderstanding of American refugee policy and the experience of refugee communities who were forced from their homes. Transnational ties are not uncommon for immigrants, especially for refugees, who often have direct ties to relatives in their countries of origin. Moreover, groups have the right to fly flags over public buildings as a matter of free speech. Just as the Ku Klux Klan had the right to protest the Martin Luther King holiday at the Ohio Statehouse in 1996, Somalis have the right to honor their old country based on the laws of their new one (Ortega 1996).

As Table 6.1 demonstrates, the *Columbus Dispatch* ran more positive (62.2 percent) than negative (37.8 percent) letters to the editor. The newspaper also appears to have made a concerted effort to include the perspectives and reactions of Somalis to stories about their community. In general, this can be interpreted as a sign that on a certain level, there is a good deal of respect for Somalis among *Columbus Dispatch* readers and the editors who select letters to print. Many negative letters, meanwhile, stemmed from misconceptions about Somalis or interpretations of American legal protections.

Overall, in terms of the ratio of positive to negative letters, the positive were more numerous.

The Twin Cities

The principal newspaper in the Twin Cities is the Minneapolis *Star Tribune*. The St. Paul *Pioneer Press* is another regional newspaper, although the circulation of the *Star Tribune* is considerably larger. Using LexisNexis, a search of letters to the editor from January 1, 2000, through May 2015 in the *Star Tribune* and *Pioneer Press* using the search term "Somali" resulted in two letters in the *Pioneer Press* and seventy-two in the *Star Tribune*. Different databases were used for the two regions, because neither database included both of the principal newspapers for Columbus and for the Twin Cities. The St. Paul *Pioneer Press* articles were not coded because of the newspaper's small sample size. As with the letters garnered from the *Columbus Dispatch,* the *Star Tribune* articles were coded as positive or negative. Ten of the seventy-two articles were eliminated, because they mentioned the term "Somali" only in passing.

As Table 6.1 illustrates, more letters appeared in the *Star Tribune* compared to the *Columbus Dispatch.* This is likely due to the larger size of the Somali community in Minneapolis, but it could also be interpreted as a higher level of Somali social incorporation resulting from the large proportion of positive letters (73.8 percent). As with the *Columbus Dispatch,* a significant number of letters to the editor did not appear in the *Star Tribune* until 2006. The *Star Tribune* included six positive articles written by Somalis, which is less than the eight such letters in the *Columbus Dispatch,* although given the small sample size, not notably different than what we see in Columbus.

The vast majority of positively coded letters fall into the category of appreciation for the diversity brought by Somalis to Minnesota and clarification about misconceptions in news articles. Andy Brehm starts his letter with the statement:

> Minnesota should be proud that it is home to the United States'
> largest Somali-American population, which includes some of our

most innovative, patriotic and hardworking citizens. (Brehm 2014)

Ayah Helmy was compelled to write in response to an article about crime among Somalis. Her comments respond to a previous article and correct misconceptions:

> The Somali community is comparable to the Vietnamese community that occupied the Riverside area previously. When it first arrived, it faced the same problems that the Somali community does. And poverty, lack of resources and lack of education always breed crime. The Somalis are just as actively engaged with society as the Vietnamese were. The belligerent statement about their leeching social services without giving back is unfounded. Somalis work and pay taxes just like the rest of us. (Helmy 2009)

Another positive letter clarifies the reasons Somalis send money back to families. In light of the new restrictions on remittances, Michael Hindin urges elected officials to find ways to keep remittance options open. His letter was printed at a time when new restrictions on remittances were being introduced because of fears that funds were making their way into the hands of terrorist cells. Hindin's letter is also particularly interesting in that it points out that a hundred years earlier, like the Somali immigrants, his Russian relatives wanted to help relatives who had been left behind:

> Our Somali-American neighbors are living the same immigrant story, with the horrors endured by loved ones left behind. The same family values drive them to support parents and extended families in war-ravaged Somalia.
>
> Tragically, the last remaining bank that facilitated funds transfers to Somalia has succumbed to fear of prosecution under current Homeland Security and banking laws, closing this life-saving pipeline to refugees and displaced persons.
>
> We must urge our banks and regulatory agencies, via our elected officials, to create a safe means for Somali-Americans

to support their relatives. This is a moral issue and, surprisingly, a means to project a positive image of America in East Africa. (Hindin 2012)

In some ways, the detail and support for the Somali community comes through more strongly in *Star Tribune* letters compared to those in the *Columbus Dispatch*. However, negative letters are just as negative and reflect concerns about domestic security and the new diversity caused by immigration. Jo Richmond's letter expresses his concerns about requirements that employers accommodate Muslim religious observances:

My point is that these so-called employees are now part of the American workforce and it is time that they begin to assimilate and stop expecting their every whim to be coddled. (Richmond 2008)

Similar to Richmond, Rosalind Kohls comments on the concern raised in a previous article about the lack of books on Muslims in public schools:

If Muslims are concerned about the lack of books for their children, then they should get busy and write them. It is not the responsibility of non-Muslims to try to provide books written from a Muslim point of view. (Kohls 2010)

Both of these letters speak to the discomfort of some readers regarding Islam. Unfortunately, pitting Muslims against Christians reinforces a divide that contributes to religious intolerance, discrimination, and an inability to see the similarities between the religious beliefs of these and other groups.

Along the lines of security fears, several letters represent the concerns raised in negatively coded articles. Sheila Franey writes in support of a Minnesota lawmaker who wanted to eliminate funding to Somali groups in the Twin Cites because of concerns about terrorist connections:

House Minority Leader Marty Seifert is absolutely right to cut off all government funds to any group that supports our enemies. It's time to stop committing national suicide in the name of political correctness (in reality, political tyranny) by paying the cost of our own demise with taxpayer dollars. (Franey 2009)

Similarly, Connie Sambor submits a letter criticizing complaints by Somalis who claim racial profiling at the airport:

Well, cry me a river—Somali-Americans are angry about airport profiling. It's not Norwegian grandmothers who are leaving this great country to slaughter innocent victims and fight against us! If it were, I would be the first in line for profiling. (Sambor 2015)

Again, the theme of us versus them emerges in these examples. These quotations reflect a fear of security threats, a tolerance for broad generalizations about a large population, and the willingness to strip "the other" of the rights we expect as Americans.

Even with the majority of letters to the editor in both regions being classified as positive, several themes in them point to areas where Somali incorporation is weak and could be improved. In other words, the negative attitudes point to areas where greater education for the general public could increase incorporation. Specifically, education about Somali religious beliefs and culture, social service benefits for refugees, the realities of life for new migrants, and the importance of transnational family ties might eliminate some misconceptions and result in better Somali social incorporation. Rectifying misconceptions will be hard at first but could become easier, potentially exponentially, once incorporation advances.

Local Police and Law Enforcement

The quotations that open this chapter touch on the social incorporation of Somalis vis-à-vis law enforcement. On the one hand, many

Somalis have complained of discrimination and profiling by law enforcement in Columbus and in the Twin Cities (Twin Cities CAIR representative interview, April 16, 2015; Columbus CAIR representative interview, March 11, 2015). At the same time, the presence of Somali officers in the Twin Cities was routinely mentioned as a major improvement in that area by Somali respondents. In this sense, the quotations allude to not only the community's fear and frustration but also the importance of the inclusion of Somali law enforcement officials. Research on police-community relations points to minorities' fear of racial profiling as a major concern (Garofalo 1977; Hindelang 1974; Huang and Vaughn 1996; McArdle and Erzen 2001; Tyler 2005). Recent events in such cities as Ferguson, Missouri, and Baltimore, Maryland, as well as other cities where white officers have killed minority citizens, continue to fuel this distrust of the police. For this reason, calls for greater diversity on the police force are only increasing in strength and number. The underlying idea is that by diversifying the police force, cultural understanding will improve within the department and ultimately between the police and the community the officers are meant to serve and protect.

Beyond the literature on attitudes toward police, another line of research on the police as important bureaucrats for new immigrant communities offers valuable insight into the positive role of local police in immigrant incorporation (Lewis and Ramakrishnan 2007; Ramakrishnan and Lewis 2005). S. Karthick Ramakrishnan and Paul G. Lewis (2005) identify police as some of the bureaucrats who best incorporate immigrants in the community. In fact, police are often more accommodating on immigrant issues than local politicians and public housing bureaucrats. While police officers have an exceptionally challenging job in high-immigration cities where there is a high potential for language barriers and general distrust of the police, they have implemented several creative methods of communicating and working with immigrants. For example, California police officers in some of the cities the authors investigate accept Mexican consular IDs as a valid form of identification and do not report the presence of suspected undocumented immigrants (Ramakrishnan and Lewis 2005). They have also introduced community-policing techniques, such as meetings between neighborhood groups and police officers, to support migrants in their new cities (Ramakrishnan and Lewis 2005).

In reviewing the literature on minority attitudes toward police officers and the bureaucratic incorporation literature on police, it is clear that community distrust among minorities and the positive attributes toward immigrants potentially cancel one another out. However, if calls for greater diversity within police departments are met, and if police in immigrant destination cities have the ability to support incorporation, positive results may emerge. Examining local law enforcement agencies and their impact on the social incorporation of Somalis in this project revealed the significant level of pride Somali respondents had about the seven Somali police officers on the Minneapolis force. Merging these comments with the literature pointed to a potentially important aspect of Somali social incorporation. In addition, the absence of Somali officers in Columbus and a controversy about a Somali woman in Columbus who left the police academy over its unwillingness to accommodate her hijab increased the significance of local law enforcement and Somali social incorporation.

Distinguishing between local and federal law enforcement adds another important wrinkle to this analysis. Whereas views about federal officials with the FBI and DHS were uniformly negative among respondents, there was a very different attitude toward local police, at least in Minneapolis, where the majority of the Somali officers in the United States can be found. The distinction stems, it appears, from the relationships local police develop as they carry out their daily responsibilities. Especially for beat officers, contact with citizens happens often, and it is not uncommon for them to be on a first-name basis with constituents (Twin Cities police interview A, June 9, 2015). In contrast, the daily work of an agent from the FBI or DHS involves less regular community contact. This fact, combined with the reality that federal agents typically spend time in the community only when there is a crisis, appears to increase community suspicion and mistrust.

Columbus

To date, the Columbus Division of Police has never hired a Somali officer. Although several Somalis have entered the academy, every candidate has either dropped out or failed to pass necessary tests or background checks (Columbus city bureaucrat interview, June 9, 2015). Most recently, a Somali woman went through the police academy but dropped out because of the department's unwillingness to adopt a police-issued hijab. The department claims that its policy stems from concerns about the hijab's putting an officer at risk for strangulation and because it could get in the way of gas masks and helmets (Pyle and Ferenchik 2015). Interestingly, other cities, including Minneapolis and Toronto, have since attempted to recruit this young woman with promises of wardrobe accommodations (Twin Cities police interview, June 10, 2015). The virtual absence of Somali law enforcement officials in Columbus stands in contrast to the efforts underway in the Twin Cities.

The Twin Cities

As of this writing, there are seven Somali officers in the Minneapolis Police Department, with several others in the academy and poised to join the force. St. Paul has one Somali female officer who joined the department in March 2014, making national headlines because she was the first Somali woman officer in the nation and because the St. Paul Police Department adopted a snap-on hijab as part of her uniform. The adoption of the police-issued hijab sent a message about religious accommodation and gender equity. As noted in the Columbus section of this chapter, opponents of the police-issued hijab claim that it potentially compromises an officer's safety. The clip-on version is a parallel to the clip-on tie that male officers wear and represents equitable treatment based on gender and religion.

The first Somali officer joined the Minneapolis force in 2006. Before that, one Somali man served as a community service officer before officially joining the force in 2008. These first officers also helped establish the Somali American Police Association (SAPA) in 2012, a national organization that attempts to provide a network of support for Somali officers and functions as an informal police officer recruitment network (Twin Cities police interview B, June 9, 2015). One member explained:

When I got on the force, I wanted to call someone and ask them questions about the profession. I had nobody to call. When we became six [officers in Minneapolis], we decided to form a group to help others coming up. (Twin Cities police interview A, June 9, 2015)

SAPA has a formal mentoring program for aspiring police officers that is highly successful, according to the two officers interviewed for this project (Twin Cities police interview A, June 9, 2015; Twin Cities police interview B, June 9, 2015). The mentoring also grew out of SAPA's conversations about the members' abilities to inspire other young Somalis to consider a career in law enforcement. One officer explained:

I still remember the first day of law enforcement training, when this Eritrean officer came to my class. He was in uniform, and I had a chance to speak to him. It made a big difference in my confidence. Seeing someone who looks like you is really important when you're trying to do something like this. (Twin Cities police interview A, June 9, 2015)

The two Somali officers interviewed take their role as mentors seriously and view it as a national responsibility that will facilitate Somalis across the country joining the profession (Twin Cities police interview A, June 9, 2015; Twin Cities police interview B, June 9, 2015). In fact, it was through SAPA conversations that Somali officers in Minneapolis reached out to the woman in Columbus who left the academy because of the hijab policy.

Community sentiment among those interviewed was incredibly positive about the Somali police. Although not all the officers are assigned to Somali communities, several volunteered to serve in the neighborhoods where they were raised. During one of the fieldwork visits for this project, I was invited to accompany two Somali officers during their night patrol in the Cedar-Riverside area, where Somalis are highly concentrated. What was most striking during my ride-along was the excitement the officers were met with during their patrols. Adults and children approached them to shake their hands and greeted them by name. Accompanying these officers and witnessing their reception in the community reinforced comments I had collected during my own interviews. One police department official explained:

> They are celebrities, rock stars. They've gotten us into a community that often has distrust of police. They opened doors and facilitated conversations between police and the community. This has created trust and credibility with people who had an issue with law enforcement. (Twin Cities police administrative representative interview A, June 11, 2015)

One Somali respondent noted:

> The Somali officers are important here in Minneapolis but also across the country. They are asked to travel out west and to Canada [Toronto] to talk about how Minneapolis ended up with seven Somali officers in 2015 when other departments across the country have none. (Twin Cities Community member interview, April 14, 2015)

During my five-hour ride-along with the officers, one specific incident stood out as indicative of the importance of their position to the community. As we drove up to the Cedar-Riverside apartment towers where many Somalis live, we noticed a girl and her parents waiting in the parking lot for the officers. The family lived in a remote suburb of Minneapolis but came to Cedar-Riverside to report an assault on their seventeen-year-old daughter. As one of the officers explained:

> Most police would send the family back to their town to file a report. We won't do that. We'll file the report and help this family. (Twin Cities police interview, June 11, 2015)

The entire exchange between the parents and the officers happened in Somali, the family's first language. The officers translated the conversation, but even with my inability to speak with the parents, it was clear that they were relieved to work with these officers. After being escorted to the children's hospital, the family was given a blue card with their case number and instructions for moving forward with charges. All the materials were provided in the Somali language.

Beyond the community pride the Somali officers generate, several respondents noted the importance of these officers with regard to educating other officers about Somali culture. Interviews with two officers for this project confirmed that sentiment. One officer said:

Once we got here [on the police force], we started educating people about our culture. They were afraid of the unknown. People are more comfortable once they understand your experience and perspective. Later on, when they deal with people who look like me, they pause. They see that person as a human. (Twin Cities police interview B, June 9, 2015)

Another Somali officer explained:

At first they [police] don't trust you. But when you become one of them, they see you as capable. We showed them we could do a phenomenal job. I told people they could ask me anything, even if they thought it was a stupid question. I told them this was a safe way to ask their questions, and they did. (Twin Cities police interview A, June 9, 2015)

Given the current crisis in police-community relations in the United States, the presence of Somali officers takes on a more expedient meaning. Aside from the risk of racial profiling that Somalis face, their ethnicity and status as immigrants put them in a particularly precarious position. The confidence the Somali officers engender within a community that has had several traumatic police-community disputes is striking. The only complaint recorded during my interviews was against the Minneapolis Police Department, stemming from its slow pace in adopting a police-issued hijab for female officers (Twin Cites community member interview, June 11, 2015). At present, St. Paul is the only city with such a policy. One respondent said:

> The Minneapolis Police Department says they want female Somali officers and that they'll adopt a police-issued hijab once they have an officer. I'm telling them that they need the policy first, [and] then the women will come. (Twin Cities community member interview, June 11, 2015)

Similarly, the officers interviewed for this project insist that the department will be very accommodating as soon as it has a Muslim woman candidate who wishes to wear a hijab.

Interviews with Somali officers in the Twin Cities also revealed that their acceptance took a little time and was not without controversy. Misunderstandings about Muslim prayer and the ability of the Somali officers to prioritize policing obligations in the face of religious demands took time to rectify. Both officers report that the department has responded appropriately to culturally sensitive matters, but in one instance, a complaint against a Somali police candidate stemming from prayer accommodations resulted in a two-year delay in his being hired. This suggests the need for police leaders to be educated about best practices in employment so misunderstandings are avoided and individual rights are upheld.

The success of the Somali officers in the Twin Cities, especially given their absence in Columbus, is worth exploring. On the one hand, there are only 8 Somali officers in the Twin Cities—a small number considering there are 1,460 officers in the Minneapolis (830) and St. Paul (630) Police Departments combined (Twin Cities police administrative representative interview A, June 11, 2015). During interviews, two Minneapolis Police Department spokespeople emphasized the priority they place on identifying a diverse pool of police candidates. The department's recruiter, a Native American himself, spends time recruiting in five states and throughout the Twin Cities (Minneapolis Police Department representative interview, June 11, 2015). He also recruits at local cultural events, such as the Somali Independence Day celebration every July (Twin Cities police administrative representative interview A, June 11, 2015). Once candidates are recruited, early assessments help police trainers identify candidates who might need extra support to make it through the training. One police spokesperson explained:

We operate like the military. If we have a recruit who needs help with something like preconditioning, we work with them on diet, exercise, dedication, etc. As long as they're progressing, we offer the support to help them succeed. I'm not sure if other departments do this, but we have built-in supports. (Twin Cities police administrative representative interview B, June 11, 2015)

The dedication to diversity through recruiting and support systems appears to be a factor in the ability of the Twin Cities police to bring on Somali officers.

Philanthropic Support of Somalis

Another indicator of Somali social incorporation emerged during fieldwork in the Twin Cities. Several Somali respondents were connected in some way to a local foundation that provided grants to individual Somalis or that benefited the Somali community. More notably, several of the oldest or most-well-known Somali community organizations receive funding from one or more of the local foundations in the Twin Cities (e.g., Confederation of Somali Community in Minnesota [CSCM], Ka Joog, and the African Development Center [ADC]). This spurred a question about the level of philanthropic support for Somalis in the Twin Cities versus in Columbus, revealing a clear difference in philanthropic philosophies and priorities.

Columbus

Contacting several of the major foundations in Columbus made clear that the level of philanthropic support of Somali groups or individuals is virtually absent in that city. One foundation representative stated, "Somalis do not pursue grant opportunities" (Foundation representative interview, July 30, 2015). The website Charity Navigator[1] is one of the most comprehensive databases of foundations and charitable organizations in the United States. According to this website, Columbus is

---

1. See http://www.charitynavigator.org/.

home to thirty-one organizations. After searching these foundations' websites and conducting follow-up phone calls, it became apparent that Columbus's foundations do not support refugee-related efforts. Some foundations support refugee resettlement programs (e.g., Catholic Social Services and the Columbus Jewish Federation) or research on new immigrants (e.g., the Columbus Foundation), but this reflects the extent of the interaction between foundations and Somali groups and individuals.

The Twin Cities

The philanthropic community in the Twin Cities stands in stark contrast to what can be observed in Columbus. Minneapolis and St. Paul combined are home to 120 local foundations and charitable organizations, according to Charity Navigator. What is particularly striking is the number of family foundations in the region. During the early to mid-1900s, several prominent Minnesota families in the lumber business (e.g., Marbrook Foundation), the flour industry (e.g., Pillsbury Foundation), and the merchandise business (e.g., Bush Foundation) used some of their wealth to create family foundations. Beyond these family foundations, the area is also home to one of the nation's oldest community organizations, the one-hundred-year-old Minneapolis Foundation. Community foundations pool donor contributions and are generally dedicated to social issues that better the lives of people in the community. The Marbrook Foundation specifically funds projects that advance the situations of immigrants and refugees in the region. Many of the other family and community foundations also dedicate resources and look favorably on proposals aimed at supporting underserved populations, including refugees.

Interviews with representatives from five foundations that support Somali organizations or individuals revealed some common themes. First, each of these foundations places a priority on promoting the successful transition to life in Minnesota for new immigrant and refugee communities. One foundation representative explained:

> They are part of this community. They're staying and putting down roots. We have a responsibility to help people get estab-

lished so they can contribute and choose their own path. (Twin Cities foundation representative interview, June 19, 2015)

A representative from a different foundation admitted that not everyone sees these new arrivals as an asset:

They bring different food, cultures, and worldviews. For some people, this makes them uncomfortable, and they perceive refugees as a resource drag. We take a different approach. We want to help integrate folks and tap into their potential. We get it and want to see people succeed so they can help build a healthier and stronger community. (Twin Cities foundation representative interview, June 19, 2015)

This general sentiment about the value of new migrants, as well as the priority the foundations place on offering opportunities to these communities, was evident during each foundation interview.

Along similar lines, many foundations have prioritized the immigrant and refugee populations for decades. For example, the Minneapolis Foundation and the Saint Paul Foundation, both community organizations, have long sought to support new communities as they settle in the region. An e-mail message from a representative from the Minneapolis Foundation about the history of that organization's support of immigrants and refugees highlights several examples of prioritizing these groups:

The Minneapolis Foundation's commitment to immigrants to the Twin Cities stretches back to the first half of the twentieth century, when the Foundation provided support to Minneapolis settlement houses, such as the Phyllis Wheatley House, Pillsbury Settlement House, and the Wells Memorial Settlement House. These houses provided basic needs—food, shelter, and clothing—to immigrants and to minority communities. As these groups became more established, those early service organizations adapted their programs to offer education, employment assistance, and other forms of family assistance. (Twin Cities foundation representative interview, June 28, 2015)

In 1999, the Minneapolis Foundation also engaged Twin Cities residents in a public relations campaign called "Minnesota, Nice or Not?" This campaign was intended to get residents to think about whether the state is truly a "nice" and hospitable place for newcomers. As a Minneapolis Foundation representative explained:

> The campaign, which included print ads, radio spots, and bus shelter posters, asked Minnesotans to examine their attitudes and behavior toward the state's increasing population of immigrants and refugees. (Twin Cities foundation representative interview, June 28, 2015)

This campaign is especially notable, because it represents an example of the philanthropic community's pushing residents to consider the context of reception they provide to newcomers. One foundation representative summed up the context in the Twin Cities in these terms:

> The Twin Cities are like the canary in a coal mine. Everyone, with all their different cultures, has settled in this one unlikely place, and now we have to make it work. (Twin Cities foundation representative interview, June 10, 2015)

Another common and important theme that resonated throughout interviews was the outreach by foundation representatives to underserved communities. For example, the foundations solicit grant applications, hold community meetings to provide information about upcoming grants, and spend time meeting with individuals who might have needs the foundations can support. Some of the foundations have even had Somalis on staff, which helps with the language barriers faced by community organizations. One foundation representative described its outreach in these terms:

> We take this responsibility seriously. We ask ourselves who is missing [from receiving grants], and we make sure there's an awareness of the opportunities. (Twin Cities foundation representative interview, June 11, 2015)

Along the same lines, all the foundations noted their interest in creating opportunities for other grant winners to network with one another. Beyond networking, mentoring and education in areas like financial literacy were mentioned as benefits grant recipients receive along with financial support from foundations.

Added to the aforementioned factors that explain the high level of philanthropic support that Somalis receive in the Twin Cities is another common thread that emerged during interviews. Each foundation representative mentioned working with city bureaucrats and elected officials to advance his or her foundation's interests. In one example, the Bush Foundation awarded the city of Minneapolis a grant specifically aimed at strengthening collaboration between immigrant and refugee communities and the city government. In another instance, a foundation representative mentioned that the foundation's support of ADC was influenced by its connections with the city of Minneapolis vis-à-vis small-business loans for Somali entrepreneurs. The coordination with city leaders is another sign of how the public and private sectors in the Twin Cities are thoughtful about strategically supporting the Somali community.

Summary

There are many ways of measuring social incorporation, including the indicators discussed in this chapter to measure Somali social incorporation. They appear in Table 6.2 and include the region's history of refugee reception, the tenor of letters to the editor that appear in the area's principal newspaper, the inclusion of Somali police officers and community sentiment about this reality, and the role of the local philanthropic community toward supporting Somalis. Although these indicators together may not yield the perfect measure of Somali social incorporation, they are nevertheless indicative of important advances and significant obstacles. For example, the experience of the Twin Cities with earlier refugee communities created an infrastructure that responded more efficiently when significant numbers of Somalis arrived. Inclusion of Somali police in the Twin Cities has enhanced perceptions of reception among Somali respondents in this

TABLE 6.2. SOCIAL INCORPORATION				
Measures	Refugee reception	Media	Somali police	Philanthropic support
Columbus	low	moderate	low	low
Twin Cities	high	moderate	high	high

study. This is not only a sign of internal incorporation of Somalis within the police department but also a situation that increases perceptions of incorporation among Somali residents. Finally, the support of the philanthropic community in the Twin Cities, along with foundations' coordination with public- and private-sector organizations that share a concern about Somali incorporation, stands as one more example of steps toward greater Somali social incorporation. In contrast, Columbus's more recent history with refugee resettlement means that Somalis' arrival in large numbers forced the ad hoc development of a complex resettlement infrastructure. The city's total absence of Somali police officers is another area where social incorporation lags behind what we see in the Twin Cities. Similarly, the absence of philanthropic support of Somali organizations and initiatives is another area where social incorporation could stand to improve.

Although social incorporation is higher in the Twin Cities, the media analysis in this chapter demonstrates that even with the positive sentiments reflected in letters to the editor in the city's principal newspaper, major misconceptions and misinformation remain about Somalis in both regions under investigation. These are the major obstacles to social incorporation, and they exist in the Twin Cities and in Columbus. Whether the cause of misconceptions is ignorance or poor communication, educating the community about Somali culture and religion is a priority. Progress has been made, but much remains unaccomplished. Social incorporation will only improve as policy makers and the general public view these new migrants as fundamental U.S. citizens who enrich our communities.

7 /

Moving toward Incorporation

n Chapters 4, 5, and 6, the political, economic, and social incorporation of Somalis in the Twin Cities and Columbus is evaluated using
a set of common indicators for each type. My findings suggest that
Somalis in Minnesota experience relatively good political incorporation, some social incorporation, and less economic incorporation. Put
simply, overall incorporation of Somalis is generally higher in the Twin
Cities than in Columbus, although many challenges remain. After
considerable investigation, it is clear that some of the most important differences in incorporation observed between the two cities are
attributable to the unique political and cultural traditions in the Twin
Cities. Daniel Elazar's (1987) classification of Minnesota as moralistic
and Ohio as traditionalistic generally holds true in this study. Robert
Putnam's (2000) more recent research on the Social Capital Index in
the fifty states indicates that Minnesota consistently ranks very high in
social capital, while Ohio is only moderate. These important findings
suggest that Somalis would likely experience higher levels of incorporation in the Twin Cities than in Columbus. This may be the case
in terms of political incorporation, but the fact that Somalis remain a
largely marginalized community is inconsistent with the high levels of
trust or connection suggested by Putnam's research, particularly with
regard to bridging social capital that helps create trust between socially

heterogeneous groups. In fact, the research in this book makes clear that the Twin Cities and Columbus have significant room for improvement when it comes to Somali incorporation. This is especially true in terms of the economic situation of the respective Somali communities. Like other works that examine how race, ethnicity, and social capital interact (Chávez, Wampler, and Burkhart 2006; Hero 2003), this book suggests that racial and ethnic minorities may acquire social capital in ways that differ from the dominant group in a given society. For example, Maria Chávez, Brian Wampler, and Ross Burkhart (2006) conducted similar research on migrant seasonal farm workers in Idaho and identified lower levels of incorporation and bridging social capital within that community. Given the remaining obstacles that face the Somali populations in both regions under investigation, it is essential that policy makers use caution when pointing to either Columbus or the Twin Cities as positive examples of Somali incorporation, because each area has a great deal of work to do if it is to truly incorporate newcomers within its borders.

It is also worth noting that many of the findings regarding Somali incorporation likely apply to other groups, particularly new refugee and other immigrant communities across the United States. The obstacles to incorporation for these groups are significant, especially when they are visible minorities, practice unique cultural traditions, or hold religious beliefs that diverge from those of the majority. These problems are compounded and made especially challenging when a particular group consists of first-generation migrants who lack English proficiency. As previous chapters have demonstrated, these obstacles have been addressed in the case of the Somalis by taking advantage of certain factors that have increased that community's incorporation in the three key spheres: political, economic, and social. These same factors—and the benefits they offer—could be extended to other new immigrant groups in the hopes of improving their own incorporation and subsequent well-being. For example, the Somali case suggests that political incorporation could benefit from strategic electoral planning, targeted outreach by political parties, and union leadership opportunities. Increasing economic incorporation is somewhat more challenging, although public-private partnerships aimed at extending financial opportunities to new migrants show signs of promise.

Finally, social incorporation has shown signs of improvement when, for instance, members of a community are given roles in the government as street-level bureaucrats, among other positions. These represent just a few of the examples of how incorporation of new communities could be smoothly, effectively, and permanently improved.

This chapter highlights the general findings about the levels of Somali political, social, and economic incorporation contained in this book. Because each type of incorporation has implications for the other two, it is important to consider not only each type of incorporation on its own but also how it interacts with the others. Factors that contribute to or impede Somali incorporation are discussed with an eye toward policy recommendations that could increase the overall incorporation of not only Somali Americans but also other migrants, both regionally within the United States and in other liberal democratic settings.

Somali Political Incorporation

Political incorporation is a measure of a group's engagement with the political system and how well that group's interests are reflected in policy making. Chapter 4 discussed Somali political incorporation by examining six indicators of their overall political progress: electoral structure, political party outreach to Somalis, the Somali role in electoral and governing coalitions, bureaucratic outreach to Somalis, the Somali community's levels of union engagement, and the political influence of Somali community organizations. As discussed in that chapter, these six measures uniformly support the conclusion that Somali political incorporation in the Twin Cities is higher than that in Columbus, although even in the Twin Cities, the group's political incorporation still has room for improvement.

With regard to electoral structure, the local ward-based electoral structure present in the Twin Cities opened doors for geographically concentrated Somalis to elect the nation's first Somali city councilperson. This achievement was accomplished through a concerted effort on the part of a Somali-led coalition to obtain more representative wards that would give underrepresented groups a better chance of having their votes matter. In contrast, the at-large electoral structure of local elections in Columbus has been a barrier to Somali electoral influence and has diminished the likelihood of a Somali's being elected to city office. The consequences of these different electoral structures come as no surprise, especially when consulting race and ethnicity scholars, who have long demonstrated the negative consequences of at-large electoral systems for underrepresented groups (Barker, Jones, and Tate 1999; Browning, Marshall, and Tabb 1984; Groffmann and Davidson 1992; Parker 1990). Without a legal challenge to the electoral structure of Columbus, the political lot of its Somalis and any other new immigrant groups will be difficult to change. However, despite the difficulty of working within Columbus's existing electoral framework, with sufficient effort and planning, it may be possible for Somalis to make progress. This strategy would require the candidacy of a Somali state legislative candidate who could be elected from a heavily Somali district. Given reports of high Somali voter turnout, the potential is there, yet it faces two major barriers. One challenge is the discovery of a viable Somali candidate, but the other is the relative disinterest in Somalis by the two major parties. Without party support, launching a viable campaign is unlikely.

The lesson we can learn from the radically different electoral structures and outcomes seen in the Twin Cities and in Columbus is that the electoral structure of a given area is one of the first issues policy makers and other interested groups should consider when strategizing about ways to increase the political incorporation of an underrepresented group. Understanding the rules of the game and how they affect political outcomes, so to speak, provides guidance about options for change. Columbus is a case in point. In Columbus and in the Twin Cities, the other essential step is to develop a pool of candidates who are interested in vying for elective office. This process is already underway in the Twin Cities and is in its infancy in Columbus. Just as women and politics scholars have suggested that more women must run for office to win positions, so too must Somalis and other marginalized groups. But this is a two-stage process that requires the cooperation of major party leaders. Somalis must be willing to run, but the parties they would run *for* must take an interest in leadership development within the Somali community.

The second indicator of Somali political incorporation used in this book is political party outreach. In the case of Columbus, outreach to voters comes in the form of particular candidates (almost uniformly Democratic) appealing directly to the community. The party itself does not prioritize outreach to Somalis; rather, the evidence suggests that any outreach efforts are taken on by individual candidates. Meanwhile, my study found that the Columbus Republican Party is completely disengaged with Somalis, despite some ideological kinship between the party and Somalis on such issues as same-sex marriage. Minnesota differs from Ohio, in part because the Democratic-Farmer-Labor (DFL) Party, a liberal Democratic Party, dominates the state's politics. But being more Democratic does not entirely explain differences between the two with regard to outreach. Admittedly, this liberal party is historically rooted in more inclusive politics, but there are still lessons policy makers can take from its example. For instance, outreach to Democratic Party leaders in Ohio to educate them on the strategies used by Minnesota's DFL Party to collaborate with Somalis might be one way to increase the attention paid to Somali voters and constituents in Columbus. After all, the community claims to vote in high numbers and is a solid Democratic bloc. Moreover, just as the DFL Party in the Twin Cities supports and encourages potential Somali candidates for office, so too could the Democratic Party in Columbus. In the U.S. context, party-level outreach is crucial. The broader message for international communities with multiparty, proportional representation systems is that leftist parties hold the potential for more inclusive policies for new migrants and would also do well to look for minority or underrepresented candidates to include on party lists. This strategy not only holds the potential for galvanizing voters from the communities of those candidates; it also fits squarely within a liberal party's overarching philosophy of inclusion and the advancement of otherwise marginal groups.

The third indicator of Somali political incorporation included in Chapter 5 was Somali inclusion in electoral and governing coalitions. Urban politics scholars have distinguished between these two types of coalitions: the former is the coalition that forms to elect a candidate, while the latter refers to the coalition that forms once a candidate wins office. The governing coalition is more powerful, because it can shape the issues that reach the political agenda. In Columbus, Somalis have not yet been part of either an electoral coalition or a governing coalition. While one could argue that Democratic candidates in Columbus who seek the Somali vote are including them in their electoral coalitions, the attention paid to Somalis—even during elections—is minimal and does not appear to provide the community with opportunities to participate in campaigns and other preelection activities. However, there were promising signs in the 2016 mayoral election cycle: one candidate courted Somalis in his electoral coalition. In the Twin Cities, Somalis have participated in multiple electoral coalitions at the local and state levels, which has contributed to the elections of Somalis and non-Somalis alike. There is also clear evidence that Somalis are included as partners in governing coalitions. Proof of this can be seen in the fact that such issues as preserving financial remittances to overseas relatives and finding additional ways for Somalis to borrow money in accordance with religious tradition are a significant part of the political agenda within Minneapolis's City Hall.

One lesson to be gleaned from examining the electoral and governing coalitions in the Twin Cities is that candidates and coalition partners must agree on the conditions of the coalition before the election. Although campaign promises can be reversed, ways must be found to hold politicians accountable if they agree to consider, for example, the appointment of Somalis to a post in their office. Likewise, if a group cares about key policy issues, a clear postelection plan must be in place before election day. Of course, all of this is easy to recommend in the abstract. The lesson imparted by my data is that, difficult as negotiations may be, stakeholders who wish to be part of the governing coalition must reach agreements before any votes are cast.

The fourth indicator of Somali political incorporation, bureaucratic outreach, reflects the willingness of street-level bureaucrats to help advance the position of underrepresented groups. Here we see evidence of bureaucratic outreach in Columbus and in the Twin Cities, although the latter has seen much more outreach by bureaucrats as well as a higher overall number of bureaucrats who are themselves Somali. My research and interviews found that Somali community members are pleased to have advocates in the public sector and feel encouraged when Somalis serve in these positions. Research on the importance of having people who reflect your demographic characteristics serve in elective office suggests that this has significant and positive effects on a community (Tate 2003). If we assume that similar effects are observed when Somalis see other Somalis in bureaucratic positions—and the fieldwork in the Twin Cities does, in fact, suggest a similar community response—then bureaucratic appointments and hiring could serve to increase a group's political incorporation. Even when bureaucrats are non-Somalis, their responsiveness to community concerns can serve to advance Somali political incorporation.

Somali union engagement is the fifth indicator of political incorporation used in this analysis. In addition to the general advocacy work that unions engage in on behalf of their employees, these organizations also have the potential to provide leadership opportunities to members. In the Twin Cities, inclusion in unions has been not only an important stepping-stone for several Somalis within the union hierarchy but also a launching pad for public service. The relationship between the DFL Party and unions is strong, which contributes to the stronger political incorporation we see in the Twin Cities. Meanwhile, Somalis in Columbus, who are generally not unionized, claim that they are unfairly treated in warehouse jobs—an allegation that, if true, could be remedied through unionization. Meanwhile, beyond the representation and leadership opportunities provided to Somalis in the Twin Cities as a result of union membership, at least one union has taken a vocal position on an issue near and dear to many Somalis—remittances. For this reason, union engagement can contribute to Somali political incorporation in several ways, especially in states where union membership and political power are more closely linked.

Finally, our examination of the role of Somali community organizations with regard to political incorporation has yielded some very important findings. In Columbus and in the Twin Cities, these organizations are not particularly well-funded. However, the diversity of the organizations in the Twin Cities, combined with the fact that the philanthropic community has infused significant funds into some Somali community organizations, has improved the potential for Somali political incorporation in that area. In Columbus, the overlapping aims of Somali community organizations have created tension and limited their influence. For these reasons, Somalis would be wise to combine resources and unite under umbrella organizations with specific policy interests while avoiding competition between charitable organizations. This unity might have the added benefit of capturing the attention of the philanthropic community, which could be persuaded to directly support organizations in a manner similar to that seen in the Twin Cities.

Somali Economic Incorporation

Chapter 5 focused on indicators of Somali economic incorporation and the subsequent upward mobility that such incorporation allows for. In both areas under investigation in this book, Somalis struggle economically. Household income generally lags significantly behind median levels in Columbus and in the Twin Cities. Notwithstanding this similarity, there are major differences—for instance, Somali employment levels in Minneapolis exceed those of other racial and ethnic minorities. Meanwhile, in St. Paul and in Columbus, Somali employment levels are lagging relative to the rest of the population, including that of other minority groups. Although unreported self-employment might slightly depress numbers, the bottom line is that even when Somalis are employed at significant levels—as in Minneapolis, for example—their household income remains low. Despite high rates of Somali unionization in the Twin Cities, which one would expect to positively affect paychecks, household income remains near the poverty line. Moreover, Somali families are often large, thus putting a strain on whatever income *is* earned and restricting upward mobility. The economic contributions made by the Somali community in Columbus and the Twin Cities through taxes, consumer capital, productive capital, and entrepreneurial capital are significant. For this reason alone, finding ways to help this community build wealth promises to offer benefits for society at large.

The economic challenges facing Somalis point to several areas where policy makers, private-sector leaders, and educational leaders can focus some of their efforts. Occupational training opportunities and targeted recruiting of Somalis are two strategies that could lift more Somalis above the poverty line and lower unemployment rates. One of the traditional ways for racial and ethnic minorities to gain entry into the middle class is though public-sector employment (Boyd 1994; Eisinger 1986; Guajardo 1999; Parks 2011; Rumberger

1983). This same model could work in the case of Somalis and other new migrants. In the public sector, the incentive for targeted recruiting would involve highlighting the added value that Somali bureaucrats and employees bring to the table. The perfect example of this strategy is the Minneapolis Police Department and its emphasis on recruiting and hiring Somali officers. However, this strategy must be taken further. For example, the lack of Somali teachers in the public school system is one concrete example of how economic mobility could be accomplished at the same time that the general population could benefit from seeing Somalis in positions as role models and increase understanding and responsiveness to the needs of Somali students. Particularly in less racially diverse schools, having a Somali teacher could increase cultural understanding for young students and ultimately improve the social incorporation of Somalis.

Beyond the public sector, private-sector employment training programs for Somalis could be encouraged through tax credits or other incentives that help business leaders see the value in having a more diverse employee base. Mentoring of Somali employees by non-Somali colleagues might also reduce feelings of isolation, encourage collaboration, and help with upward employment mobility for Somalis. Again, the lesson from the Somali police in the Twin Cities suggests that when Somalis joined the force, they helped non-Somali officers better understand Somali culture and tradition while also improving the position of the Somali community as a whole. Given the tension in community-police relations prior to the inclusion of Somalis on the force, this change is significant. The private sector could also benefit in this way.

A shared feature of the Twin Cities and Columbus is that these cities serve as regional education hubs. Each state's respective flagship university is in these cities, as are several other colleges, universities, and community colleges. Coordination between employers and educational institutions holds the promise of identifying new paths for occupational opportunities. For example, if a school system places a premium on hiring Somali teachers, a local college or university might recruit Somali students more heavily. Under the best circumstances, the philanthropic community would also take an interest in such programs and offer to underwrite scholarships.

The targeted recruiting discussed for public- and private-sector jobs could occur relatively easily, given the dense concentration of Somalis in certain geographic areas. Somali malls also serve as important social spaces where community outreach could happen. Religious leaders and Somali high school student populations might be prime targets for outreach. For example, new job and education programs could be promoted among these constituencies. Making the most of ethnic enclaves should be seen as a first step in innovative employment and educational programs. The other component in this equation is the development of occupational and educational programs designed specifically for Somalis. This is the more challenging task, but it is worthy of creative exploration.

One positive example offering a potential model for better economic incorporation is the public-private partnership in the Twin Cities concerning Somali economic opportunities. The African Development Center (ADC), in collaboration with local politicians, has played a vital role in finding ways to provide Islamic-compliant small-business loans. Beyond the loans, ADC offers a complex web of support programs for borrowers as well as courses for first-time homebuyers. ADC's success can be seen in the low loan-default rates among its clients. As of this writing, ADC and the mayor of Minneapolis are looking for ways to expand the success they have had with small-business loans to other financial areas, such as mortgages for Somali clients. The philanthropic community has also added significant resources to ADC's budget, further demonstrating the power of the public-private partnership.

Several valuable lessons can be learned from the ADC model. First, practicing Muslims in American cities need creative lending options. The collaboration between ADC and city leaders is also a vital piece of the ADC success story. Finally, the investment in ADC by the philanthropic community has allowed for the expansion and implementation of its lending and financial training goals. Although ADC has no plans for expansion outside Minnesota, the model, provided there is a coordinated effort by multiple stakeholders, could be replicated elsewhere.

Homeownership is the fourth indicator of Somali economic incorporation. Estimates of Somali homeownership in both cities are low. Increasing access to mortgage financing is a glaring need—one that policy makers in the Twin Cities are taking seriously. There remains room for Somali leaders, Islamic and otherwise, to challenge preconceived notions about rules regulating Islamic-compliant lending among Somali immigrants. Large Somali families would likely find ownership of a modest home more affordable than renting an apartment, would have more space for large families, and would have the opportunity to build equity. Moreover, the rapid increase in rental prices in the Twin Cities has created a more tenuous situation for lower-income renters, who are often forced into surrounding suburbs where rents are lower but jobs might not be as plentiful.

Somali Social Incorporation

Somali social incorporation is the final measure considered in this book. This concept is tied to perceptions of inclusion as well as the context of reception by the receiving community. In comparing Columbus and the Twin Cities, four measures of social incorporation were selected that highlight some noteworthy differences between the two regions: each region's history of welcoming refugees, letters to the editor about Somalis in each region's principal newspaper, the role of Somali police, and support of the local philanthropic community for Somali-based projects.

The Twin Cities area receives moderate to high marks on all four measures of social incorporation. The area's history of welcoming refugees, most recently the Hmong, means that a well-established infrastructure for refugee support services existed prior to the Somali population increase. This history set the stage for a relatively smooth transition for Somali refugees upon arrival, particularly in terms of the resettlement infrastructure already established in the Twin Cities. In Columbus, the arrival of large numbers of Somalis helped that city create a new refugee infrastructure that will help other refugee communities in years to come. Until the Somalis' arrival, Columbus was not a major refugee destination. Since the 1990s, the web of services and agencies hosted by the city has evolved and matured. One lesson learned from the different refugee reception stories is that once well-functioning structures are established, the process of refugee resettlement becomes easier for new communities that arrive.

Beyond the historical influences, a media analysis of letters to the editor about Somalis in the local newspaper provides a means to gauge public opinion about Somalis. Because of an absence of public opinion data on attitudes toward Somalis, and in an effort to provide some sense of public attitudes toward that community, letters to the principal newspapers' editors over a fifteen-year period were analyzed. An analysis of letters in the *Star Tribune* reveals that 73.8 percent were positive, suggesting a substantial amount of support for Somalis, at least among a subsection of the newspaper's readership. Columbus's local newspaper, the *Columbus Dispatch,* printed a significant ratio (62.2 percent) of supportive letters to the editor about Somalis during the period under review. Although not as high as the percentage observed in the Twin Cities, this measure reveals a general level of positive sentiments about Somalis. Taken as a whole, these letters shed some light on attitudes toward Somalis and a hint of their reception in the communities.

In contrast to what the letters to the editor tell us, the inclusion of Somali police officers in the Twin Cities represents a sign of Somali perceptions of their social incorporation. The immense pride Somali respondents take in these officers is noteworthy. The mutual respect the officers show for the citizens they work with is similarly impressive. Somali concerns about the ways federal law enforcement agents and organizations interact with their community stand in stark contrast to their sentiments about the local police. As discussed in Chapter 5, public opinion about the police, particularly in communities of color, is often quite negative. The story of Somali police in Columbus is virtually nonexistent, with the exception of the story about the female police academy student who was refused the option of wearing a snap-on hijab. The promising narrative in the Twin Cities—although the actual number of Somali officers is still small—demonstrates the potential for improved police-community relations if Columbus is able to add Somali police to its force. Police leaders would be wise to consider the value added by having Somali officers and work to eliminate barriers to their employment. In addition, targeted recruiting would go a long way toward reaching the goal of Somali inclusion.

The final measure of social incorporation involves the investment of the local philanthropic community in Somalis. Local foundations play a pivotal role in supporting the Somali community in the Twin Cities, which became apparent soon after research for this project was underway. More important is the fact that these organizations also coordinate with local government and community organizations to maximize their influence. However, the local philanthropic community is virtually absent from the Somali incorporation story in Columbus. Although part of the philanthropic situation in the Twin Cities is unique to that area and to its long-standing local foundations, adoption of similar priorities by foundations in Columbus is not an outrageous proposition. Many of the foundations in Columbus are committed to community improvement and might just need some encouragement to prioritize refugee communities. Lessons from the Twin Cities offer concrete examples of how these efforts could pay off.

Altogether, the level of social incorporation of Somalis in Columbus is low. These findings echo many of the comments made by Somali respondents in Columbus, who insist that life is better for Somalis in the Twin Cities. As noted at the opening of this chapter, we must cautiously accept the findings about higher levels of Somali social incorporation in the Twin Cities, with the caveat that social incorporation is difficult to measure *and* that even in this better case, incorporation is not complete by any means. The indicators selected in this book represent the few quantifiable options available, but it is easy to see that Somalis in the Twin Cities and in Columbus are residentially segregated, live on the economic margins, and are scrutinized by authorities and the public for perceived terrorist connections. These realities suggest that social incorporation, even in the Twin Cities, may in reality be quite a bit lower than the indicators reveal. Still, the indicators point to several areas where positive change can begin. Prioritizing the recruitment of Somali police holds the promise of lifting more Somalis out of poverty while simultaneously increasing the Somali community's perceptions of inclusion. Likewise, working with philanthropic leaders to demonstrate the reasons that prioritizing new refugee communities is a worthy investment could have positive results.

One of the biggest threats to Somali social incorporation is the current attention paid by authorities to alleged Somali terrorist connections and recruiting. The skepticism and frustration expressed by respondents about federal investigations in their community raise serious concerns about the effectiveness of these efforts and highlight a lack of trust. Somali respondents are worried about the discrimination they face as members of a suspect community, often sharing concerns that parallel those of federal agencies that wish to prevent further recruiting in their community. The trust between Somalis in the Twin Cities and local law enforcement authorities stands in stark contrast to comments respondents made about federal law enforcement. Here a lesson can be learned about the significance of ongoing community outreach and trust building. A related idea is that diversifying the employment base might also increase institutional cultural understanding. With federal agencies responsible for Countering Violent Extremism (CVE) programs in cities across the country, these community ties take on a new level of significance.

Toward Guiding Principles for Policy Makers

From the general incorporation findings summarized in the previous sections of this chapter, a number of specific recommendations can be made for policy makers interested in best practices. With regard to increasing the political incorporation of marginalized groups, examining the unique ramifications of the electoral system on the community is essential. Once the specific implications are determined, strategies for eliminating barriers can be pursued. These strategies could involve challenging the existing system in the courts or working within this system to run candidates from the marginalized group and galvanize voters from that community.

Political parties should also be educated about the benefits associated with outreach to a new candidate and voter base. Inclusion within a party can result in the mobilization of specific voters who may be able to influence the outcome of elections. Of course, convincing a political party to reach out to a new group requires knowledge of how sentiments held by group members will align with party interests.

Considering ways to increase union membership and leadership opportunities for marginalized groups is another logical opportunity for contributing to political incorporation. Because unions increase collective power and voice, they provide a vehicle for laborers to collectively express their interests. Given the connections we typically see between unions and political parties, boosting unionization could go hand-in-hand with the goal of increasing party involvement among marginalized communities. Of course, union power varies from place to place and must be considered in the calculation.

Assessing the organizational strengths of a community is essential for policy makers interested in the political incorporation of marginalized groups. Taking stock in the number of community groups and their goals, missions, and resources will provide essential information about organizational overlap, funding sources, and opportunities for collaboration. Organizations can also do this on their own, but policy makers could contribute to these efforts by identifying public- and private-sector funding sources. They could also provide information on grant writing if an organization lacks this type of connection. Along these same lines, local philanthropic groups should also be consulted to determine whether their goals align with the goals of the various community organizations. When connections are identified, introductions should be forthcoming.

Finally, policy makers must consider the power and importance of street-level bureaucrats who are in regular contact with the members of a marginalized community. In addition to the important role these bureaucrats play in the daily lives of individuals and communities, their understanding of the interests of the group is valuable. When these bureaucrats are also members of the marginalized group, there is even more of a chance that trust building between the community and government will take place, especially when the bureaucrat has some influence over governmental decision making.

Economic incorporation is tied to educational and occupational opportunities. For underrepresented groups at or below the poverty line, attention must be paid to areas where doors can be opened for them. For example, college scholarships and targeted recruiting of high school students for internships in the public and private sectors, mentoring programs, summer employment, and college admission are just some of the ways doors can be opened. Incentives that could involve tax breaks or other benefits represent innovative ways of encouraging employment in the private and public sectors. Creating new routes for underrepresented groups would not only elevate them economically but also increase their visibility in the broader community. This visibility might also reduce stereotypes and increase positive interactions between members of the marginalized group and the majority population.

Policy makers interested in economic incorporation would also be wise to investigate potential opportunities for public-private partnerships to elevate a community. Examples include banking and loan programs, mortgage-financing options, scholarships and grant programs, or other endeavors that could target the specific areas of economic underincorporation within a particular community. Examples from the Twin Cities in this book provide some methods for how this can be done.

Finally, when it comes to social incorporation, policy makers must first evaluate the situation of the group within the larger society. If there is evidence of marginalization, investigating the propensity toward stereotyping and misunderstandings by the dominant society should be considered. Educating the public through elementary and secondary educational curricula about the group is one way to reduce the tendency toward generalizations. Media outlets and government-sponsored information could also be directed toward clarifying information about a group and offering an accurate portrayal of their experience. Returning to a point made previously, prioritizing the hiring of qualified members of the marginalized group for public positions could also go a long way toward increasing perceptions of legitimacy and provide children from the marginalized community with role models who could serve as inspirations and mentors.

All of these examples provide some specific considerations for policy makers, but there is no substitute for building trusting and sustainable relationships. This rule applies to the relationships not only between policy makers and marginalized communities but also among policy makers across the country and at various levels of government. Regular contact among policy makers to discuss best practices and ways of solving vexing problems could facilitate the incorporation of new immigrant communities.

Incorporation Interactions

The three types of incorporation addressed in this book are interrelated and mutually reinforcing: progress in any one of the areas of incorporation can produce concomitant improvements in the two other areas. For example, with greater levels of political incorporation of Somalis in the Twin Cities, there is evidence that policy makers take seriously the challenges the community faces with regard to their economic incorporation. The current attention by public and private entities to creating new paths for Islamic-compliant financing is a concrete example of how political incorporation can spill over into economic incorporation. We have also observed how progress in terms of social incorporation can improve economic incorporation through the employment of Somali police officers in the Twin Cities. In this instance, these officers have served to improve community morale, expand cultural sensitivity within the police organization, and offer a chance at upward mobility for those employed in the public sector. The inverse is also true: reduced levels of incorporation in one area can also hamper or prevent gains in the other two areas. In Columbus, for example, the generally lower levels of social and political incorporation are likely tied to the economic marginalization of Somalis. However, there are positive ways to alter this relationship. For instance, in the Twin Cities, where the economic situation is similarly bleak, other factors unique to that area help compensate for economic incorporation.

One lesson we can learn from this study of incorporation is that advances become progressively easier over time. For example, after the first Somali has run for public office in an area, there is a greater likelihood that others will follow. Similarly, the unionization of Somalis can lead to leadership opportunities that are ultimately linked to political ones. The differences between overall incorporation levels in the Twin Cities versus those in Columbus provide a nice contrast and a promising forecast provided that policy makers, community leaders, and private-sector actors coordinate their efforts to increase Somali incorporation. Because each area of incorporation is interconnected, small steps toward incorporation in one area can have positive effects in the other areas.

Another lesson is that incorporation advances become progressively easier over time. An important part of the Twin Cities narrative is the region's history of welcoming refugees in previous decades. In Columbus, which lacked a strong refugee resettlement infrastructure, the establishment of such a structure with the arrival of Somalis has facilitated an easier transition for future newcomers to the region. Now that Columbus is experiencing a surge in Nepalese refugees, the infrastructure that has already been established can better serve these newcomers as they begin their new life. Similarly, the employment or election of the first Somali to any post creates opportunities for others to imagine the possibilities for themselves and their community. In the Twin Cities, the relatively rapid increase in the number of Somalis running for public office is one example of how this phenomenon works. Despite differences within the electoral structure in Columbus, backing Somali candidates for political positions holds the promise of helping members of the community realize their individual potential as representatives and also raising awareness of the concerns of the Somali community. In this example, Somalis must be motivated but also actively recruited and embraced by the political party. This is certainly a challenge given the current situation in Columbus, but it also suggests that these relatively simple steps could greatly increase political incorporation for years to come. Another example involves public-sector employment. Whereas it seems like a daunting task to dramatically increase the number of Somali teachers in the public schools, the lesson of Somali police recruitment and its benefits suggests that this is an attainable and worthy goal. As noted earlier, cooperation between different stakeholders is the key to these innovations. Once they are created, more can be built on this foundation. Again, the overarching lesson is that although the initial steps toward incorporation may seem daunting, because they represent a change from the past, once the framework is created, incorporation is easier.

Another overarching lesson of this research is the mutually beneficial implications for Somalis and the community at large when incorporation levels increase. The shared interest in incorporation can be seen from a number of vantage points. If we value the concept of participatory democracy, the political incorporation of Somalis brings us closer to realizing the ideals that underpin our political system. Somalis are already doing their part at the ballot box, at least according to the high levels of voter turnout that respondents in this project often reported. However, if they experience informal barriers to other forms of political incorporation, this should be viewed as an area in need of improvement. Along the same lines, social incorporation advances via Somali inclusion in public-sector employment or through the investment by foundations in innovative Somali-based projects could promote more intercultural understanding and interactions. Finally, the economic uplifting of the Somali community holds the promise of reducing levels of community poverty and creating a better quality of life for all residents.

Appendix A

Challenges of Immigrant Incorporation in New Destinations

Somalis in the Twin Cities and Columbus

Interview Questionnaires

Professor Stefanie Chambers

Policy Maker Interview Questions
1. Why has X city (Columbus or Twin Cities) become a new immigrant destination for Somalis?
2. Are there specific city employees or elected officials who have been instrumental in helping the Somali community in city X (Columbus or the Twin Cities)?
   (probe for specific examples)
3. Is there more that could be done by the city or state to help Somalis in X city (Columbus or Twin Cities)?
   (probe for specific examples)
4. How are Somalis faring politically in city X (Columbus or the Twin Cities)?
   (probe about challenges and successes)
5. How are Somalis faring economically in city X (Columbus or the Twin Cities)?
   (probe about challenges and successes)
6. How are Somalis faring socially in city X (Columbus or the Twin Cities)?
   (probe about challenges and successes)
7. In terms of housing, can you discuss the benefits and challenges associated with having a large Somali community in city X (Columbus or the Twin Cities)?

Somali Community Member Interview Questions
1. What brought you or your family to city X (Columbus or the Twin Cities)?
2. Are there specific city employees or elected officials who have been instrumental in helping the Somali community in city X (Columbus or the Twin Cities)?
   (probe for specific examples)

3. Is there more that could be done by the city or state to help Somalis in X city (Columbus or the Twin Cities)?
   (probe for specific examples)
4. How are Somalis faring politically in city X (Columbus or the Twin Cities)?
   (probe about challenges and successes)
5. How are Somalis faring economically in city X (Columbus or the Twin Cities)?
   probe about challenges and successes)
6. How are Somalis faring socially in city X (Columbus or the Twin Cities)?
   (probe about challenges and successes)
7. In terms of housing, can you discuss the benefits and challenges associated with having a large Somali community in city X (Columbus or the Twin Cities)?

Police Administrative Interview Questions

1. Please explain the process by which the Minneapolis Police Department hired Somali officers?
2. Why was having Somali officers on the force a priority?
3. What impact have the officers had on community policing?
4. Are there efforts underway to hire more Somali officers?

Police Officer Questions

1. Why did you decide to join the Minneapolis Police Department?
2. Do you believe your presence on the police force has helped your fellow officers understand Somali Americans in a new way?
3. How has the Somali community responded to your position as a law enforcement official?
4. Has your inclusion on the police force had a noticeable impact on Somali interest in joining the police force?

Philanthropic Community Interview Questions

1. Has the X Foundation awarded any grants to Somalis or Somali organizations that specifically try to better the lives of Somali Americans in city X (Columbus or the Twin Cities)?
   1a. If yes, could you provide a few examples?
2. Can you describe any initiatives or programs at the X Foundation that specifically target the Somali or refugee community in city X (Columbus or the Twin Cities)?
   2a. If yes, can you provide specific examples?
3. If the X Foundation is dedicated to supporting Somali Americans, can you describe how this emphasis came about?

Appendix B

Immigrant Incorporation in New Destinations

Somalis in the Twin Cities and Columbus

Interview Consent Form

Participant's name:

Mailing address:

I agree to be interviewed for this project on Somali incorporation in Columbus, Ohio, and Minneapolis/St. Paul, Minnesota. Data from this interview are for use in a forthcoming book on the topic.

My participation in this project is entirely voluntary, and I may withdraw at any time. I understand that all of my comments will remain anonymous and that I will be identified in this project only by category (for example, town committee member, community activist, union representative, city bureaucrat, police officer). The only exception is for elected and appointed officials who are identified by their public positions—for example, Mayor Smith, Chief Jones.

I am aware that the tape recording of my interview will be destroyed as soon as the interview is transcribed. I also understand that I can decline to have my interview recorded. Finally, I understand that an edited transcript of the interview will remain with Professor Stefanie Chambers of Trinity College and be destroyed one year from now (on or about April 2016).

Any exceptions to this agreement must be listed below. [*For example, the participant may wish to delay the public release of the interview for a certain period of time; participant can ask that certain information not be included in the transcribed interview or notes; participant can decline to have any quotations included in the book*]:

Participant's signature _____

Date _____

Appendix C

Columbus Somali Incorporation Interviews

Columbus Academic Interviews

February 27, 2014: female—College Professor in Ohio*

Columbus Community Interviews with Subjects
Who Are Also Public School Graduates

July, 24, 2013A: female—small-business owner in Somali mall
July, 24, 2013B: female—works at small business in Somali mall
June 27, 2014A: female—college student at Ohio State
June 27, 2014B: female—college student at Ohio State
June 27, 2014C: male—works as tutor for Somali kids
March 11, 2015: female—applying for grad school

Who Are Also Public School Teachers/Former Teachers

July 24, 2013: male—traditional public school in Columbus
July 25, 2013: male—charter school in Columbus
June 27, 2014: female—Westerville Schools (suburb)

Somali Businesspeople

June 27, 2014: female—works for corporate bank
June 28, 2014A: male—home health care business
June 28, 2014B: male—childcare business

TOTAL COLUMBUS INTERVIEWS = 49, plus 7 follow-ups = 56

*Indicates that the respondent is not Somali.

Note: When multiple follow-up interviews were conducted with the same respondent, only the first two interviews were calculated in the total number of interviews.

June 28, 2014C: male—transportation business
July 25, 2014: male—home health care business
March 3, 2015: male—home health care business

Others

March 4, 2014A: male
March 4, 2014B: male
March 4, 2014C: male
March 5, 2014: female
March 5, 2014, and March 10, 2015: male
March 6, 2014A: male
March 6, 2014B: male
June 26, 2014A: male
June 26, 2014B: female
June 26, 2014C: male
June 26, 2014D: female
March 11, 2015: male
March 12, 2015A: male
March 12, 2015B: male

Leaders of Community Organizations
(Somali and Non-Somali Organizations)

July 26, 2013A: male
July 26, 2013B, March 9, 2015, March 10, 2015, and October 15, 2015: male
July 26, 2013C: male
June 26, 2014A, and March 11, 2015: female
June 26, 2014B, March 8, 2015, and June 26, 2013: female
June 27, 2014A: male
June 27, 2014B: male
March 11, 2015: male—Council on American-Islamic Relations*

Somalis Working in the Media

June 19, 2013: female
June 27, 2013: female
June 28, 2014, and March 10, 2015: female

Bureaucrats

June 9, 2013, June 17, 2013, and July 26, 2013: male—city bureaucrat
July 24, 2013: male—city bureaucrat*
December 26, 2013: male—state bureaucrat
June 28, 2014: male—U.S. Department of Homeland Security

Foundation Representatives

July 30, 2015: male—Columbus philanthropic representative

Resettlement Agency Representatives

June 26, 2014, and June 12, 2015: female
June 1, 2015: female*
October 16, 2015: female

Elected Officials

June 29, 2012: Mayor Michael Coleman*

Appendix D

Twin Cities Somali Incorporation Interviews

Twin Cities Academic Interviews

June 2, 2014: male*
June 3, 2014: male*
July 1, 2014: female
July 10, 2014, and April 14, 2015: female

Twin Cities Community Interviews with Subjects
Who Are Also Public School Graduates

June 2, 2014A: male—community college student
June 2, 2014B: male—working in retail
June 2, 2014C: male—starting college
June 2, 2014D: female—working for a community organization
June 3, 2014A: male—working for a community organization
June 3, 2014B: female—working for a community organization
June 3, 2014C: female—volunteering at community organization and in
    college

Who Are Also Public School Teachers/Former Teachers

April 24, 2014, June 1, 2014, and April 13, 2015: male
June 4, 2014: female
June 9, 2015: male

Somali Businesspeople

June 2, 2014, and April 15, 2015A: female—African Development Coalition
    (in book—ADC representative, not as community interview)

TOTAL TWIN CITIES INTERVIEWS = 65, plus 13 follow-ups = 78

*Indicates that the respondent is not Somali.

Note: When multiple follow-up interviews were conducted with the same respondent, only the first two interviews were calculated in the total number of interviews.

June 3, 2014A: male—daycare center owner
June 3, 2014B: male—home health care business
July 11, 2014: female—owns shop in Somali mall
April 15, 2015B: a male—African Development Coalition (in book—ADC representative, not as community interview)
June 11, 2015A: male—transportation business
June 11, 2015B: male—transportation business

Others

April 14, 2014: male
May 24, 2014: female
May 31, 2014, June 4, 2014, and April 12, 2015: male
June 1, 2014A: female
June 1, 2014B: female
June 4, 2014A: male
June 4, 2014B, and April 13, 2015A: female
June 4, 2014C, and April 12, 2015: female
June 8, 2014: male
July 9, 2014: male
July 11, 2014A: male
July 11, 2014B: male
February 10, 2015: female
April 15, 2015: female
April 16, 2015: male

Leaders of Community Organizations (Somali and Non-Somali Organizations)

June 3, 2014A: male
June 3, 2014B: male
June 5, 2014, and April 15, 2015: male
August 5, 2014: female
April 15, 2015: male
April 16, 2015: male—Council on American-Islamic Relations

Bureaucrats and Political Strategists

June 2, 2014, March 17, 2015, April 14, 2015, and June 9, 2015: male—mayor's office and former labor leader
July 11, 2014: male—Congressman Keith Ellison representative
September 9, 2014, and March 6, 2015: male Democratic-Farmer-Labor Party representative*
March 21, 2015: male—political strategist*

Religious Leader

June 5, 2014, and July 11, 2014: male—also public school teacher
July 12, 2014: male
June 12, 2015: male

Union Leader

July 11, 2014, and April 16, 2015: male

Foundation Representatives

June 10, 2015: female*
June 11, 2015: female*
June 19, 2015: male*
June 28, 2015: female*

Police Leadership Interviews

June 11, 2015A: male*
June 11, 2015B: male*

Somali Police Officers

June 9, 2015A: male
June 9, 2015B: male
June 9, 2015C, and June 10, 2015: male
June 11, 2015: male

Resettlement Agency Representatives

June 4, 2014: male

Elected Officials

June 5, 2014, and April 14, 2015: male—Abdi Warsame
June 24, 2014: male—Mohamed Noor
July 11, 2014, and April 8, 2015: male—Mayor R. T. Rybak*
July 31, 2014: female—Mayor Betsy Hodges*

References

Abdi, Cawo Mohamed. 2007. "Convergence of Civil War and the Religious Right: Reimagining Somali Women." *Signs: Journal of Women and Culture in Society* 33 (1): 183–207.

———. 2014. "Threatened Identities and Gendered Opportunities: Somali Migration to America." *Signs* 39 (2): 459–483.

Alba, Richard, and Nancy Foner. 2009. "Entering the Precincts of Power: Do National Differences Matter for Immigrant Minority Political Representation?" In *Bringing Outsiders In: Transatlantic Perspectives on Immigrant Political Incorporation,* edited by Jennifer L. and John H. Mollenkopf, 277–293. Ithaca, NY: Cornell University Press.

Alex-Assensoh, Yvette M. 2004. "Taking the Sanctuary to the Streets: Religion, Race, and Community Development in Columbus, Ohio." *Annals of the American Academy of Political and Social Science* 594 (1): 79–91.

Ali, Ihotu. 2011. "Staying Off the Bottom of the Melting Pot: Somali Refugees Respond to a Changing U.S. Immigration Climate." *Bildhaan: An International Journal of Somali Studies* 9 (11). Available at http://digitalcommons.macalester.edu/bildhaan/vol9/iss1/11.

Allen, Ryan. 2010. "The Bonding and Bridging Roles of Religious Institutions for Refugees in a Non-gateway Context." *Ethnic and Racial Studies* 33 (6): 1049–1068.

Aptekar, Sofya. 2009. "Organizational Life and Political Incorporation of Two Asian Immigrant Groups: A Case Study." *Ethnic and Racial Studies* 32 (9): 1511–1533.

Barker, Lucius J., Mack H. Jones, and Katherine Tate. 1999. *African Americans and the American Political System.* 4th ed. Upper Saddle River, NJ: Prentice Hall.

Becker, Jessie. 2014. "Kahn Will Represent University Area." *Minnesota Daily,* November 5. Available at http://www.mndaily.com/news/metro-state/2014/11/05/kahn-will-represent-university-area-again.

Berman, Hyman, and Linda Mack Schloff. 2014. *Jews in Minnesota.* St. Paul: Minnesota Historical Society Press.

Bloemraad, Irene. 2006. *Becoming a Citizen: Incorporating Immigrants and Refugees in the United States and Canada.* Berkeley: University of California

Borgerding, Tom. "Columbus Somalis Gain U.S. Citizenship, Head for the Polls." *WOSU News,* October 29, 2008. Available at http://delta.wosu.org/site/news/2008/10/29/columbus-somalis-gain-u-s-citizenship-head-for-the-polls/.

Boyd, Robert L. 1994. "The Allocation of Black Workers into the Public Sector." *Sociological Focus* 27 (1): 35–51.

Brandl, John E. 2000. "Policy and Politics in Minnesota." *Daedalus: Minnesota—A Different America?* 129 (3): 191–220.

Brehm, Andy. 2014. "Readers Write (Oct. 2): Invasive Species, Somali Community, Transgender Students, Cycling Assault, Security, Fleetwood Mac." *Star Tribune,* October 2. Available at http://www.startribune.com/readers-write-oct-2-invasive-species-somali-community-transgender-students-cycling-assault-security-fleetwood-mac/277822731/.

Bronfenbrenner, Kate, and Dorian T. Warren. 2007. "Race, Gender, and the Rebirth of Trade Unionism." *New Labor Forum* 16 (3): 142–148.

Browning, Rufus P., Dale Rogers Marshall, and David H. Tabb. 1984. *Protest Is Not Enough.* Berkeley: University of California Press.

Burstein, Rachel. 2012. "How Labor Won in Ohio." *Dissent* 59 (3): 34–37.

Caeiro, Alexandre. 2004. "The Social Construction of Sari'a: Bank Interest, Home Purchase, and Islamic Norms in the West." *Die Welt des Islams* 44:351–375. Available at http://www.academia.edu/957992/CAEIRO_The_Social_Construction_of_Shari_a_Bank_Interest_Home_Purchase_and_Islamic_Norms_in_the_West.

Callen, Chris D. 2009. "Somali Flag above the Statehouse Is Wrong." *Columbus Dispatch,* July 9. Available at http://www.dispatch.com/content/stories/editorials/2009/07/09/Callen_ART_07-09-09_A12_49EDHDM.html.

Carlson, Benny. 2007. "Hard Workers and Daring Entrepreneurs: Impressions from the Somali Enclave in Minneapolis." In *The Role of Diasporas in Peace, Democracy, and Development in the Horn of Africa,* by Benny Carlson, 179–188. Lund, Sweden: Lund University. Available at http://citeseerx.ist.psu.edu/viewdoc/download?doi=10.1.1.458.2296&rep=rep1&type=pdf#page=179.

Chambers, Stefanie. 2006. *Mayors and Schools: Minority Voices and Democratic Tensions in Urban Education.* Philadelphia: Temple University Press.

Chambers, Stefanie, Diana Evans, Anthony Messina, and Abigail Williamson, eds. Forthcoming. *The Politics of New Immigrant Destinations: Transatlantic Perspectives.*

Chambers, Stefanie, and William E. Nelson. 2014. "Black Mayoral Leadership in New Orleans: Minority Incorporation Revisited." *National Political Science Review* 16: 117–134.

Chambers, Stefanie, and Will Schreiber-Stainthorp. 2013. "Michael Coleman: The Midwestern Middleman." In *21st Century Urban Race Politics: Representing Minorities as Universal Interests,* edited by Ravi K. Perry, 133–162. Bingley, UK: Emerald Group Publishing.

Chávez, Maria L., Brian Wampler, and Ross E. Burkhart. 2006. "Left Out: Trust and Social Capital among Migrant Seasonal Farmworkers." *Social Science Quarterly* 87 (5): 1012–1029.

Chemelecki, Lisa. 2003. "Jockeying for Power." *Lewiston Sun Journal,* December 14.

Citizens Committee for Fair Redistricting. 2012. Letter to Barry Clegg, chair of the Minneapolis Chapter Commission. January 27. Available at http://www.minneapolismn.gov/www/groups/public/@clerk/documents/webcontent/wcms1p-085467.pdf.

City of Columbus. 2013. "Community Relations Commission." Available at http://columbus.gov/Templates/Detail.aspx?id=65002.

Cockayne, James, and Liat Shetret. 2012. *Capitalizing on Trust: Harnessing Somali Remittances for Counterterrorism, Human Rights and State Building.* Global Center on Cooperative Security. Available at http://globalcenter.org/wp-content/up loads/2012/07/CapitalizingOnTrust.pdf.

Cohen, Jeffrey, and Nidia Chavez. 2013. "Latino Immigrants, Discrimination and Reception in Columbus, Ohio." *International Migration* 51 (2): 24–31. Available at http://www.academia.edu/3087119/Latino_Immigrants_Discrimination_and_Re ception_in_Columbus_Ohio.

Corrie, Bruce P. 2008. "A New Paradigm for Immigrant Policy: Immigrant Capital. A Case Study of People of Mexican Origin in Minnesota." *William Mitchell Law Review* 35 (1): 283–308.

Curnutte, Mark, and David Berman. 2013. "KKK Tries to Recruit New Members in Ohio." *Cincinnati Inquirer,* October 1. Available at http://www.usatoday.com/story/ news/nation/2013/10/01/kkk-tries-to-recruit-new-members-in-ohio/2905427/.

Da'ar, Omar. 2012. *Economic Impact of African Development Center of Minnesota in the Twin Cities.* Available at http://www.adcminnesota.org/files/ADC_Economic_Im pact_Analysis_4-12.pdf.

Dahl, David S. 1988. "Minneapolis/St. Paul: An Agricultural Hub." *Rangelands* 10 (3): 111–113.

Darcy, Robert, Susan Welch, and Janet Clark. 1994. *Women, Elections, and Representation.* 2nd ed. Lincoln: University of Nebraska Press.

de Graauw, Els. 2008. "Nonprofit Organizations: Agents of Immigrant Political Incorporation in Urban America." In *Civic Hopes and Political Realities: Immigrants, Community Organizations, and Political Engagement,* edited by S. Karthick Ramakrishnan and Irene Bloemraad, 323–350. New York: Russell Sage Foundation.

de la Puente, Manuel. 1990. *The Census Undercount of the Hispanic Population.* Center for Survey Methods Research, Bureau of the Census.

Delton, Jennifer. 2001. "Labor, Politics, and African American Identity in Minneapolis, 1930–50." *Minnesota History* 57 (8): 418–434.

DeRusha, Jason. 2011. "Good Question: Why Did Somalis Locate Here?" *CBS Minnesota,* January 19. Available at http://minnesota.cbslocal.com/2011/01/19/good-question -why-did-somalis-locate-here/.

Eisinger, Peter K. 1973. "The Conditions of Protest Behavior in American Cities." *American Political Science Review* 67 (1): 11–28.

———. 1986. "Local Civil Service Employment and Black Socioeconomic Mobility." *Social Science Quarterly* 67 (1): 169–175.

Elazar, Daniel J. 1987. *Exploring Federalism.* Tuscaloosa: University of Alabama Press.

Elazar, Daniel Judah, Virginia Gray, and Wyman Spano. 1999. *Minnesota Politics and Government.* Lincoln: University of Nebraska Press.

Elder, Laurel. 2004. "Why Women Don't Run: Explaining Women's Underrepresentation in America's Political Institutions." *Women and Politics* 26 (2): 27–56.

Elliott, Andrea. 2009. "A Call to Jihad, Answered in America." *New York Times,* July 11. Available at http://www.nytimes.com/2009/07/12/us/12somalis.html?page wanted=all&_r=0.

Ellison, Keith. 2014. "Ellison, Paulsen, Duffy Applaud Passage of Money Remittances Improvement Act." Press release, May 6. Available at https://ellison.house.gov/

media-center/press-releases/ellison-paulsen-duffy-applaud-passage-of-money-remittances-improvement.

Erikson, Robert S., John P. McIver, and Gerald C. Wright. 1987. "State Political Culture and Public Opinion." *American Political Science Review* 81 (3): 797–813.

Etzioni, Amitai, and Fred DuBow. 1970. *Comparative Perspectives: Theories and Methods.* Boston: Little, Brown.

Fennelly, Katherine. 2006a. "Latinos, Africans and Asians in the North Star State: Immigrant Communities in Minnesota." In *Beyond the Gateway: Immigrants in a Changing America,* edited by Elzbieta M. Gozdziak and Susan F. Martin, 111–135. *Migration and Refugee Studies Series.* Lanham, MD: Lexington Books.

———. 2006b. *State and Local Policy Responses to Immigration in Minnesota.* Report to the Century Foundation, July 8. Available at http://archive.hhh.umn.edu/people/kfennelly/pdf/slp_immigration_in_mn.pdf.

———. 2008. "Prejudice toward Immigrants in the Midwest." In *New Faces in New Places: The Changing Geography of American Immigration,* edited by Douglas S. Massey, 151–178. New York: Russell Sage Foundation.

———. 2012. "Immigration in the Midwest." *Scholars Strategy Network.* Available at https://www.scholarsstrategynetwork.org/sites/default/files/ssn_basic_facts_fennelly_on_immigration_in_the_midwest_1.pdf.

Fennelly, Katherine, and Myron Orfield. 2008. "Impediments to Integration of Immigrants: A Case Study in Minnesota." In *America's Twenty-First-Century Gateways: Immigrant Incorporation in Suburban America,* edited by Audrey Singer, Caroline Brettell, and Susan Hardwick, 200–224. Washington, DC: Brookings Institution Press.

Forrest, Tamar Mott, and Lawrence Brown. 2014. "Organization-Led Migration, Individual Choice, and Refugee Resettlement in the U.S.: Seeking Regularities." *Geographical Review* 104 (1): 10–32.

Franey, Sheila. 2009. "Funding Our Enemies." *Star Tribune,* April 25.

Fuchs, Ester R. 1992. *Mayors and Money: Fiscal Policy in New York and Chicago.* Chicago: University of Chicago Press.

Garjeex, Abdisalam M. 2000. "Immigrants from Somalia Could Use a Helping Hand." *Columbus Dispatch,* January 3.

Garofalo, James. *Public Opinion about Crime: The Attitudes of Victims and Nonvictims in Selected Cities.* Rockville, MD: U.S. Department of Justice, Law Enforcement Assistance Administration, National Criminal Justice Information and Statistics Service, 1977.

Gilbert, Lauren. 2009. "Citizenship, Civic Virtue, and Immigrant Integration: The Enduring Power of Community-Based Norms." *Yale Law and Policy Review* 27:335–397.

Gilman, Rhoda. 2000. "The History and Peopling of Minnesota: Its Culture." *Daedalus: Minnesota—A Different America* 129 (3): 1–29.

Golden, Shannon, Elizabeth Heger Boyle, and Yasin Jama. 2010. "Achieving Success in Business: A Comparison of Somali and American-Born Entrepreneurs in Minneapolis." *CURA Reporter* 40 (1–2): 43–51.

Golden, Shannon, Yasin Garad, and Elizabeth Heger Boyle. 2011. "Experiences of Somali Entrepreneurs: New Evidence from the Twin Cities." *Bildhaan: An International Journal of Somali Studies* 10 (1). Available at http://digitalcommons.macalester.edu/bildhaan/vol10/iss1/9.

Gray, Jane. 2004. "U.S. Needs to Take Care of Refugees." *Columbus Dispatch,* January 3.

Greenblatt, Alan. 2013. "For Somali Immigrants, All Politics Really Is Local." *NPR*, October 29. Available at http://www.npr.org/blogs/itsallpolitics/2013/10/29/241632965/for-somali-immigrants-all-politics-really-is-local.

Groffman, Bernard, and Chandler Davidson. 1992. *Controversies in Minority Voting: The Voting Rights Act in Perspective*. Washington, DC: Brookings Institution Press.

Guajardo, Salomon A. 1999. "Workforce Diversity: Monitoring Employment Trends in Public Organizations." *Public Personnel Management* 28 (1): 63–85.

Hatcher, Jessica. 2015. "Ending Somali-US Money Transfers Will Be Devastating, Merchants Bank Warned." *The Guardian*, February 6. Available at http://www.theguardian.com/global-development/2015/feb/06/somali-us-money-transfers-merchants-bank-remittances.

Healy, Sally, and Mark Bradbury. 2010. "Endless War: A Brief History of the Somali Conflict." *Conciliation Resources*. Available at http://www.c-r.org/accord-article/endless-war-brief-history-somali-conflict#sthash.6Y6PpQnc.dpuf.

Hein, Jeremy. 2006. *Ethnic Origins: The Adaptation of Cambodian and Hmong Refugees in Four American Cities*. New York: Russell Sage Foundation.

Helmy, Ayah. 2009. "Readers Write for Saturday, April 18." *Star Tribune*, April 17. Available at http://www.startribune.com/readers-write-for-saturday-april-18/43201762/.

Hero, Rodney E. 2003. "Social Capital and Racial Inequality in America." *Perspectives on Politics* 1 (1): 113–122.

Hindelang, Michael J. 1974. "Public Opinion Regarding Crime, Criminal Justice, and Related Topics." *Journal of Research in Crime and Delinquency* 11 (2): 101–116.

Hindin, Michael. 2012. "Somali Diaspora." *Star Tribune*, January 10.

Hirsi, Ibrahim. 2014. "Somali-American Officers Bridge Gap between Police and Community." MinnPost.com, September 25. Available at https://www.minnpost.com/community-sketchbook/2014/09/somali-american-officers-bridge-gap-between-police-and-community.

Hirsi, Jibril. 2009. "The Somali Community Is a Promising Economic Powerhouse in Ohio." *SomaliCAN Outreach Newsletter*, August. Available at http://somalican.org/yahoo_site_admin/assets/docs/Somali_Community_in_Ohio.20374400.pdf.

Hochschild, Jennifer L., and John H. Mollenkopf. 2009. *Bringing Outsiders In: Transatlantic Perspectives on Immigrant Political Incorporation*. Ithaca, NY: Cornell University Press.

Hopkins, Daniel J., Van C. Tran, and Abigail Fisher Williamson. 2014. "See No Spanish: Language, Local Context, and Attitudes toward Immigration." *Politics, Groups, and Identities* 2 (1): 35–51.

Horst, Cindy. 2004. "Money and Mobility: Transnational Livelihood Strategies of the Somali Diaspora." Available at http://dare.uva.nl/record/1/425118.

———. 2006. "Connected Lives: Somalis in Minneapolis, Family Responsibilities and the Migration Dreams of Relatives." *United Nations High Commission for Refugees*, July. http://www.unhcr.org/44b7b6912.html.

———. 2008. "A Monopoly on Assistance? International Aid to Refugee Camps and the Role of the Diaspora." *Afrika Spectrum* 43 (1): 121–131.

Horst, Cindy, Marta Bivand Erdal, Jørgen Carling, and Karin Fathimath Afeef. 2014. "Private Money, Public Scrutiny? Contrasting Perspectives on Remittances." *Global Networks* 14 (4): 514–532.

Horst, Cindy, and Nick Van Hear. 2002. "Counting the Cost: Refugees, Remittances and the

'War against Terrorism.'" *Forced Migration Review* 14:32–34. Available at http://www .fmreview.org/sites/fmr/files/FMRdownloads/en/FMRpdfs/FMR14/fmr14.13.pdf.

Huang, Wilson W. S., and Michael S. Vaughn. 1996. "Support and Confidence: Public Attitudes toward the Police." *Americans View Crime and Justice: A National Public Opinion Survey,* 31–45. Thousand Oaks, CA: Sage.

Hunker, Henry. 1996. "Columbus: The Capital City." In *A Geography of Ohio,* edited by Leonard Peacefull, 159–164. Kent, OH: Kent State University Press.

———. 2000. *Columbus, Ohio: A Personal Geography.* Columbus: Ohio State University Press.

International Crisis Group. 2008. *Somalia Conflict History.* Available at http://www .crisisgroup.org/en/publication-type/key-issues/research-resources/conflict-his tories/somalia.aspx.

Jones-Correa, Michael. 2005. "The Bureaucratic Incorporation of Immigrants in Suburbia." Paper presented at the Conference on Immigrants to the United States. New York Sources and Destinations, New York. February. Available at http://www .princeton.edu/csdp/events/JonesCorrea051007/Jones-Correa051007.pdf.

Judd, Dennis R., and Todd Swanstrom. 2015. *City Politics.* London: Routledge.

Kane, Lucile M. 1961. "Rivalry for a River: The Twin Cities and the Mississippi." *Minnesota History* 37 (8): 309–367.

Kohls, Rosalind. 2010. "Teachers Should Worry about All Students." *Star Tribune,* December 30.

Lee, Taeku, S. Karthick Ramakrishnan, and Ricardo Ramírez. 2007. *Transforming Politics, Transforming America: The Political and Civic Incorporation of Immigrants in the United States.* Charlottesville: University of Virginia Press.

Lefrak, Mikaela. 2014. "A Massachusetts Mayor Wants to Say 'No' to More Refugees." *Global Nation.* Available at http://www.pri.org/stories/2014-06-24/massachusetts-mayor-wants-say-no-more-refugees.

Lewis, Paul G., and S. Karthick Ramakrishnan. 2007. "Police Practices in Immigrant-Destination Cities: Political Control or Bureaucratic Professionalism?" *Urban Affairs Review* 42 (6): 874–900.

Locke, Steven P. 2006. "In This Age of Information, the True Nature of Islam Can't Be Papered Over." *Columbus Dispatch,* July 8.

Lor, Yang. 2009. "Hmong Political Involvement in St. Paul, Minnesota and Fresno, California." *Hmong Studies Journal* 10:1–53.

Marrow, Helen B. 2009. "Immigrant Bureaucratic Incorporation: The Dual Roles of Professional Missions and Government Policies." *American Sociological Review* 74 (5): 756–776.

———. 2011. *New Destination Dreaming: Immigration, Race, and Legal Status in the Rural American South.* Redwood City, CA: Stanford University Press.

McArdle, Andrea, and Tanya Erzen, eds. 2001. *Zero Tolerance: Quality of Life and the New Police Brutality in New York City.* New York: New York University Press.

McClain, Paula D., and Joseph Stewart Jr. 2010. *"Can We All Get Along?": Racial and Ethnic Minorities in American Politics.* Boulder, CO: Westview Press.

McEnroe, Paul. 2015. "Minneapolis FBI Refused to Use Somali Outreach for Spying." *Star Tribune,* February 28. Available at http://www.startribune.com/minneapolis-fbi-refused-to-use-somali-outreach-for-spying/290150151/.

Meier, Kenneth J., and Laurence J. O'Toole. 2006. "Political Control versus Bureaucratic Values: Reframing the Debate." *Public Administration Review* 66 (2): 177–192.

Nardulli, Peter F. 1990. "Political Subcultures in the American States: An Empirical Examination of Elazar's Formulation." *American Politics Research* 18 (3): 287–315.

Nelson, William E., Jr. 2002. *Black Atlantic Politics*. Albany: State University of New York Press.

Newport, Frank. 2009. "State of the States: Importance of Religion." Gallup, January 28. Available at http://www.gallup.com/poll/114022/state-states-importance-religion.aspx.

Newshour. 2015. "The American Dream Is Alive in the Twin Cities, but Not for Everyone." *PBS News Hour,* March 18. Available at http://www.pbs.org/newshour/bb/american-dream-alive-twin-cities-everyone/.

Office of Refugee Resettlement. 2013. *Annual Report to Congress*. Available at http://www.acf.hhs.gov/sites/default/files/orr/arc_2013_508.pdf.

Office of the Assistant Secretary for Planning and Evaluation (OASE). 2010. *2010 HHS Poverty Guidelines*. Available at https://aspe.hhs.gov/2010-hhs-poverty-guidelines.

Orozco, Manuel, and Julia Yansura. 2013. *Keeping the Lifeline Open*. OxFam America. Available at https://www.oxfamamerica.org/static/media/files/somalia-remittance-report-web.pdf.

Ortega, Janice. 1996. "Antiracist Protest Counters Ohio Klan Rally." *The Militant* 60 (5). Available at http://www.themilitant.com/1996/605/605_23.html.

Otiso, Kefa, and Bruce Smith. 2005. "Immigration and Economic Restructuring in Ohio's Cities, 1940–2000." *Knowledge Bank*. Available at http://hdl.handle.net/1811/31917.

Park, Robert E. 1928. "Human Migration and the Marginal Man." *American Journal of Sociology* 33:881–893.

Parker, Frank R. 1990. *Black Votes Count: Political Empowerment in Mississippi after 1965*. Chapel Hill: University of North Carolina Press.

Parks, Virginia. 2011. "Revisiting Shibboleths of Race and Urban Economy: Black Employment in Manufacturing and the Public Sector Compared, Chicago 1950–2000." *International Journal of Urban and Regional Research* 35 (1): 110–129.

Perry, Ravi K., ed. 2013. *21st Century Urban Race Politics: Representing Minorities as Universal Interests*. Bingley, UK: Emerald Group Publishing.

Portes, Alejandro, and Rubén G. Rumbaut. 2006. *Immigrant America: A Portrait*. 3rd ed. Berkeley: University of California Press.

Portes, Alejandro, and Min Zhou. 1993. "The New Second Generation: Segmented Assimilation and Its Variants." *Annals of the American Academy of Political and Social Science* 530 (1): 74–96.

Putnam, Robert D. 2000. *Bowling Alone: The Collapse and Revival of American Community*. New York: Simon and Schuster.

Pyle, Encarnacion, and Mark Ferenchik. 2015. "Somali Police Recruit Leaves Class over Head-Scarf Rule." *Columbus Dispatch*, April 28. Available at http://www.dispatch.com/content/stories/local/2015/04/28/head-scarves-debated-after-somali-police-recruit-exits.html.

Ramakrishnan, S. Karthick, and Irene Bloemraad. 2008. *Civic Hopes and Political Realities: Immigrants, Community Organizations, and Political Engagement*. New York: Russell Sage Foundation.

Ramakrishnan, S. Karthick, and Paul George Lewis. 2005. "Immigrants and Local Governance: The View from City Hall." San Francisco: Public Policy Institute of California.

Rao, Maya. 2013. "First Somali Elected to Mpls. City Council." *Star Tribune,* November 6. Available at http://www.startribune.com/first-somali-elected-to-mpls-city-council/230761041.

Richmond, Jo. 2008. "Somali Case May Show 'e pluribus unum' Is Passe." *Star Tribune*, September 11.

Risjord, Norman K. 2005. *A Popular History of Minnesota*. St. Paul: Minnesota Historical Society Press.

Roble, Abdi, and Doug Rutledge. 2008. *The Somali Diaspora: A Journey Away*. Minneapolis: University of Minnesota Press.

Romero, Mary. 1992. "Ethnographic Evaluation of Behavioral Causes of Census Undercount of Undocumented Immigrants and Salvadorans in the Mission District of San Francisco." *Ethnographic Evaluation of the 1990 Decennial Census Report* 18:89–41.

Rumberger, Russell W. 1983. "Social Mobility and Public Sector Employment." Stanford: Stanford University, California Institute for Research on Educational Finance and Governance.

Salhani, Justin. 2015. "The Tricky Business of Combating the Islamic State in Minneapolis–St. Paul." *Think Progress*, May 4. Available at http://thinkprogress.org/world/2015/05/04/3654349/tricky-business-combating-islamic-state-minneapolis-st-paul/.

Samatar, Ahmed. 2008. "Beginning Again: From Refugee to Citizen." *Bildhaan: An International Journal of Somali Studies* 4 (1). Available at http://digitalcommons.macalester.edu/bildhaan/vol4/iss1/5.

Samatar, Hussein. 2005. "Experiences of Somali Entrepreneurs in the Twin Cities." *Bildhaan: An International Journal of Somali Studies* 4 (1). Available at http://digitalcommons.macalester.edu/bildhaan/vol4/iss1/9.

Sambor, Connie. 2015. "Somalis Simply Shouldn't Be Upset." *Star Tribune*, March 8.

Schmidt, Ronald. 2015. "Race and Politics." In *Routledge Handbook of Interpretive Political Science*, edited by Mark Bevir and R.A.W. Rhodes, 367–380. New York: Routledge.

Senf, Dave. 2003. "Minnesota's Recipe for an Expanding Economic Pie: Four Parts More Labor and Three Parts Higher Productivity." *Minnesota Economic Trends*, December 2001/January 2002. Available at www.mnwfc.org.

Shane, Scott. 2015a. "From Minneapolis to ISIS: An American's Path to Jihad." *New York Times*, March 21. Available at http://www.nytimes.com/2015/03/22/world/middleeast/from-minneapolis-to-isis-an-americans-path-to-jihad.html.

———. 2015b. "6 Minnesotans Held in Plot to Join ISIS." *New York Times*, April 20. Available at http://www.nytimes.com/2015/04/21/us/6-somali-americans-arrested-in-isis-recruiting-case.html.

Silk, Mark, and Andrew Walsh. 2008. *One Nation, Divisible: How Regional Religious Differences Shape American Politics*. Vol. 9. Lanham, MD: Rowman and Littlefield.

Singer, Audrey, and Jill H. Wilson. 2006. "From 'There' to 'Here': Refugee Resettlement in Metropolitan America." Brookings Institution. Available at http://www.brookings.edu/research/reports/2006/09/demographics-singer.

Slifer, Anne. 2004. "Assistance Priorities Are Way out of Wack." *Columbus Dispatch*, July 19.

Sonenshein, Raphael J. 1997. "Post-incorporation Politics in Los Angeles." In *Racial Politics in American Cities*, edited by Rufus P. Browning, Dale Rogers Marshall, and David H. Tabb, 41–61. New York: Longman.

Sullivan, Lucas, and Rick Rouan. 2015. "Ginther Era Begins in Columbus." *Columbus Dispatch*, November 4. Available at http://www.dispatch.com/content/stories/public/2015/election/columbus-mayor.html.

Tam Cho, Wendy K. 1999. "Naturalization, Socialization, Participation: Immigrants and (Non-) Voting." *Journal of Politics* 61 (4): 1140–1155.

Tate, Katherine. 2003. *Black Faces in the Mirror: African Americans and Their Representatives in the U.S. Congress.* Princeton, NJ: Princeton University Press.

Temple-Raston, Dina. 2015. "For Somalis in Minneapolis, Jihad Recruiting Is a Recurring Nightmare." NPR.org, February 18. Available at http://www.npr.org /2015/02/18/ 387302748/minneapolis-st-paul-remains-a-focus-of-jihadi-recruiting.

Thao, Mao. 2009. "Immigrant and Refugee Mental Health." *Wilder Research*, February. Available at http://www.wilder.org/Wilder-Research/Publications/Studies/Immigrant %20and%20Refugee%20Mental%20Health%20-%20Best%20Practices%20in%20 Meeting%20the%20Needs%20of%20Immigrants%20and%20Refugees/Immi grant%20and%20Refugee%20Mental%20Health%20-%20Best%20Practices%20 in%20Meeting%20the%20Needs%20of%20Immigrants%20and%20Refugees,%20 Snapshot.pdf.

Treuhaft, Sarah, Angela Glover Blackwell, and Manuel Pastor. 2011. *America's Tomorrow: Equity Is the Superior Growth Model.* PolicyLink.org. Available at http://www .policylink.org/sites/default/files/SUMMIT_FRAMING_SUMMARY_WEB.PDF.

Tyler, Tom R. 2005. "Policing in Black and White: Ethnic Group Differences in Trust and Confidence in the Police." *Police Quarterly* 8 (3): 322–342.

Vang, Chia Youyee. 2008. *Hmong in Minnesota.* St. Paul: Minnesota Historical Society.

Voyer, Andrea M. 2013. *Strangers and Neighbors: Multiculturalism, Conflict, and Community in America.* Cambridge: Cambridge University Press.

Wade, Richard C. 1959. *The Urban Frontier.* Cambridge, MA: Harvard University Press.

Waters, Anita. 2012. "Racial Formation and Anti-Somali Ideologies in Central Ohio." *Bildhaan: An International Journal of Somali Studies* 12 (1). Available at http:// digitalcommons.macalester.edu/bildhaan/vol12/iss1/10.

Waters, Mary C. 1999. *Black Identities: West Indian Immigrant Dreams and American Realities.* New York: Russell Sage Foundation; Cambridge, MA: Harvard University Press.

Waters, Mary C., and Tomás R. Jiménez. 2005. "Assessing Immigrant Assimilation: New Empirical and Theoretical Challenges." *Annual Review of Sociology* 31:105–125.

Weber, Laura E. 1991. "'Gentiles Preferred': Minneapolis Jews and Employment 1920–1950." *Minnesota History* 52 (5): 166–182.

Wilkins, David E., and Heidi Kiiwetinepinesiik Stark. 2010. *American Indian Politics and the American Political System.* Plymouth, UK: Rowman and Littlefield.

Williams, Brandt. 2013. "Abdi Warsami Makes History, Wins Seat on Minneapolis City Council." Minnesota Public Radio. Available at http://blogs.mprnews.org/cit ies/2013/11/abdi-warsame-city-council/.

Williamson, Abigail F. 2011. "Beyond the Passage of Time: Local Government Response in New Immigrant Destinations." Ph.D. diss., Harvard University.

Wolford, Russell, and Patricia Wolford. 2000. "Columnist's Picture of Africa Is off the Mark." *Columbus Dispatch,* September 2.

Yuen, Laura. 2015. "Twin Cities Leaders Take Anti-extremism Efforts to White House." MPRnews, February 14.

Yusuf, Ahmed Ismail. 2012. *Somalis in Minnesota.* St. Paul: Minnesota Historical Society Press.

Index

Stefanie Chambers is Charles A. Dana Research Associate Professor of Political Science at Trinity College in Hartford, Connecticut. She is the author of *Mayors and Schools: Minority Voices and Democratic Tensions in Urban Education* (Temple).